Literary Conceptualizations of Growth

Children's Literature, Culture, and Cognition (CLCC)

The overarching aim of the CLCC series is to promote new theoretical approaches in the realm of children's literature research on the one hand, and to emphasize a non-Anglo-American focus, bringing in exciting research from other areas, on the other hand. In addition, the new book series will present research from many linguistic areas to an international audience, reinforce interaction between research conducted in many different languages and present high standard research on the basis of secondary sources in a number of languages and based in a variety of research traditions. Basically the series should encourage a cross- and interdisciplinary approach on the basis of literary studies, media studies, comparative studies, reception studies, literacy studies, cognitive studies, and linguistics. The series includes monographs and essay collections which are international in scope and intend to stimulate innovative research with a focus on children's literature (including other media), children's culture and cognition, thus encouraging interdisciplinary and multidisciplinary research in this expanding field.

For an overview of all books published in this series, please see
http://benjamins.com/catalog/clcc

Editors

Volume 2

Literary Conceptualizations of Growth. Metaphors and cognition in adolescent literature
by Roberta Trites

Literary Conceptualizations of Growth

Metaphors and cognition in adolescent literature

Roberta Trites
Illinois State University

John Benjamins Publishing Company

Amsterdam / Philadelphia

The paper used in this publication meets the minimum requirements of the American National Standard for Information Sciences – Permanence of Paper for Printed Library Materials, ANSI z39.48-1984.

Library of Congress Cataloging-in-Publication Data

Trites, Roberta Seelinger, 1962-
Literary Conceptualizations of Growth : Metaphors and cognition in adolescent literature
          / Roberta Seelinger Trites.
p.   cm. (Children's Literature, Culture, and Cognition, ISSN 2212-9006 ; v. 2)
Includes bibliographical references and index.
1. Discourse analysis, Literary. 2. Literature--Psychology. 3. Psychology and literature.
          4. Metaphor. 5. Cognition. I. Title.
P302.5.T75   2014
809'.89283--dc23   2014011669
ISBN 978 90 272 0156 0   (Hb ; alk. paper)
ISBN 978 90 272 6996 6   (Eb)

John Benjamins Publishing Co. · P.O. Box 36224 · 1020 ME Amsterdam · The Netherlands
John Benjamins North America · P.O. Box 27519 · Philadelphia PA 19118-0519 · USA

I dedicate this book to all of my Ph.D. students,
without whom this work would not have been possible.

Table of contents

Introduction

Why is growth such a prevalent concept in adolescent literature? This project, *Literary Conceptualizations of Growth: Metaphor and Cognition in Adolescent Literature*, grew out of questions about adolescent maturation left unanswered in my earlier work on adolescent literature. In *Disturbing the Universe: Power and Repression in Adolescent Literature*, I argue that adolescent literature isn't as much about growth as it is about teaching adolescents either to conform to societal pressures or die (Trites 2000). That is, although characters like Holden Caulfield initially appear to be iconoclasts and rebels who refuse to conform, by the end of most novels about adolescents — including *Catcher in the Rye* — the rebellious protagonist has either "matured" into some level of conformity or has died. (Two characters in S.E. Hinton's *The Outsiders*, Johnny and Dallas, provide examples of the latter case.) In other words, adolescent literature initially appears to empower teenagers, but empowerment proves to be something of an illusion in many novels because so frequently, teenaged characters demonstrate to teen readers that the only true form of empowerment comes from growing up and leaving adolescence behind. It's certainly logical that we must all mature, but the message to young readers is a consistent one: "there is something wrong with your subject position as a teenager. Grow up and become someone else." In that sense, adolescent literature is the only genre written with the subversive ideological intent of undermining the reader's subject position. (As a counter-example, think of women's literature — which certainly is not written for the purpose of teaching women how to outgrow being women!)

But in *Disturbing the Universe*, I did not ask the question *why*? That is, why do authors focus stories so frequently on adolescent characters who grow? And why do literary critics spend so much time analyzing that growth — frequently relying themselves on metaphors of growth in their own analyses? *Literary Conceptualizations of Growth* posits that perhaps our own cognitive structures are responsible for the pervasiveness of growth as both a metaphor and a narrative pattern in adolescent literature. The purpose of this book is therefore not to define adolescent literature or examine the Young Adult (YA) novel as a genre; that work has been undertaken by, among others, Nikolajeva (1996, 2000), McCallum (1999), Cadden (2000), Trites (2000, 2007), Coats (2004), and Waller (2009). Rather, the purpose of this book is to examine *how* growth is conceptualized in literature and in literary criticism. In order to understand the cause(s) and effect(s) of these conceptualizations, I rely on one of the disciplines that analyzes conceptualization as a cognitive process: cognitive linguistics.

Cognitive linguistics

Cognitive linguistics emerged from the broad interdisciplinary movement in cognitive science begun in the 1950s that involved scholars who employed methodologies from psychology, linguistics, computer science, anthropology, and philosophy as a way of better understanding cognition. The earliest cognitive scientists were reacting against behaviorists, who tended to dominate some fields of psychology in the 1950s with their assumptions that all behaviors are learned, but too much about unconscious thought, instinctive behaviors, and the nature of consciousness itself were left unanswered by behaviorism. Cognitive scientists strove to explore *all* aspects of thought, not just those that were influenced by learned behaviors. Initially, these early cognitive scientists argued that brains were like computers, so they believed that if they could understand the brain's coding, they could understand cognition; eventually, however, they acknowledged this analogy to be flawed. Brains are living, mutable, and infinitely complex; they are not coded in binary systems like computers are. Therefore, "today's cognitive scientists tend to concentrate instead on the more organic metaphor the 'embodiment' of mind, that is, of the mind's substantive indebtedness to its bodily, social and cultural contexts" (Hart 2001:315). Moreover, cognitive scientists, and especially those in the subdiscipline of cognitive linguistics, examine how language usage affects our thinking. Cognitive linguists focus, among other things, "on the figurative phenomena of metaphor, metonymy, image schemata, 'fields', 'frames', and other 'integrative mental spaces' (as they are called), and the gradient structures and prototypical bases of semantic categories, all of which contribute to recasting human reason into a set of highly imaginative — not logical but figural — processes" (Hart 2001:315). In other words, cognitive linguists acknowledge that language usages — even such rhetorical devices as metaphor and metonymy — shape, define, and limit how conceptualizations occur.

Furthermore, cognitive linguists acknowledge that categorization is fundamental to the cognitive process of conceptualization. Our concepts — and the processes by which we conceptualize — depend on the ability to categorize objects or ideas. Gregory Murphy, a cognitive psychologist who explores the relationship between cognition and language, explains it this way: "Our concepts embody much of our knowledge of the world, telling us what things are and what properties they have"; for example, we know the difference between "chair" and "not-chair" when we enter a new room, or when we meet a "bulldog" we know it is a member of the category "dog" but not "cat" (Murphy 2002:1). Murphy calls concepts "the glue that holds our mental world together.… in that they tie our past experiences to our present interactions with the world, and because the concepts themselves are connected to our larger knowledge structures" (1). We cannot think without categorizing, nor can we think without concepts.

Cognitive linguists, such as George Lakoff and Mark Johnson (1980), have thus traced how conceptualization is affected by various linguistic phenomena, but especially metaphors. They argue that we conceptualize the world in ways that are influenced by our embodiment, and they maintain that the language we use shapes how we conceive ideas and process them:

> [M]etaphor is pervasive in everyday life, not just in language but in thought and action. Our ordinary conceptual system, in terms of which we both think and act, is fundamentally metaphorical in nature.
>
> The concepts that govern our thought are not just matters of the intellect. They also govern our everyday functioning, down to the most mundane details. Our concepts structure what we perceive, how we get around in the world, and how we relate to other people. Our conceptual system thus plays a central role in defining our everyday realities. (1980:3)

Lakoff and Johnson therefore argue that such cognitive structures as metaphors and their influence on conceptualization can and should be studied in terms of both language and thought.

For example, the concept of *growth* is defined first by categorization, but also second, in metaphorical terms. That which is growing exists in the category of "that which is animate" not in the category "that which is inanimate" or "that which is dead." Human growth also involves the embodied nature of the brain; brains are housed within organic bodies that grow, mature, and die, just as all organic beings gestate, grow, decline, and die. Indeed, both the English words "maturation" and "growth" have their origins in agricultural metaphors of plant growth: the verb "to mature" entered English via the influence of Middle French (and therefore Latin) on Middle English: *maturare* in its Latin transitive sense means "to ripen, finish in good time," while "to grow," in its oldest usage in English, emerged from Middle Dutch's *groeyen* or *groyen*, with the denotation "to manifest vigorous life; to put forth foliage, flourish" (Mature, v. 2012; Grow, v. 2012). Human conceptualizations of growth and maturation in England during the Middle Ages were thus clearly influenced by plant growth and its importance in sustaining human life through agriculture. Thus, it would seem that more than a millennia ago, speakers of English conceived of growth in metaphorical terms: people grow like plants grow.

Today, metaphors of growth surround us. We employ so many metaphors of growth in our daily lives that we don't even notice many of them. We say that a project grew out of another project when we mean one project developed from

another; we say that Americans have a growing sense of anxiety about the economy when we mean they have an increasing sense of anxiety; we say that we're
growing bored when we mean we're getting bored or becoming bored. We tell
school children to "grow their minds" when we want them to think in new and
difficult ways, and we tell irritating people to "grow up" when they are acting immature, even if they are already adults — which we also refer to metaphorically as
being a "grown-up." These metaphorical conceptualizations of growth may well
be inescapable because we are neurologically wired to think in terms of our own
growth. That is, after all, what our brains do for many years of our lives: grow —
and then, if we live long enough, eventually decline.

Cognitive linguistics has influenced the study of metaphor in literature in a
field sometimes referred to by the name "cognitive poetics" that often focuses on
poetry. Narrative theorists have also been influenced by cognitive linguists (and
its related subdiscipline, cognitive poetics) to pay attention to the ways that narratives, such as novels, intersect with cognition and language. Psycho-emotional
growth, for example, provides an easily recognizable narrative pattern in the
Bildungsroman, the novel of transition from youth to adulthood. But there is more
to understanding literature than simply understanding metaphors or the patterns
of narrative structure. How, for example, do the cognitive processes of memory
and repetition figure in the creation and reception of narrative? How does the brain
actually come to recognize and understand stock characters, narrative formulae,
and narrative conventions? How does language-use limit and enhance narrative
understanding? And how does narrative affect our cognitive ability to recognize
larger cultural narratives at work in our lives? Cognitive literary theorists, including Mark Turner (1991), David Herman (2002), Alan Richardson (2004), Lisa
Zunshine (2006), and Monika Fludernik (2010) explore these very ideas.

Within the field of children's and adolescent literature, cognitive literary
theory is also gaining increased attention. For example, Margaret Mackey (2010,
2011, 2012) has explored the influence of embodiment and memory on the cognitive perception of children's literature in a series of essays that has appeared
in *Children's Literature in Education*. Karen Coats (2011) also traces the relationship between embodiment and cognition in an elegant exploration of metaphors
of the body as container. John Stephens (2011) investigates the relationship between cognition and narrative patterns called *scripts* in his article "Schemas and
Scripts," work that is further explored in a specific multicultural context by Sung-
Ae Lee (2011). Marek Oziewicz (2007, 2011) has also relied on cognitive literary
theory to explore conceptualizations of justice, particularly in terms of scripts.
Maria Nikolajeva (2012) examines the cognitive creation of empathy in multi-
media texts in "Reading Other People's Minds through Word and Image," while
Bettina Kümmerling-Meibauer demonstrates this process at work in the YA novel

in her article "Emotional Connection" (2012). Kümmerling-Meibauer (2011) also explores the role of cognition in the emergent literacy of young children. Lydia Kokkola (2013) examines how competing cognitive conceptualizations of innocence and sexuality influence knowledge production in adolescent literature. Not only do these critics demonstrate the usefulness of cognitive literary theory (including cognitive poetics and cognitive narratology) to children's and adolescent literature, but — taken as a whole — they also show how influential the idea of embodied cognition is to literature written for youth.

Narrative cannot happen without cognition, so it seems inevitable that cognitive narratology would emerge as the intersection between cognitive linguistics and narrative theory. "Cognitive narratology can be defined as the study of mind-relevant aspects of storytelling practices, wherever — and by whatever means — those practices occur" (Herman 2011:2). Thus, although narrative theory focuses largely on texts alone, cognitive narratology focuses on the interrelationship between cognition and textual structures. Although my work focuses more on the reception of text than on its creation, cognitive narratology offers insight into both how narrative structures involving growth emerge and are perceived. I should, however, offer a caveat: while this text is informed by cognitive literary theory, it is not intended to be a primer in how cognitive literary theory, particularly cognitive narratology, is meant to work. Rather, *Literary Conceptualizations of Growth* is an exploration of how literary conceptualizations of growth are enacted in novels about characters living through a phase of life that is typically associated with growth: adolescence. I rely on cognitive literary theory in this exploration because these theorizations are fundamental to my explanation of how and why adolescent literature is so invested in concepts of growth.

Brain science

We know that cognition changes during adolescence; indeed, the brain may well change more during adolescence than any other stage after our births except for the first six months of life.[1] According to Blakemore and Choudhury, two areas of the

---

1. Adolescence is a discursive and socially-situated construct; that is, it is a language-driven concept that changes based on context, including era. Various definitions offered by experts in contemporary Euro-American contexts emphasize biophysical age and puberty: adolescence is "post-pubertal youth" (Adams & Berzonsky 2006:xxi); "Adolescence, in modern industrial societies, is the transition from childhood to adulthood. It lasts from age 11 or 12 until the late teens or early twenties" (Papalia, Olds & Feldman 2006); "Adolescence is thus a modern — and even postmodern — concept that acknowledges the unique space between childhood and full adulthood" (Christenbury, Bomer & Smagorinsky 2009:4). Perhaps the most practical and least

brain develop with particular rapidity following puberty: the parietal lobe, which is involved with integrating sensory data, and the frontal lobe, which is the center of executive functioning (2006: 296–297). Increases in both the white matter and the thickening of the neurons' protective layer of myelin in the prefrontal cortex make it possible for adolescents to process information more quickly than they did as children; the neural pruning that immediately follows the onset of puberty allows adolescents to process information more efficiently (Steinberg 2005: 70). Thus, the changes triggered by puberty include — among other brain functions — increased executive functioning skills, increased social cognition, increased processing efficiency, increased risk-taking, and decreased negative mood regulation.

The frontal lobe experiences perhaps more changes than other lobes of the brain during adolescence. The frontal lobe pertains to an understanding of narrative because it is involved in both social cognition and executive function. *Executive function* includes "selective attention, decision-making, voluntary response inhibition and working memory" (Blakemore & Choudhury 2006: 301). Understanding a narrative depends on selective attention, some degree of decision-making, and a good measure of memory. Social cognition, which also occurs in the frontal cortex, includes such issues as self-awareness, perspective-taking, emotion- and facial recognition, and a "theory of mind, that is the ability to understand other minds by attributing mental states such as beliefs, desires, and intentions to other people" (Blakemore & Choudhury 2006: 302). Premack and Woodruff argue that "[a]n individual has a theory of mind if he imputes mental states to himself and others" (1978: 515). Frith, Happé, and Simmons build on this definition to argue that in order to "mentalize," or understand and represent other people's thoughts, "we need to be able to represent mental states, such as belief and desire, if we are to understand and predict other people's behaviour. The term 'theory of mind' (Premack & Woodruff 1978) is often used to refer to the (quite unconscious) ability to attribute mental states, and to use these invisible postulates to explain behaviour in everyday life" (Frith et al. 1994: 109–110). Following the work of Frith and her colleagues, Blakemore and Choudhury argue that "The ability to take another's perspective is crucial for successful social communication" (2006: 302). That ability is also crucial for humans to understand narrative — and during adolescence, frontal lobe activities increase our ability to understand perspective complexly: "[P]uberty represents a period of synaptic reorganisation and as a consequence the brain might be more sensitive to experiential input at this period of time in

---

contextually-situated definition is offered by Lerner and Steinberg, which describes adolescence as nothing more or less than "the second decade of life" (2004: x). I must note, however, that all literary characters are discursive and are therefore not necessarily subject to the biophysical conditions that psychological definitions of adolescence imply.

the realm of executive function and social cognition" (Blakemore & Choudhury 2006:307). Thus, what we know about cognitive development of the adolescent brain provides us with information both about how adolescents process what they read and why they can read at a more complex level following puberty than they can prior to puberty.

Laurence Steinberg argues that it is essential that we understand adolescence as a stage of life that is vulnerable "specifically because of gaps between emotion, cognition and behavior" (2005:69). As he observes, many changes in the brain are central to "the regulation of behavior and emotion and to the perception and evaluation of risk and reward," and there is a disconnect "between the adolescent's affective experience and his or her ability to regulate arousal and motivation" (69–70). He emphasizes the significant changes (and increases) in adolescents' ability to reason, process information, and master particular cognitive skills that create a sense of expertise (70). In effect, the increases in information processing, executive functioning skills and social cognition have particular bearing on adolescent literature because literary concepts of growth are often implicated in the increased complexity of teenaged characters' thinking and their social relationships.

Growth

Literary Conceptualizations of Growth is an exploration of the processes by which maturation is represented specifically in adolescent literature. The study is inflected by cognitive literary theory and by cognitive linguistics and its influence on experiential philosophy; the history of ideas also proves to be germane to the examination of how critics, scholars, and philosophers have historically constructed the concept of growth. This study, then, has two interrelated goals: to examine how concepts of growth manifest themselves in adolescent literature and to interrogate how growth serves as a cognitive concept that structures our ability to think about adolescence as literary critics.

Chapter 1 introduces rudimentary concepts in cognitive linguistics (such as the idea of the *embodied metaphor*) as basic tools for exploring in Chapter 2 more complex embodied narrative concepts involved in patterns of growth (such as *schema*, *script*, and *sequence*). Chapter 3 investigates the cognitive locus of *cultural narratives* that affects maturation. Chapter 4 provides a specific case study of the cognitively embedded nature of cultural narratives. I turn in Chapter 5 to an exploration of how authors use these concepts in sophisticated explorations of growth as epistemologically and ontologically experienced. Cognitive linguistics situates itself as a mediated site between philosophical explorations of ontology and epistemology; Lakoff and Johnson refer to their philosophy as "experientialism," arguing that all epistemology and ontology are dependent on embodied experiences (1980:226). The conceptualization of growth — especially as it is depicted in adolescent literature — is thus implicated in the embodied metaphors, scripts, and cultural narratives that demonstrate the experiential nature of both *being* and *knowing*. The book concludes in Chapter 6 with an archaeology of the concept of growth, as Foucault (1994) uses the term archaeology, tracing the concept of growth both in terms of the history of ideas and in terms of how critics of literature for the young themselves rely on emplotments that are informed by cognitive concepts of growth. In sum, *Literary Conceptualizations of Growth* argues that maturation, as it is conceptualized within adolescent literature, links cognition inviolably to embodiment with significant epistemological, ontological, disciplinary, and cultural implications.

In all cases, the youth novels and films I examine are English-language texts for one very practical reason: metaphors are used uniquely within each language. Some languages allow for metaphors to be translated with precision; others require a shift in metaphor that could well alter the original meaning and/or the cognitive effect of the reading process. Because so much of what I am doing here requires me to analyze closely the relationship between metaphor and conceptualization, I think it prudent to base my analyses in the language I know best. I have, however, tried to select novels that represent a broader range than just those written in the U.S., so I have also included narratives written by authors from Australia, Canada, New Zealand, and the U.K. These novels are not discussed in chronological order; rather, they have been selected to represent various ideas at work in the cognitive narratology of growth. While I have chosen those novels — and in Chapter 4, films — that I think best support my effort to interrogate growth as a concept, all of the texts are necessarily limited by the context in which they were created.

Growth is a powerful and fundamental concept within adolescent literature and children's literature. Although I limit my study to adolescent literature because I seek to interrogate, among other things, how traditions of the *Bildungsroman* influence our field, much of the work here can also be extrapolated to children's literature. How we think about growth influences how we experience growth — and what we tell adolescents about their own growth, in turn, has significant ramifications for their own conceptualizations of maturation. As historian Robert Nisbet once noted, "No occupation or discipline can make do without its metaphors.... Even so, metaphors must be watched; they can be treacherous" (1970:351).[2]

---

2. Material on pages 28–31 is reprinted by permission of the Publishers from "Images of Growth: Embodied Metaphors in *Adventures of Huckleberry Finn*," forthcoming in *Representing Children in Chinese and U.S. Children's Literature*, edited by Claudia Nelson and Rebecca Morris (Farnham: Ashgate, 2014). Copyright © 2014

Acknowledgements

My first acknowledgements must go to the scholars whose intellectual interests have stimulated me to explore conceptualizations of growth: Susan L. Stewart and Melissa Sara Smith. Their dissertations and our subsequent conversations have shaped my interests for the better part of a decade now.

I am also grateful to Margaret Mackey, John Stephens, Karen Coats, Michelle H. Martin, and Bruce Hawkins, who all encouraged me, in different and significant ways, to explore cognitive linguistics and literary theory. Each of the members of ISU's 2012 seminar on cognitive narratology in children's literature also influenced this project, so I thank Ayla Goetsch, Melanie Goss, Karly Grice, Jordana Hall, Amy Hicks, Meghann Meeusen, Miranda Mills, Niall Nance-Carroll, Susana Rodriguez, Christine Stewart, and Elizabeth Williams. Emily Woster, Beth Pearce, Mpale Mwansasu-Silkiluwasha (my sister!), and Hari Adhikari also provided me with interesting and fruitful lines of thought. Laura Berk and Sam Catanzaro guided me toward various studies in the field of psychology, for which I am grateful.

I would like to thank those members of the Children's Literature Association who have created professional opportunities that have allowed me the space in which to expand this project. Jonathan Klassen of Soochow University in Taiwan, Claudia Nelson of Texas A & M University, and Rosemary Ross Johnston of University of Technology, Sydney, have been particularly supportive in this regard. I also thank Betsy Hearne, Mike Cadden, Claudia Mills, Jan Susina, Mary Moran, Lynne Vallone, Kenneth Kidd, Yoshida Junko, Jean Webb, Jackie Stallcup, Annette Wannamaker, Paula Connolly, Kate Capshaw, Mark West, Lissa Paul, Leona Fisher, Beth Marshall, Teya Rosenberg, Marilynn Olson, Lisa Rowe Fraustino, Annette Wannamaker, Jackie Stallcup, Jennie Miskec, Gwen Tarbox, Kathy Kiessling, and Carly Armstrong. Special thanks to Kara Keeling and Scott Pollard for always being available for a good meal and an even better glass of wine. Joseph W. Campbell and Billie Jarvis-Freeman deserve special recognition for both their friendship and for working with me in a life-changing independent study one lovely summer.

The editors of Benjamins Children's Literature, Culture, and Cognition series include Bettina Kümmerling-Meibauer, Maria Nikolajeva, Nina Christensen, and Elina Druker. I am especially grateful to Professor Kümmerling-Meibauer for inspiring me to draft the manuscript and submit it to this series.

Various dear friends have also been willing to offer both intellectual advice and emotional support, so I thank Pam Riney-Kehrberg and Susan Burt for their almost daily support in the development of this project over the last three years. The friends who have kept me going with coffee and walks and music and beer include April Schultz, Kass Fleisher, Karen Khusro, Rick Martin, Tak Cheung, Jim Stanlaw, Scott Jordan, Sally Parry, Bob McLaughlin, Sue Sprecher, Barb Heyl, Judi

Sevel, and Pat and Dick Witzig. Becky and Jim Skibo have sustained my faith in more than one institution, and because of Jim, I will always think of this as the book that grew by "magic." Illinois State University staff members Diane Smith and Peggy Haycraft have provided both efficient and loving support. Without ISU librarians Julie Derden, Jean MacDonald, and Maureen Brunsdale, nothing would be possible. And two ISU deans also deserve special mention: Greg Simpson, Dean of Arts and Sciences, and Dane Ward, Dean of Libraries.

Most of all, I am indebted to my wonderful and intellectually invigorating family: my husband, George F. Seelinger, and our delightfully engaging children, George H., John, and Katharine. These three Seelinger children were all teenagers when I both began and finished the first draft of this project, so it is to be noted that their adolescences very likely had a great deal to do with stimulating my scholarly interest in adolescent growth.

CHAPTER 1

Growth, cognitive linguistics, and embodied metaphors

As a literary term, *adolescent literature* refers to both creative works, such as fiction or drama or poetry, and the critical study or literary criticism of those creative works. Additionally, in both senses of the term, adolescent literature is closely linked to children's literature, particularly around issues of growth. Because growth is arguably one of the most salient features of fiction for young people, the idea of growth gains much consideration in the criticism that attempts to define literature written for youth.

In this chapter, I will first provide some background information for my argument, including a review of the literary theory dealing with growth and basic definitions of the *Bildungsroman* and terms related to that pivotal concept. My goal in this section is to establish the pervasiveness of the concept of *growth* within adolescent literature. Next, I give the reader a brief overview of important concepts in cognitive linguistics that help explain the prevalence of growth as a concept in fiction about adolescence. This section is a general introduction to basic ideas from the field of cognitive linguistics and is not necessarily specific only to adolescent literature, although L.M. Montgomery's *Anne of Green Gables* (1908) supplies examples that are particularly germane. In the third section, I examine the metaphors literary critics themselves use to describe growth in adolescent literature to demonstrate that literary critics are as influenced by embodied conceptualizations of growth as literary artists are. Finally, as an example of how to employ a cognitive reading of adolescent literature, I conclude this chapter by analyzing the embodied metaphors at work in a canonical American novel about adolescence, Mark Twain's *Adventures of Huckleberry Finn* (1885). Ultimately, I hope to demonstrate that cognitive conceptualizations of growth are a major factor in the genre of adolescent literature (literature about adolescence) and its subgenre, the Young Adult (YA) novel, which is written for and marketed directly to adolescents.

Background and review of the literature

Critics of both adolescent literature and children's literature frequently observe how a protagonist's growth shapes the plot of novels about young people. It should be noted that most of the critics I include in the following literature review adhere to a standard convention of the field in considering adolescent protagonists to be residing within the broader scope of a general category of literary study called "children's literature" — a convention to which I have also adhered, as in my book, *Waking Sleeping Beauty* (Trites 1997). Thus, many observations about "children's literature" in what follows can also be considered to apply to adolescent literature. For example, like me, Vandergrift (1980), Lukens (1982), Wolf (1985), Stephens (1992), Russell (2001), Nikolajeva (2002), and Natov (2003) also do not distinguish children's literature from adolescent literature when they are evaluating the tendency of protagonists to grow in fiction for the young. That said, this chronological review of the literature reveals how prevalent the concept of growth is within the study of adolescent (and children's) literature.

Rebecca Lukens believes growth figures prominently in novels for the young because it is fundamental to the human condition: "In life the development of a person's character or personality is a matter of growth and change" — so, "character development means showing the character … with the complexity of the human being"; ergo, well-developed characters *must* grow (1982: 30, italics in the original). Lukens is participating in a bias that assumes literary characters written for a young audience "must" grow as inevitably as preadolescent and adolescent readers themselves do. In a similar vein, Kay Vandergrift argues: "Main characters … are three-dimensional complex individuals who *grow*, change, and develop as a result of the events of story" (1980: 110, italics added). Also writing in the 1980s, Virginia Wolf concludes that "[a]ll great children's literature [is] about *growing* up" (1985: 299, italics added).

John Stephens considers "the most pervasive theme in children's fiction" to be "the transition within the individual from infantile solipsism to maturing social awareness" (1992: 3), while Robyn McCallum also assumes that growth is a defining factor of adolescence. She argues that adolescent fiction invariably interrogates subject-formation because "ideas about and representations of subjectivity are always inherent in the central concerns of this fiction: that is in the concerns with personal *growth* and *maturation*, and with relationships between the self and others, and between individuals and the world, society or the past" (1999: 256, italics added). According to McCallum, literary adolescence is inflected by the conventional wisdom that adolescence marks a time of growth that includes changing self-perception: "Concepts of personal identity and selfhood are formed in dialogue with society, with language, and with other people, and while this dialogue is ongoing, modern adolescence — that transition stage between childhood and adulthood — is usually thought of as a period during which notions of selfhood undergo rapid and radical transformation" (1999: 3). Thus, both Stephens and McCallum write about adolescence as a time of transition that involves growth.

David Russell asserts that "In most children's stories, the protagonist is a *dynamic* character, that is, one who changes throughout the narrative, usually toward greater maturity" (2001: 58, italics in the original). Similarly, Nikolajeva calls "inner growth" the "foremost goal" of children's novels that are character-oriented rather than plot-oriented; the culmination of the master plot in children's literature, she argues, occurs when the typical protagonist has "found a treasure or gained knowledge and maturity" (2002: 160). She also acknowledges that "[i]n character-oriented narratives, we expect the character to obtain new — presumably higher — moral qualities, *mature* spiritually, gain knowledge and insights, and so on" (2002: 64, italics added). Similarly, Roni Natov identifies "the central question of much of children's literature" as a response to the following question: "How can we *grow* up without losing the spontaneity of our natural responses?" (2003: 101, italics added).

Alison Waller identifies growth as an end-goal in both realism and fantasy in YA literature: "the conventions of teen realism foreground social problems and a concern with the teenage protagonist's solutions through interpersonal *growth*. A fantastic realist text might cover similar ground but pay more attention to the relationship between what is real and unreal, shifting interpretive activity from social reality to metaphysical questions" (2009: 12, italics added). Thus, *growth* does seem to be a central issue for both children's and adolescent literature. However, although many of the conceptualizations of growth I am exploring in this text pertain to both children's and adolescent literature, I am limiting my focus to adolescent literature for both purposes of economy and out of a recognition that growth in children's literature is depicted in more diverse and less formulaic ways than in the *bildungsroman*-influenced genre of the YA novel.

The *Bildungsroman* provides the narrative pattern that has had the greatest influence on adolescent literature — although the term is frequently misused (Trites 2000: 10–15). Manfred Engel identifies the *Bildungsroman* as being derived from the *Entwicklungsroman*, the novel of development, as are the *Erziehungsroman* (the novel of education) and the *Künstlerroman* (the novel of artistic development) (2008: 265). All of these genres have in common the concept of "*Bildung*" as "a process of organic or quasi-organic development" (Engel 2008: 264); the *Bildungsroman* is thus necessarily a novel "of character" and "of development" and "not a process of social or biological determination but a process of formation" (265–266). That is, the *Bildungsroman* is focused on the interior or spiritual growth of one character. According to Jerome Buckley, "By the time [the protagonist of the *Bildungsroman*] has decided, after painful soul-searching, the sort of accommodation to the modern world he can honestly make, he has left his adolescence behind and entered upon his maturity" (1974: 18). Typically, the *Bildungsroman* involves maturation into adulthood or an embarkation into adulthood.

Critics such as Maria Nikolajeva aptly separate *bildungsroman*-influenced novels that focus on character growth from series books in which the protagonist's maturation would be detrimental to the publication (and subsequent sales) of sequels: "There are in fact protagonists who do not evolve or mature, do not gain any material wealth or moral improvement. The protagonists of formulaic fiction normally do not change, physically or spiritually.... The absence of change is dictated by the nature of the genre" (2002:65). Series books, such as the Nancy Drew books or Sweet Valley High novels, are focused more on plot than on character. Because these books do not depict character growth, they are not the subject of this study. Rather, I focus herein on those novels that appear to be participating in the traditions of the *Bildungsroman* by privileging insights into a character's interior growth, whether it is psychological, emotional, creative, or ethical.

This constant presence of growth as an idea in adolescent literature leads me to ask two questions: how is growth privileged in the theories of adolescent literature? and, more important, why? — by which I mean, why do so many authors produce texts that privilege growth, and why have literary theorists been so interested in this pattern for more than a century? In other words, why should that be? Why is attention to growth so prevalent in adolescent literature?

For most of my academic life, I have assumed that European traditions of the *Bildungsroman* have influenced adolescent literature to focus on the interior life and psychological growth of the individual. Certainly, I still consider that to be one factor responsible for the proliferation of this pattern. But cognitive literary theory has led me to believe that we write novels about growth because our embodied brains *know* growth. We understand intuitively what growth is because we have witnessed the growth of plants, animals, and other people — and far more significantly, we have experienced our own physical, emotional, and cognitive growth. *Literary Conceptualizations of Growth: Metaphors and cognition in adolescent literature* thus relies on cognitive literary theory — and particularly on the study of cognitive linguistics and cognitive narratology — to explore cognitive conceptualizations of the idea of growth within the field of adolescent literature.

Cognitive linguistics and embodied metaphors

George Lakoff and Mark Johnson define cognitive science as the "discipline that studies conceptual systems" (1999:10); Gilles Fauconnier identifies "[m]eaning construction [a]s a cornerstone of cognitive science" (2003:2). Some cognitive scientists study, for example, "the active (and largely unconscious) mental processing that makes behavior understandable" (Richardson 2004:1). As a subdiscipline of cognitive science, cognitive linguistics is invested in examining how human beings think and communicate by creating language categories that affect conceptualization — and cognitive linguists also explore how the language of those conceptualizations, in turn, alters cognition. Moreover, cognitive linguists recognize the brain as embodied; that is, all brains are housed in a body and therefore dependent upon that embodiment, because all thought resides within a body. Cognitive linguists therefore acknowledge the cultural situatedness of cognition because human thought, both conscious and unconscious, is influenced and constructed by the cultures in which individuals live and the language that they employ (Hart 2001: 315).

Cognitive linguists are thus aware of two related issues: language use is embodied, and culturally-inflected language use affects how we think about things or *conceptualize*. Cognitive linguistics, then, focuses on the relationship between cognitive conceptualization and language. In the rest of this chapter, I will explore the various ways that the concept of *growth* is affected by the language that literary critics and authors use, with a particular emphasis on how embodiment interacts with the conceptualization of growth.

According to Lakoff and Johnson, one of the most fundamental and primary acts of cognition required for any animal species to survive is the ability to *categorize*. They argue that the ability to categorize is essential for evolutionary survival: humans, like most animal species, depend on their ability to identify at a minimum two important categories: food and not-food (1999: 17). The ability to distinguish prey from not-prey and safety from danger are also essential for survival. Lakoff and Johnson describe how dependent cognitive categorization is on our embodiment: "Categorization is therefore a consequence of how we are embodied. We have evolved to categorize; if we hadn't, we would not have survived" (1999: 18). Because most humans perceive the world through four or five senses, we tend to create categories based on those perceptions. "Categorization is thus not a purely intellectual matter, occurring after the fact of experience. Rather the formation and use of categories is the stuff of experience. It is part of what our bodies and brains are constantly engaged in" (Lakoff & Johnson 1999: 19). We categorize; therefore, we think — and we think; therefore, we categorize. The following two fundamental principles are central to cognitive linguistics: all thought (both conscious and unconscious) is embodied, and all thought depends on categorizations that are influenced by that embodiment.

This embodied ability to categorize affects how we form concepts and how concepts, once formed, in turn shape our subsequent ability to perceive the world. Lakoff and Johnson argue that concepts "are crucially shaped by our bodies and brains" (1999: 22), and they use as one example the idea of spatial-relations concepts. We understand such concepts as "here" and "there," for example, in relationship to where our bodies are positioned at any given moment. We understand such concepts as "in front of" the classroom or "at the back of the cupboard" because our own bodies have fronts and backs (Lakoff & Johnson 1999: 30). In a more complex example, we also understand the idea of containers through our bodies — because we know what it means to be full when we eat or to empty our bladders. Indeed, Lakoff and Johnson argue that the English word "*in*" relies on a "container schema" of "a bounded region in space" that includes three structures: "an inside, a boundary, and an outside" (1999: 31–32).[1] Our ability to conceptualize the relationship between "in" and "out" depends on our bodies both having those boundaries and being able to experience them perceptually by seeing and/or feeling how containers — from cups to football stadiums — have interiors, boundaries, and exteriors. Thus, embodiment is inherent in a concept as basic as *in*.

The inherently embodied ability to conceptualize, Lakoff and Johnson argue, leads to a proliferation of concepts that are, effectively, metaphors. That is, we rely on linguistic concepts to help represent the knowledge we have gained cognitively from living as embodied beings. In *Metaphors We Live By*, Lakoff and Johnson demonstrate how metaphors structure the way people think: "Our concepts structure what we perceive, how we get around in the world, and how we relate to other people. Our conceptual system thus plays a central role in defining our everyday realities" (1980: 3). Our brains store language in a cognitive process that proves to shape — and even structure — our perceptions because "metaphor resides in thought, not just in words" (Lakoff & Turner 1989: 2).

Cognitive linguists contend that this process of structuring our understanding of abstract concepts in terms of embodiment begins in childhood. Our physical experiences of living in the world shape our language. For example, many speakers of English learn in childhood to equate metaphors of physical vision with metaphors of cognitive understanding, particularly if they are sighted.[2] This is demonstrated when people say such things as, "Yes, I *see* that" or "The argument *looks* different from my *point of view*" (M. Johnson 1990: 108). In Chinese a similar metaphor occurs when the character "ming" (bright) is combined with the character "bai" (white) to indicate the idea of understanding something clearly or with clarity: 明白 míngbái. Speakers of English are thus by no means the only people who conceptualize thought in terms of vision. These are embodied metaphors; that is,

---

1. For more on the body-as-container within children's literature, see Coats (2011).

2. For a Disability Studies critique of Lakoff and Johnson, see Amy Vidali, who argues that "they are ableist in assuming that bodies have particular physical/cognitive/sensory experiences and related metaphorical expressions" (Vidali 2010: 34). This position, of course, privileges the effect of language usage on individuals, as opposed to examining how language, including metaphor usage, develops in communal and cultural contexts. As Vidali notes: "A disability approach to metaphor critiques the obvious and subtle implications for disability" (46).

"seeing clearly" is a metaphor for understanding that arises from the embodied ability to — literally — see. According to Lakoff and Johnson (1980), the embodied metaphors we use affect our cognition because when we apply one embodied concept to another unrelated, abstract concept, both concepts become linked in our cognition — as vision and understanding are for most speakers of English. In this example, "vision" is the *source domain* because it is the conceptual domain from which we are drawing the metaphorical expression; "understanding" is the *target domain* because that is the concept that we are trying to explain by making the comparison (Lakoff & Johnson 1980: 48).

This process of mentally applying one conceptual category from a source domain to a target domain is called *mapping*. Mapping inevitably entails applying one concept to another; that is, we map one concept onto another, as we do when we map the perception of sight onto the cognitive concept of understanding. According to Fauconnier, "mappings between domains are at the heart of the unique human cognitive faculty of producing, transferring, and processing meaning" (2003: 1); moreover, most mappings occur on an unconscious level (2003: 1–2). "A mapping, in the most general mathematical sense, is a correspondence between two sets that assigns to each element in the first a counterpart in the second" (Fauconnier 2003: 1). To clarify, when we think of one idea in terms of another, we change the nature of how we are thinking about that primary idea. Cognitive linguists sometimes refer to these ideas or concepts as *domains*; a domain thus refers to "any sort of conceptualization: a perceptual experience, a concept, a conceptual complex, an elaborate knowledge system, etc." (Langacker 2006: 31). When we map one domain onto another, we change how we have conceptualized that idea. And we are rarely aware when we map one concept (or domain) onto another.

Additionally, when we map one domain onto another, we may change how we understand it. For example, our sense that UNDERSTANDING IS VISION alters our ability to think about understanding in different terms.[3] In English we don't, for example, have metaphors about smelling a strong scent that equates with understanding. Thus, we don't say, "I *smell* what you mean," but we do say, "I *see* what you mean." An example of a playful parody of this mapping occurred when American hippies in the 1960s said, "I feel you," as a way of saying, "I see what you mean" — but the entailment UNDERSTANDING IS TOUCHING has not maintained the cultural dominance that UNDERSTANDING IS VISION has. Cognitive linguists call mapping one concept onto another in a limiting way an *entailment*; that is,

---

3. Herein, I will rely on the conventions established by Lakoff and Johnson in *Metaphors We Live By* (1980). In cognitive linguistics, metaphorical statements are set in all caps, and I will italicize metaphorical words that refer to embodiment in quotations. All italicizations are mine, unless otherwise noted.

when we think about one domain or concept in terms of another, we define, limit, and structure how we can subsequently think about it (Lakoff & Johnson 1980: 92–93). Frequently, our embodiment influences entailments; our conceptualizations are defined by and even limited by our embodied perceptions of the world.

Literature provides many examples of sighted characters mapping the embodied act of seeing onto the conceptual act of understanding. A highly visual character, such as Anne Shirley, in Lucy Maud Montgomery's *Anne of Green Gables*, is one obvious example. Anne frequently claims to "see" something when she means that she understands it. When she pauses to think about something, she says "let me *see*" (Montgomery 2004: 19, 20, 36, 203, italics added), and when she can't understand something, she says, "I don't *see* why" (83, 225, 242, italics added). Anne, and her bosom friend, Diana, and Anne's guardian Marilla all three use the embodied metaphor "I don't *see* how" when they mean "I don't know how" (227, 203, 220, italics added). Marilla first explains that she understands Matthew is determined to adopt the orphaned Anne by saying, "Matthew was terrible set on it. I could *see* that, so I gave in" (9, italics added). Anne explains earnestly to Matthew what an affliction her red hair is, "Now you *see* why I can't be perfectly happy" (18, italics added). In this use of the word "see," Matthew can both literally view the redness of Anne's hair and metaphorically understand why it makes her unhappy.

Significantly, when Marilla begins to grow physically blind, Anne makes a decision to sacrifice her own dreams — the ambitions she has been "*look*[ing] forward to" achieving in order to become Marilla's caretaker (275, italics added). Anne tells her guardian, "When I left Queen's my future seemed to stretch out before me like a straight road. I thought I could *see* along it for many a milestone. Now there is a bend in it" (293, italics added). In this construction, she overtly connects thinking and seeing: "I *thought* I could *see*." Preparing her for this type of sacrifice has been her dedicated teacher, Miss Stacy, who has agreed to "stay and *see* you through," making her own sacrifices to help those she loves — and Miss Stacy is the teacher who has taught Anne to become a better writer through an economy of words, which Anne has gotten so used to now that she can perceive her writing differently: "I *see* it's so much better" (238, 246 italics added). Anne understands well that her duty lies at Green Gables and that she can still continue her ambition to be a writer, in part because her writing has improved. But she uses an embodied metaphor of vision to define her growth, some variation on the phrase, "I see." Anne has mapped sight so thoroughly onto understanding that she can no longer separate the two concepts in her own speech — or how she articulates her own cognitive processes.

Lakoff and Johnson (1999) demonstrate that the metaphors we use shape how we process and conceptualize information, and they show how our thought processes are shaped by language use from a very early age. Children's earliest experience of metaphor comes from a process called *conflation*, in which they learn to associate a physical feeling — such as being held — with a metaphor, as we tell a child when we say in English, "I am holding you in my heart" (Lakoff & Johnson 1999: 46). We know what it is to be physically held; we have learned that the concept "heart" serves metaphorically as the site in our bodies in which we store emotions. Thus, we understand the embodied metaphor of being *held in someone's heart*. These types of experiences throughout our childhoods lead to conflations that, in turn, cause us to participate in a widespread use of metaphors. Moreover, cognitive linguists have demonstrated that "The 'associations' made during the period of conflation are realized neurally in simultaneous activations that result in permanent neural connections being made across the neural networks that define conceptual domains" (Lakoff & Johnson 1999: 46). That is, throughout our childhoods, as we learn to think about concepts in certain terms, our brains neurally structure these concepts in subsequent years, so that our cognition continues to be bound by the associations we learned in our childhoods. One example would be the concept that "UP IS GOOD"; in English, we employ such phrases as "things are looking *up*" or "I feel *up*beat," using physical directionality to talk about emotional cheer (Lakoff & Johnson 1980: 50). As we grow, our cognition continues to build around these types of embodied associations, which in turn serves to structure our conceptualizations. As Lakoff and Johnson put it, "We acquire a large system of primary metaphors automatically and unconsciously simply by functioning in the most ordinary of ways in the everyday world from our earliest years. We have no choice in this" (1999: 47).

Take, for example, the spatial relationship involved in the embodied metaphor of *growing up*. We refer to children as "growing up" because they literally do grow upwards in space. When my elder son grew thirteen centimeters (five inches) in one year, I was not being particularly metaphorical in saying, "My son is growing *up*." He literally was growing upwards. But in the 1970s, when my mother disciplined my teenaged self by telling me, "Oh, grow *up*," she was using an embodied metaphor. I had already achieved my full height of 171 centimeters (5'7"), so I had no way to grow "upwards" anymore. Instead, my mother had mapped the spatial relationship of upwards growth onto the concept of maturation to create an embodied metaphor: growing up. We use the same embodied metaphor when we distinguish children from "grown-ups." We usually don't mean something like, "this group of adults is physically taller than those short children"; we mean "this group of older people is more mature than that group of younger people." Nonetheless, we have still employed an embodied metaphor that is spatial.

The entailments on that phrase "grown up" are legion. For example, we imply that growth is desirable when we tell an adolescent, as my mother did, to "just grow up." In addition, the idea of growth being good is linked to another set of spatial metaphors, "UP IS GOOD," which creates a complex set of associations. It is good to be able to grow tall enough to reach the light switch or sit in the front seat of a car or qualify to ride the roller coaster at the amusement park. And it is also good to be grown up enough that other people depend on one's maturity, reliability, and logic — which is what we mean when we compliment a colleague by saying behind her back, "She is so sane. She is such a *grown-up!*" The spatial metaphor "UP IS GOOD" entails the embodied metaphor of "GROWING UP" in such a way that *not* growing up has negative connotations. We accuse immature people of refusing to grow up; Peter Pan is their poster child precisely because he refuses to "grow up." Accusing an adult of not having grown up is a complicated metaphor — and a stinging insult.

Growth is a complicated concept, but as I hope to demonstrate, our understanding of this concept is sometimes entailed by the way we map embodiment onto the concept of growth. Moreover, the complex nature of the growth metaphor affects the field of adolescent literature because, unlike children's literature, adolescent literature is a genre in which it is almost always assumed that maturation is both necessary and positive.[4] Children's literature allows for texts that celebrate childhood without insisting on the protagonist's growth, and, too, being a child in children's literature is often described with positive metaphors. For example, Jonathan Cott asserts that "Children's literature … helps us to wake up" (1981:xxii), while Jerry Griswold analyzes children's literature in terms of "lightness" (2006:75–100) and "aliveness" (2006:103–122). Hollindale describes children's literature in terms of "childness," which he defines as "the quality of being a child — dynamic, imaginative, experimental, interactive and unstable. It is by our childness that we grow" (1997:46). Hollindale — like Cott and Griswold — demonstrates that existing in a life stage called "childhood" is often celebrated in children's books. But with the notable exception of certain series books, adolescent literature — whether written about adolescents and marketed to adults or focused on teenagers in a YA novel — is a genre saturated with conceptualizations of growth that imply growth is inevitable, necessary, sometimes painful, and must lead to adulthood.

Embodied metaphors of growth in literary criticism

As I have noted, the embodied metaphor of *growing up* permeates adolescent literature, as do a number of other embodied metaphors. Children and adolescents grow in many ways, including physically and psychologically — that is,

---

4. Melissa Sara Smith (2010) notes an exception when she analyzes the nostalgia (and grief) about growing up inherent within adolescent literature.

both emotionally, and cognitively. Even those forms of growth that are not visible, however, such as emotional and cognitive growth, are still embodied experiences because they occur within that part of the human body referred to as *the brain*. Perhaps this is why many authors represent these types of maturation with embodied metaphors that compare mental growth processes to physical experiences — that is, many authors map embodiment onto maturation by employing embodied metaphors to describe psychological growth in children's and adolescent literature. This tendency to structure growth, and especially psychological growth, in embodied terms serves at least two purposes: authors can use discourse — that is, language itself — to help readers perceive psychological growth by supplying physical images that readers readily understand. Even more important, these embodied metaphors reveal the interconnection between mind and body. Since all brains are embodied, so is all growth — whether that growth is physical or psychological. And because we have so thoroughly internalized embodied metaphors as part of our cognitive structure, most authors for young people cannot help but employ images of embodiment to describe maturation metaphorically. Herein, I analyze those metaphors used to describe maturation that emerge from our bodies. That is, I will examine a wide variety of embodied metaphors of growth, first as they are deployed by various literary critics and then in the next section as they are deployed in one fictional example, Mark Twain's *Adventures of Huckleberry Finn* (1885). As with my earlier example from *Anne of Green Gables*, I employ *Huckleberry Finn* both because it is widely known and because embodied metaphors recur throughout the text. But first, I explore the embodied metaphors on which literary critics rely as a way to demonstrate how frequently concepts of psychological growth are entailed by embodiment.

One fairly common metaphor of adolescent growth in literary criticism is the idea that growth itself is a journey. Mark Turner analyzes the relationship between "progress" and "journey" with the specific metaphor "MENTAL PROGRESS IS A JOURNEY" (1991: 204). Lakoff and Johnson analyze the metaphor, "LONG-TERM ACTIVITIES ARE JOURNEYS" (1999: 193), arguing that this metaphor proliferates because we have no way of thinking about the passage of time in any other way than by employing metaphors (1999: 166). The journey is an embodied, physical process — the body itself moves from point A to point B — but maturation does not, literally, require that anyone take a trip anywhere. As Lakoff and Turner point out, the common metaphor that LIFE IS A JOURNEY sets up the following metaphorical expectations:

- The person leading a life is a traveler.
- His purposes are destinations.
- The means for achieving purposes are routes.

- Difficulties in life are impediments to travel.
- Counselors are guides.
- Progress is the distance traveled.
- Things you gauge your progress by are landmarks.
- Choices in life are crossroads.
- Material resources and talents are provisions. (Lakoff & Turner 1989: 3–4)

Lakoff and Turner invite us to recognize that the metaphor LIFE IS A JOURNEY allows for the fact that there are many types of journeys and many types of destinations, so the metaphor can be used flexibly, depending on the context; moreover, the complexity of the journey is enhanced by "the structure of our knowledge of journeys and our ability to map from that structured knowledge to a conception of life" (61).

Critics of the genre of the *Bildungsroman* (sometimes referred to as the coming-of-age novel) thus impose these metaphors of embodied journeys onto the idea of maturation frequently, although they also rely on other embodied metaphors as well. For instance, in the 1820s, Karl Morgenstern, the first known critic to use the term *Bildungsroman*, implied the genre involves a passage or journey through time because it portrays "the *Bildung* of the hero in its beginnings and growth to a certain stage of completeness" (Labovitz 1987: 2). In explaining the frequency with which journeys occur within the *Bildungsroman*, Susanne Howe observes that the pattern, which includes the motif of "man and his meeting with the world," makes a compelling plotline because "it implied the gaining of experience — usually the author's own — at the hands of the world, and therefore it involved action, travel" (1966: 1).[5] Critics often describe this metaphorical journey in terms of stages that must be visited or traveled through. As Tennyson observes, in the mid-1860's, Wilhelm Dilthey defined the *Bildungsroman* as a novel that "examines a regular course of development in the life of the individual; each of its *stages* has its own value and each is at the same time the basis of a *higher stage*" (Tennyson 1968: 136, italics added). Dilthey adds to the metaphor of a journey the notion of ascent; positive growth is both outwards and upwards (because, UP IS GOOD). Melitta Gerhard also wrote in 1926 about the *Bildungsroman* as if it were a physical journey: the novel centers around a character's "gradual maturing and growth in the world, in whatever way the goal of his *journey* may be construed" (Tennyson 1968: 138, italics added).[6] Following in 1958, Hans Heinrich Borcherdt

---

5. Although not specifically writing about the *Bildungsroman*, Jerry Griswold demonstrates how reliant on Joseph Campbell's monomyth the archetypal connection between "journey-quest" and "growth" is (1992: 4). See also Stephens and MacCallum (1998: 101–108).

6. I rely on G.B. Tennyson for his translations of Dilthey, Borcherdt, and Gerhard because his German is far more proficient than mine.

described the *Bildungsroman* as "a reasonably *direct line* from error to truth, from confusion to clarity, from uncertainty to certainty, from, as the Germans have it, nature to spirit" (Tennyson 1968: 137, italics added). Morgenstern's early definition of the *Bildungsroman*, as subsequently developed by Dilthey, Gerhard, Borcherdt, and Tennyson, captures the sense of development as a staged journey, while also demonstrating the tendency for us to think of human lives as something that can be metaphorically sculpted or organically grown:

> Briefly stated, Dilthey's main points about the *Bildungsroman* are five: (1) the idea of *Bildung*, or formation, cultivation, education, shaping of a single main character, normally a young man; (2) individualism, especially the emphasis on the uniqueness of the protagonist and the primacy of his private life and thoughts....; (3) the biographical element....; (4) the connection with psychology, especially the then-new psychology of development; and (5) the ideal of humanity of the full realization of all human potential as the goal of life. (Tennyson 1968: 136)

In Dilthey's terms, spiritual *Bildung* is "formation" and "cultivation"; it is the "shaping of a single main character." Tennyson himself also adds some interesting embodied metaphors to the mix when he writes that the *Bildungsroman* is "the novel of harmonious *cultivation* of the whole personality," but he considers the most interesting novels in this genre to be those which portray how "the protagonist comes to a *deeper* understanding of life" (1968: 142, 140, italics added). Like Dilthey, Tennyson depicts growth with the metaphor of plant cultivation, but he also demonstrates the tendency that other critics display of depicting the human body or human mind as a container that needs to be filled, implying that the goal is for the character to have a "deeper" understanding and more knowledge, as if knowledge is a fluid poured into the empty vessel of the adolescent's empty but awaiting brain. Martin Swales actually writes about the genre as if it is alive: "the *Bildungsroman* is a novel genre which derives its very *life* from the *awareness* both of the given experiential framework of practical reality on the one hand and of the creative potential of human imagination and reflectivity on the other" (1978: 5); various German novels "constitute the transmission of a particular kind of fictional concern which is, as it were, the *breeding ground* for the high points of the German contribution to the novel form" (6); "the *Bildungsroman* figures as a *vital* fictional medium" (7, italics added in all cases).

In sum, many scholars of the *Bildungsroman* are unable to write about growth without relying on metaphors that involve either human embodiment as a container or humans who are embodied as artist or farmer or traveler.

Critics of adolescent (and children's) literature also rely on the journey metaphor in their own writing. G. Robert Stange writes that the genre involves "a young man of talents who *progresses* from the country to the city, *ascends* in the social hierarchy, and *moves* from innocence to experience" (1954: 10, italics added). John Rowe Townsend observes the ubiquity of the journey (as well as the microcosm) in literature for the young: "It may be noted that the themes of all these three books — the dangerous journey, as in *The Pilgrim's Progress*; the desert island, as in *Robinson Crusoe*; and the miniature or other imaginary world, as in *Gulliver* — have served for innumerable later books, both children's and adult, and are by no means worn out" (1983: 28). James Johnson describes the adolescent hero as someone who undergoes a "*metamorphosis*," experiencing a "*transitional period*" with a mind "half-child, half-adult"; the genre emphasizes "*flight and attempted escape* as a consequence of realizing one's *bodily* and spiritual *isolation*" in an "unending *search* for the meaning of existence" (1959: 4, 7 italics added). Mordecai Marcus considers the journey to be inevitable because the protagonist experiencing initiation must undergo a transformation with a specific directional orientation: "this *change* must *point or lead him towards* an adult world" (1960: 222, italics added). According to David Peck, the initiation "takes us *from* the protected and ideal world of childhood *into* the real and often discouraging … world of adulthood…. In every case there is a *loss* of innocence and a consequent *gain* of experience" (1989: xix, italics added). In an article entitled "The *Journey* Inward," Anne Scott MacLeod, traces the increasing tendency of YA authors in the 1960s and 1970s to focus on inward growth rather than external quests in novels that depict "getting *through* the teen years to the equally undefined *territory beyond*" (1997: 126, italics added). Moreover, Kent Baxter traces how often since the turn of the twentieth-century adolescence has been depicted as a "*path* by which the child becomes an adult" (2008: 11, italics added). The journey metaphor is pervasive in the literary criticism of adolescent literature.

Buckley, who has written what is probably the most-cited definition of the *Bildungsroman* pattern in English, describes the *Bildungsroman* in terms of the journey (1974: 17–18), but he also writes about growth in terms of embodied processes such as sculpting and art: "Insofar as the word *Bildung* itself is related to *Bild* and *Bildnis*, it may connote 'picture' or 'portrait' as well as 'shaping' or 'formation'" (13–14). Sculpting and painting are both embodied processes that require brains, arms, and hands to work together to create the finished product. He also demonstrates the tendency to add metaphors of constraint to those that depict growth. For example, "As he reaches maturity the hero of the *Bildungsroman* … will typically feel his *bondage*, the multiple *constraints* of living" (281, italics added).[7]

Metaphors of constraint are frequent, too, in feminist accounts of female development. Indeed, Barbara White considers constraint and conflict to be the *sine qua non* of the fiction of female development:

---

7. Lakoff and Turner identify the following metaphors as common in literature: LIFE IS BONDAGE and LIFE IS A BURDEN (1989: 23, 25).

> There is a constant sense of *deja vu* [sic] when girls envy their brothers, when they express outrage at being molested by a man, when they try to avoid doing housework, or when they say they feel *enclosed, imprisoned, stuffed in a sack, or under a bell jar.* In novel after novel the protagonist is in conflict over her gender identity.... In her rebellion against growing up female the adolescent heroine is usually *besieged* from within and without. She is *hampered* both by the strength of social institutions designed to prepare her for a subordinate role and by her own inner conflicts and passivity. (1985: 137, italics added)

White's metaphors of constraint even incorporate the bellicose image of besiegement. Lissa Paul is similarly direct in her metaphors of entrapment: she uses the metaphor of constraint to describe females in children's and adolescent literature as physically, linguistically, and economically entrapped (1987: 187–188).

The journey metaphor is nonetheless still present in the literary criticism of female development: "Plot elements from the *Bildungsroman* may be put to a different use; for instance, the *journey*, which in the *Bildungsroman* is a vehicle for *vertical* development, may become in the novel of adolescence an *oscillation* from side to side" (White 1985: 13, italics added). Together with Annis Pratt, White also identifies female growth as shrinking: they argue that the most conservative fictions of female development commend the protagonist for "'growing *down*' rather than 'growing *up*'" (Pratt 1981: 14, italics added). The growth of the hero is "halted," with the female *Bildungsroman* "trac[ing] the heroine's growth *up* to her physical maturity to the *neglect of her potential* for further development," so according to Esther Kleinbord Labovitz, the nineteenth-century female protagonist is on a foreshortened journey in which her growth is always stunted; her "*quest* for self-development ... *disappears* by virtue of the ambivalent endings (1987: 5, italics added). Focusing on post-colonial novels, Christine Wick Sizemore defines the female *Bildungsroman* as "the young girls' *search* for adult roles amid ... conflicting demands" (2002: 21, italics added). Elizabeth Abel, Marianne Hirsch, and Elizabeth Langland (1983) define female development in terms of the journey, albeit an interior-oriented voyage in which the search involves introspection; their book devoted to the topic is entitled *The Voyage In*. All of these feminist critics depict growth by relying on metaphors of physical movements, such as growth up or down, (or growth that is halted), oscillation, and/or the journey, the voyage, the quest, or the search.

In Patricia Meyer Spacks' analysis, adolescence — especially female adolescence — involves a dynamic of power and powerlessness in the context of inter-generational conflict, such that the female adolescent character becomes a metaphor for the "twentieth-century phenomena of alienation and experienced powerlessness for all ages, all conditions: the adolescent girl thus provides a metaphor for her elders as well as, on occasion, a target for their vindictiveness"

(1981: 52). In Spacks' model, growth is conducted in competition with controlling adults, so maturation becomes a matter of *"winning* and *losing,"* although "[t]he adolescent can win only conditionally as long as he or she remains adolescent" (195, 196, italics in the original). According to Spacks, adolescence is defined in terms of "[e]xploration, becoming, growth, pain" (4) — all of which are embodied metaphors, and at least one of which, exploration, also ties into the notion of growth as a journey. Girls gain power with their sexuality; boys with their ability to increase their capital gains (196) — but adult authors include adolescents in novels not necessarily written for young readers to "[expose] the *barrenness* of the adult world" (288, italics added). Spacks piles metaphors on metaphors: growth involves gaining or losing something; girls themselves are metaphors for powerlessness; adolescents are contrasting metaphors for the barren landscape of adulthood.

Other critics demonstrate that males, too, experience growth as constraint and loss — as an almost tangible sense of lost freedom, which Buckley observes: "quiet intuition may restore as much of [the protagonist's] *lost freedom* as is still recoverable" (281, italics added). For Leslie Fiedler, growth is not an upward trajectory; it is a downward fall from grace, which he describes in terms that demonstrate his immersion in Judeo-Christian ideology: "An initiation is a *fall* through knowledge to maturity; behind it there persists the myth of the Garden of Eden, the assumption that to know good and evil is to be done with the joy of innocence and to take on the *burdens* of work and childbearing and death" (1958: 22, italics added). And I myself, for all I have insisted in an earlier work (Trites 2000) that adolescent literature is defined in terms of adolescents becoming adults more by learning about social structures of power than by growth, even I have written about the genre using an ongoing series of embodied metaphors about forms of containment, such as "curtailment" (14), "prison" (24), "pressure" (43), "powerless[ness]" (27, 76, 79, 119), and "repression" (16, 55, 141).

Geta Leseur makes a compelling case for the black *Bildungsroman* as a genre particularly given to issues of constraint, loss, darkness, and even blindness. In a study entitled *Ten is the Age of Darkness*, Leseur argues that the black *Bildungsroman* shares with the white *Bildungsroman* the same narrative patterns of journey, education, dealing with parents, finding a mate, and a vocation. But in the black *Bildungsroman*, the hero finds a guide or mentor who teaches the youth "a philosophy of darkness" (1995: 18).

> As the hero or heroine reaches maturity, each will typically feel *bondage*, the multiple *constraints* of living, often represented by the *pressures* of the cruel city. The creative *vision*, however, restores freedom, and the child's questioning sense of outward things is *parent* of the understanding child; the *quickened* imagination *outlives* the troubled "season of youth." (1995: 20, italics added)

Leseur acknowledges that gender affects the genre: "The Black boy who *discovers* himself discovers that he is *isolated* in an alien society, where the *journey* to manhood is painful and will continue to be so, as long as he resides in a racially charged society" (100, italics added), while the black female *Bildungsroman* "depict[s] woman's internal struggle to *unravel* the immense complexities of racial identity, gender definition, and the *awakening* of their sexual being" (101, italics added). Leseur demonstrates that protagonists in these novels are invariably "poised for *travel* to another life" (194, italics added); motifs of being beaten permeate the genre: the protagonists are not only "*beaten* in the old slave tradition," but they are also "metaphorically 'beaten up' in their lives" (199, italics in the original). Thus, although the literary critic of the traditional (white, male) *Bildungsroman* frequently depicts growth employing both positive and negative metaphors of embodiment, critics writing about marginalized groups (people of color, women) tend to employ more negative than positive images of embodiment. In these cases, metaphors of growth represent the limitations of human embodiment — and of human growth.

Nevertheless, as Barbara White observes, novels about growth rarely focus solely on physical maturation. "It is significant that of the major themes critics have identified in the novel of adolescence, only one — obsession with physical change — has any direct relation to biological maturation" (1985: 14). Fictions of female development have a greater emphasis on embodiment — both as maternal body (White 1985: 17) and as a body situated within the "green world" of nature (Pratt 1981: 17). Katherine Dalsimer defines physical maternity as the most significant aspect of female development. "These works of literature suggest that at every phase of female adolescence, and in every aspect — from the beginning changes in the contours of the body, in the *awakening* of sexual feeling, in the forming of new friendships and in love, in the making of those choices that will define, for that individual, her womanhood — all of these developments take place in the context of this continuing relationship" with the mother (1986: 140, italics added). Fictions of female development require the female to be aware of herself — and her mother — as a reproducing body. Yet when Pratt (1981) and Dalsimer (1986) talk about maternity, they are speaking literally, not figuratively, about reproduction. Their metaphors, however, tend to involve the type of physical metaphors that critics also use to describe male patterns: women *awaken* to sexual feeling (Dalsimer 1986: 140, italics added); the "literary tradition" of female novels is "a *barren* one" (White 1985: 21, italics added); the self has "*roots*" in a plant metaphor that evokes the idea of maturation as a process of cultivation (Pratt 1981: 1, italics added).

Thus, critics describing literary patterns of adolescent growth typically rely on one or more of the following embodied metaphors: (1) growth occurs while living a life as if it followed a path on a journey, often in quest of a goal; (2) growth involves filling a life (particularly the mind) as if it were a container; (3) growth entails cultivating a life as if it were a plant; (4) growth can be a matter of molding or forming a life as if it were a sculpture; (5) growth is moving upwards, as if a life could ascend into the sky or heavens; (6) growth is like awakening, as if infancy and/or childhood are times of unconsciousness or sleep; (7) growth comes from experiencing a revelation, as if life could be perceived as a visible object; or — in more negative terms, (8) growth is a sort of freeing from imprisonment, as if childhood is a cage (or conversely, increased constraint, as if adulthood represents imprisonment); or (9) as a loss, as if growth is a sacrifice or shrinking or a matter of losing something specific, such as innocence. All of these metaphors share in common their basis in the physical experience of the human body. Bodies go on journeys; bodies are containers that can be filled and emptied. Bodies grow upwards, as do plants, and although we need tools to sculpt or planes to fly, we also understand these metaphors on a visceral level.[8] We know what it is to wake and sleep; many people know what it is to see; we know what it is to be caged and to gain or lose something. These are not the only metaphors for growth on which literary critics rely (growth as a "season" would be an alternative example), but taken together, the metaphors I have traced here demonstrate how embodiment affects our conceptualizations of growth — both literal human growth and the discursive growth of narrative patterns such as that of the *Bildungsroman*. Clearly, literary critics have a pronounced tendency to conceptualize maturation in terms of human embodiment.

Fiction as an example: *Adventures of Huckleberry Finn*

Mark Twain's *Adventures of Huckleberry Finn* contains perhaps the most famous U.S. example of an adolescent whose physical and embodied journey equates to his psychological growth. Huckleberry Finn, who has been raised as a social outcast, feels uneasy with the mores of middle class society in the nineteenth-century pre-Civil War South. Eventually, he helps a friend — Jim — escape from slavery. They float on a raft down the Mississippi River, hoping to take a steamboat north to freedom while experiencing many feuds, frauds, and betrayals. When Jim is recaptured into slavery, Huck decides to help his friend escape a second time, even though he believes this means sacrificing his soul for eternity. Huck's old friend Tom Sawyer, who turns up in the final chapters of the novel and proves to be more of a hindrance than a help in Jim's escape, finally reveals, however, that Jim has been free all along because his owner — Miss Watson — manumitted him,

---

8. Lakoff and Turner identify "PEOPLE ARE PLANTS" as a "basic metaphor" (1989: 5–6).

prompted by feelings of guilt that she once tried to sell him downriver. Jim has achieved his goal: he has attained freedom. But Huck can never attain the freedom he desires, which is freedom from human cruelty and corruption. As the novel ends, he flees to the Western territories, hoping to avoid the civilizing influences of middle-class society. During his journey down the river, however, he has grown out of being the type of callous lad who would play tricks on a slave to being the type of young man who would help that slave escape to freedom.

At the beginning of the novel, Huck accepts the conventional wisdom of his racist culture, most notably when he still believes that Miss Watson's moral pronouncements are valid. But she commits the betrayal that provides Huck with his traveling companion when she tries to sell her slave, Jim. Huck solidifies their relationship when he first insists that Jim flee. In this urgent message to Jim, Huck employs an embodied metaphor: "Git up and hump yourself, Jim!" (Twain 2002:75). The transitive nature of the reflexive colloquial verb "hump" demonstrates its inherent embodiment: Jim's brain needs to "hump" his body — that is, curve his back in hard work — to get the rest of his body moving (Hump, v. 2013). Significantly, Huck immediately joins his own physical plight to Jim's: "There ain't a minute to lose. They're after us!" (75). In point of fact, no one is after Huck since the town believes his dead body lies drowned in the Mississippi River. These embodied metaphors of flight, however, contribute to the primary metaphor of growth as a journey. That metaphor continues right up to the novel's conclusion, when Huck decides he will "light out for the Territory ahead of the rest" (362). In this instance, "light out" is another metaphor for escape, this time with its origin in the idea of lightening a load (Light, v. 2012). Huck will physically journey to the Western territories, but he will do so in rapid flight — as if the faster he travels, the lighter he will feel. When Huck urges Jim to escape literal slavery early in the novel by "humping it" and when Huck himself escapes the metaphorical confinement of societal conventions by "lighting out" at the end of the novel, Huck perceives freedom in terms of embodied escape. The metaphor is a compelling image that joins the concept of *freedom* with the physical ability to run away from confinement, whether that confinement is the literal embodied imprisonment of slavery or the metaphorical confinement of societal strictures.

Twain's tendency to use the colloquialism "a body" when he means "a person" further underscores how Huck's embodiment structures his perceptions and conceptualizations. For example, aboard the sinking steamboat *The Walter Scott*, Huck listens to a band of thieves and expresses his fear entirely in embodied terms: "a body couldn't breathe and hear such talk" (83). Listening to these murderous thieves, Huck is so afraid that he refers to himself as "a body" unable to breathe in the presence of such a fearsome conversation. Soon thereafter, in one of his earliest moral dilemmas, Huck has an internal debate about whether or not to reveal he is harboring a runaway slave. When he decides he cannot betray Jim, he thinks, "I see it warn't no use for me to try to learn to do right; a body that don't get *started* right when he's little, ain't got no show" (127, italics in the original). Twain's use of the colloquial term "body" as a metonym for the whole person demonstrates Huck's sense of his morality as embodied. The body cannot be separated here from its moral decisions — or its actions. Later, when he watches two rapscallions, the Duke and the King, take advantage of a young woman named Mary Jane and her family, he thinks, "It was enough to make a body ashamed of the human race" (210). Here, Huck blends his cognitive perceptions with embodied emotions, demonstrating again how Twain uses language to represent the inviolable relationship between Huck's mind and body.

Huck's understanding of religion also plays a role in his experience of morality — and moral growth — as embodied. He understands his spirituality in very literal and embodied terms. Early in the novel, he discusses the afterlife with Jim's owner, Miss Watson. They debate the relative merits of heaven and hell as if they were actual places to which the body journeys after life. Huck is bored enough that he says to her, "I wished I was there" in hell (3) — which shocks Miss Watson (3). She describes heaven as a place where "all a body would have to do there was to go around all day long with a harp and sing, forever and ever" (4). Her definition of life after death is as embodied as Huck's, what with the image of playing harps and singing, but he then reinforces the idea of spiritual growth as occurring on an embodied journey: "I couldn't see no advantage in *going* where she was going, so I made up my mind I wouldn't try for it" (4, italics added). The notion that hell is a physical place to which one journeys is echoed in the novel's most famous passage, when Huck decides "All right, then, I'll *go* to hell" (271, italics in the original). Several layers of irony accrue to this passage: most readers trained to read for irony are aware that Huck will not go to hell for helping a friend escape an institution as heinous as slavery. Most readers also understand that this decision marks Huck's moment of greatest psychological growth. Significantly, however, Huck represents his initial moral decision, "not to try" to go to heaven in terms of an embodied journey, just as he expresses his final moral decision in the active terms of going on a journey. He will physically and spiritually *go* to hell for his friend. Just as his journey down the river represents his overall growth, his decision about journeying to hell represents his spiritual growth — even though he, ironically, believes himself to be a moral back-slider. Huck then describes spiritual growth in another embodied metaphor, this time as a matter of cleanliness. As he decides whether to help Jim escape from slavery, he feels "good and all washed clean of sin for the first time I had ever felt so in my life" (269). He again feels cleansed when he meets people who assume that he is Tom Sawyer, "it was like being born again, I was so glad to find out who I was" (282). In this instance, Huck experiences rebirth in terms of an entirely new embodiment, as if his identity is solely a matter of his physical being.

Although the journey represents the most frequently employed metaphor for Huck's psychological growth in *Adventures of Huckleberry Finn*, many other images, such as rebirth and cleansing, also provide metaphors for his maturation. In yet another series of embodied metaphors, Huck presents growth as being a matter of work, that is, of physical labor. He asks, "[W]hat's the use you learning to do right, when it's troublesome to do right and ain't no trouble to do wrong, and the *wages* is just the same? I was stuck. I couldn't answer that. So I reckoned I wouldn't bother no more about it, but after this, always do whichever come *handiest* at the time" (127, italics added). When Huck uses the term "wages," he doesn't literally mean that he will be paid for his efforts; he is employing a metaphor that means here "consequences"; rather, he recognizes that the consequences of doing right will cause him as much emotional turmoil as doing wrong. The metaphor is reinforced when Huck uses the metaphor "handiest." The *Oxford English Dictionary* associates the term "handy" with manual labor that is done by hand (Handy, adj. 2012). Thus, Huck implies that moral decision-making is a matter of hard, manual labor. Huck also associates morality with a physical ailment that makes him sweat. At one point, he feels so guilty his conscience makes him feel "feverish" and "scorched" (123); eventually, Huck's "conscience got to stirring me up hotter than ever" (124). Huck's moral decision-making leads him to experience metaphorical fevers, scorching, and heat in a way that anticipates his eventual decision to go to the burning flames of hell for Jim's sake. Nevertheless, the terms are embodied, equating as they do a concept such as feeling guilty with a literal feeling of fever.

Huck's growth also includes embodied images of risk-taking, physical safety, and sight. For example, he thinks, "I reckon a body that ups and tells the truth when he is in a tight place, is taking considerable many resks; though I ain't had no experience, and can't say for certain; but it looks so to me, anyway; and yet here's a case where I'm blest if it don't look to me like the truth is better, and actuly *safer*, than a lie" (239, italics in the original). Again, Twain has used the word "body" to mean "a person," but Huck's dilemma makes him feel as if he is in a "tight place." Thus, the concept of a moral dilemma is embodied here as physical entrapment, and he conceptualizes resolving the problem as a matter of vision — "it looks so to me" — with an embodied metaphor that is used twice in the same passage. Huck's goal is to feel safety from risk, and he cannot explain that concept without tying it to his embodiment.

Conclusion

Repeatedly in *Adventures of Huckleberry Finn*, Huck explains his perceptions and experiences in conceptual terms that rely on his own embodiment. The concept of maturation is mapped onto a physical journey; the concept of redemption is mapped onto cleansing; the concept of moral decision-making is mapped onto physical labor; the concept of escaping social strictures is mapped onto physical escape. Huck cannot explain his world without using his body to do so. Lakoff and Johnson (1980) would argue that this is because, through language, his cognition is shaped by his embodied experiences. But Huck, of course, does not really have a body. He is a discursive construct — nothing more than a conceptualized character whose expression manifests itself in language alone. Twain, however, has himself relied on the embodied nature of cognition to create this character — and he knows that his readers will understand these embodied metaphors because they have experienced the conflation of mapped concepts of growth in their own language development.

Even more important for the purposes of studying adolescent literature, Twain relies on embodied metaphors in the way he represents Huck's maturation. Adolescents experience growth in very embodied ways: puberty triggers physical changes in the body that have a profound emotional effect on most people as they change from children into adolescents and then adults. Perhaps one reason that authors who write for adolescents rely on embodied metaphors to represent maturation includes the inherently embodied experience of puberty. More significant, however, are the ways that language structures our cognition so that we describe our perceptions and experiences in terms of what we know viscerally. I would argue that this is a form of epistemology that is fundamental to the adolescent experience: as children and adolescents, we know the world through our bodies and because of our bodies. Moreover, our language has structured our cognition to describe many concepts in terms of our embodiment. As a result, we understand growth — both physical change and psychological maturation — in embodied terms. Authors for children and adolescents rely on the brain's preconditioned neuro-circuitry when they map embodiment onto concepts of growth. In sum, we know everything that we know through our bodies, so our epistemology is embodied, perhaps during adolescence in very unique ways. We also use language to express what we know — and we frequently use that language to map embodied concepts onto abstract concepts.

At its most basic level, cognitive linguistics affords us the opportunity to interrogate how the metaphors we employ manipulate our epistemologies — a concept I will explore at greater length in Chapter 5. The embodied metaphors of growth that proliferate in literary criticism, however, demonstrate how impossible it is to separate psychological growth from embodiment (as it is represented discursively) in literary studies. At one level, these embodied metaphors of journey and plant cultivation and sculpting and awakening and constraint seem to belie the discursive nature of fiction, but at another level, they affirm it. Our ability to conceptualize growth is dependent on our concepts of embodiment and the language we use to think about that embodiment. Metaphors of growth demonstrate how we use the language of embodiment to ground fictional processes both cognitively and physically. Lakoff and Johnson maintain that we do so because we have no other way of knowing the world than our bodies (1980: 3). We understand fictional growth because of our own experiences with embodied growth, both physically and psychologically.

CHAPTER 2

Sequences, scripts, and stereotypical knowledge

As I have demonstrated in Chapter 1, conceptualizations about growth are often influenced and shaped by embodied metaphors. In this chapter, I will examine the relationship between embodiment and narrative structure, specifically how cognition affects various aspects of narrative, because the interplay between cognition and narratives about maturation is significant.

No one creates a text without employing either hands or mouth (or both); no one experiences a text without perceiving it through eyes or ears or fingertips. Even more important, no one experiences textuality without filtering it through memories specific to that individual but influenced by his or her cultural context — and those memories often trigger emotional responses. Cognitive narratologist David Herman defines "memory, perception, emotion" as three functions of *mind*; all are required in the process of storytelling (2007: 312). F. Elizabeth Hart describes how "the architecture and contents of the brain/mind" lend themselves to the epistemological study of "what constitutes literary knowledge and knowing" (2001: 319). How our brains process knowledge affects what our minds perceive in literary texts. The cognitive study of narrative, then, insists on a *rapprochement* between embodiment and post-structural theories of discourse. David Herman puts it this way: cognitive narratology specifically bears "on the traditions of in-quiry that locate the mind not in the heads of solitary thinkers but rather in socio-communicative activities unfolding within richly material settings" (2007: 308).

Most important to the field of adolescent literature, cognitive literary theory confronts and redefines the post-structural emphasis on discourse that has had such tremendous influence on the study of adolescent literature. Discourse is al-ways already culturally situated, and it tends to be studied as an external force, one that acts upon people to shape their subjectivities. Cognitive narratology, however, insists that the functioning of the human brain also plays a role in cultural produc-tion. That is, human thought is shaped by both external (discursive) and internal (cognitive) forces. As Karen Coats argues, *childhood* is a discursive construct — as is *adolescence* —, but *children* and *adolescents* are embodied individuals — and our field does well to recognize how such discursive concepts are inevitably linked to embodiment (2001: 148–153).

In other words, cognitive narratology provides a way to explore narrative as the product of embodied beings while it simultaneously affects those embodied beings, specifically allowing us to investigate how embodiment influences both the author's discursive creation of story and its subsequent meaning-making as a function of the reader's cognition in terms of language use, memory, perception, and emotion. Herein, I will explore three aspects of cognition pertinent to maturation in adolescent literature — stereotypical knowledge, sequences, and scripts — all of which are both biophysically and culturally situated. Gene Luen Yang's *American Born Chinese* (2006) demonstrates how complex the relationships between stereotypical knowledge and scripts of growth are, while Margaret Mahy's *Memory* (1987) and Jay Asher's *Thirteen Reasons Why* (2007) openly problematize memory and its cognitive role in the storying process. At stake are interpretive strategies that acknowledge embodied adolescent growth within the culturally-defined discourses of adolescent literature.

Sequences, scripts, and stereotypical knowledge

A concept linking embodiment to cognition is the idea of *scripts* as a function of *experiential repertoires*. According to Herman, our brain stores repeated physical actions as "structured repertoires of expectations about current and emergent experiences" that occur in two types: *static repertoires* and *dynamic repertoires* (2002:89). Objects that remain stable over time constitute the domains of our static repertoires, so this type of memory helps us distinguish a container from a plant or an adolescent from an adult. Dynamic repertoires, on the other hand, involve how we use domains to understand processes. Relying on the discourse of computer science, cognitive narratologists refer to processes, or any short series of events, as a *sequence*. For example, entering a house and eating porridge are typical sequences that involve predicable processes. Events in a sequence happen in a standard order: first someone is outside a house; then in the sequence, she crosses the threshold. In a second sequence, she enters the house. Each process, each movement, each action comprises a sequence.

Scripts, then, are dynamic repertoires comprised of a series of sequences. According to Marek Oziewicz, "scripts are kinds of memory structure, paradigmatic stories, serving as a way 'to store knowledge that we have about certain situations'.... They form the basis of human understanding" (2011:35); Oziewicz draws this definition from the context of Knowledge Structure Theory, an Artificial Intelligence (AI) theory advanced by Roger Schank. A script "is a structure that describes an appropriate sequence of events in a particular context.... a script is a predetermined, stereotyped sequence of actions that defines a well-known situation" (Schank & Abelson 1975: 151). Entering a house and sitting in three different chairs, for example, involves several sequences (entering, sitting, standing, sitting again, etc.); eating from three bowls of porridge involves three more sequences. But we know one particularized version of the script this way: "Goldilocks entered the house. First she sat in three chairs; then she ate from three bowls of porridge." A script is "how a sequence of events is expected to unfold.... Scripts represent a sequence of events that take place in a time sequence" (Mercadal 1990: 255). From the perspective of cognitive narratology, the idea that the process is unfolding in an *expected* way is central to the idea of the script.

Moreover, dynamic repertoires are one of the brain's many forms of shorthand: rather than remembering the details of every set of behaviors we've ever experienced (such as going to the dentist or the events of every school day), we remember standard procedures conceptually and in generalized terms. Neurotypical brains store *stereotypical knowledge* about routine processes as a matter of efficiency (Herman 2002: 89). We don't remember every event that happens every time we go to the grocery store, for example, but we do remember the pattern of the grocery store: arriving outside the store, entering the store, getting a shopping cart, etc. Herman describes "stereotypical knowledge" as events that are repeated in such a way that we do not need to remember every repetition of the action. For example, most school days have a predictable pattern, so our brains store "the events of a typical school day" as "stereotypical knowledge" rather than remembering every single minute and day that we spend in school (Herman 1997: 1047–1048). Standard metaphorical mappings, such as "GROWTH IS A JOURNEY," are thus also a form of stereotypical knowledge. Cognitive narratologists, as Herman defines himself, argue that our brains rely on this shorthand as a matter of cognitive efficiency, so that we need not store in our memories every event or detail of every concept that we experience (2007: 306). Rather, we remember most concepts as stereotypical knowledge — that is, as generalized patterns of conceptualization, such as "GROWTH IS A JOURNEY" or "MAKING A MORAL DECISION IS LABOR."

Cognitive narratologists argue that embodied experiences, such as shopping or attending school, influence our ability to understand narratives because our brains know how to transform the basic unit (or "domain") of dynamic repertoires into story scripts that are tied to concepts. Thus, scripts are "knowledge representations" stored in the neurological cells of memory as finite groupings of causally and chronologically ordered actions; we learn stories because we remember certain events as sequentially standardized (Herman 2002: 90). Scripts can be as short as "what happens at a 4-way STOP sign" or as long as a fully-developed narrative pattern, such as "what happens in a standard love triangle." Our brains understand, for example, that stories with three characters — such as "The Three Bears" — will involve a series of dynamic repertoires (sitting in chairs, eating porridge) that are organized by a script that I call "the Script of Three." That is, we know from experience that the third character or third action in many groupings of three will be the character who changes the pattern, in this case, eating porridge that is "just right" or finding Goldilocks in bed: "And there she is!" Moreover, as John Stephens argues, anticipating and completing the script within a narrative enhances the reading experience: "When readers recognize the beginning sequence of a script, they anticipate what is to come and derive satisfaction from how the text expands the script by completing or varying the expected pattern" (2011:15). All narratives rely on readers' cognitively stored scripts, but the scripts can be varied to create an infinite number of story-lines.

Stephens demonstrates additionally that within the cognitive category of experiential repertoires, scripts are comprised from *schemas*, which he defines as follows: "Generally, a schema consists of a network of constituent parts, and the stimulus evokes the network and its interrelations, especially what is normal and typical about that network.... Whereas a schema is a static element within our experiential repertoire, a script is a dynamic element, which expresses how a sequence of events or actions is expected to unfold" (2011:14). By way of example, Stephens describes either a dog on a frayed leash or a running cat as a schema stored in our memories; when the dog breaks the leash and chases the cat, we experience a script of stereotypical knowledge: what happens when "*dog chases cat*" (14–15, italics in the original). Stephens' use of the term "schema" corresponds to Herman's term "static repertoire." Both are ways of identifying static concepts stored in the brain as stereotypical knowledge.

Cognitive narratologists are effectively employing Vladimir Propp's basic idea of a story function by expanding it to ask how linguistic and semiotic phenomenon within the story, such as metaphors and cultural narratives, influence the reader's "co-creat[ion]" of a text (Herman 2002:98). Vladimir Propp ascribes to the dramatis personae of a fairy-tale a *function*; that is, the function is an analysis of what a character does in the way that that character "performs the same action" in every tale (1968:20). The issue is a structural one, according to Propp; that is, it is a "structural feature" (22), and he identifies his work as "morphology," that is, the study of parts (xxv). Lévi-Strauss identifies Propp's idea of the function as the "constituents of the tale," the "various plot actions" as those specific actions work together to create the plot (1984:170). A function is "act, behavior, action" (76); moreover, "[a] function is designated simply by the name of an action: 'interdiction,' 'flight,' and so forth" (170). Where Propp's idea of the "function" differs from cognitive narratology's idea of the "script" is in where the analysis lies. Propp identifies function only as a textual feature and does not acknowledge the necessity of human cognition for the function to be recognized. In other words, Propp does not acknowledge that the memory of stereotypical knowledge is essential for a reader to recognize what he calls *function* (but a cognitive narratologist would call *script*, acknowledging the role of human cognition in the completion of story-meaning.)

So how, specifically, does embodiment affect the reader's ability to discern dynamic repertoires strung together to create scripts? All scripts rely on an individual's cognitive acts of perception and memory, which acts are both embodied in a brain. For example, what some critics call archetypes — for example, the monomyth of quest and initiation — are effectively stored in the brain as scripts. But that monomyth could not exist without embodied understandings of conceptual domains, such as birth, death, and rebirth; nor could it exist without a cultural dynamic that privileges that particular set of scripts. In cognitive narratology, scripts gain significance both in how they rely on stereotypical conceptual knowledge and how they vary that pattern. The narratological study of scripts in adolescent literature, then, might well analyze the intersection between standard scripts (such as "love triangles") and how the embodied adolescent characters involved will influence the adolescent reader's cognitive experience of that script. When readers bring to the text an expectation that an adolescent character will grow, they are using their own stereotypical knowledge (stored in their memories) to anticipate a script of maturation, one that has likely been influenced by the pattern of the *Bildungsroman*.

As early as the mid-1980s, some critics were puzzling through a basic understanding of scripts without necessarily employing that term. Lois Kuznets, for example, analyzes a series of novels that "produced only a layer of realism imposed upon a stereotypical structure, which in turn rested upon an archetypal base" (1984–85: 148). Citing her work, Perry Nodelman draws the conclusion that the "apparent sameness" of children's and adolescent novels results from a recurring set of themes in children's fiction, especially those that explore opposing ideas, such as "freedom and constriction, home and exile, escape and acceptance" (1985: 20). Kuznets and Nodelman are demonstrating two of the principles of scripts: scripts rely on stereotypical knowledge, and authors change or vary the script to affect the reader's specific emotional responses. However, scripts are usually based in embodied experience. Our memories store stereotypical knowledge based on what our bodies do. Thus, Nodelman (1985) can perceive repeated themes such as freedom/constriction or home/exile, but he does not identify that authors depend on child and adolescent readers to understand those scripts as a function of embodied stereotypical knowledge. Young readers know from embodied experiences what constriction is; they also know from their bodies what it means either to be at home or away from it. Authors for the young thus rely heavily on embodiment and visceral memory when they string scripts together to create narratives with protagonists who grow, which novels such as *American Born Chinese, Memory*, and *Thirteen Reasons Why* demonstrate.

Scripts and stereotypical knowledge in *American Born Chinese*

If we were to reduce scripts to their lowest common denominator, we would consider them to be our brain's very efficient way of storing processes as stereotypical knowledge. And at their most basic level, we could use the concept of scripts to analyze those aspects of any story that rely on the brain's stereotypical knowledge for the completion of the story. For example, myriad scripts intertwine to create the three subplots of Gene Yang's *American Born Chinese*, which combines the Chinese myth of the Monkey King with stories about a lonely second-generation Chinese-American boy, Jin, and an American boy, Danny, who is embarrassed by his Chinese cousin, Chin-Kee. The novel is depicted in graphic narrative form, which complicates even further how scripts are intertwined in the story because some of the scripts are told pictorially while others are told alphagraphically — and most of the scripts rely on a multi-media combination of both visual and alphagraphic semiotics.

The story opens with a picture of gods and goddesses having a dinner party, and that picture itself contains many scripts based in stereotypical knowledge. In one quadrant of the page, a sequence of women smiling over peaches appears. In another quadrant, a man smiles menacingly at a pretty woman. Two different conversations are occurring: "Your peaches are looking especially plump today, my dear," one old man tells a young woman attending the party, and a war god gloats to another, "I don't mean to boast, but that thunderstorm I put together last night impressed even myself" (Yang 2006: 7). The sequences in this picture are easy to identify because we have basic stereotypical knowledge about what happens at parties and even more narrow ideas, like what peaches are — what they taste like and how to eat them. We also understand that a script is occurring: the old man is making a sexual innuendo as he flirts with the pretty young woman, while in another testosterone-laden act, the war god is verbally sparring with another warrior. Yang is relying on so many forms of stereotypical knowledge in this one picture alone that to count them all would be tedious, but he knows as an author that he does not need to spell out for his readers what peaches are or how alpha-male behavior unfolds. He knows he can trust readers to supply that information from their own stereotypical knowledge.

Indeed, on the next few pages, ideas of masculinity and dominance take on increasing significance, as the Monkey King decides to journey to heaven to join the other deities in their party. Following a fairly predictable script, he is denied entrance to the party, ostensibly because he has no shoes, but really because he is a monkey. The Monkey King responds in typical alpha-male fashion, by wreaking havoc on the other party-goers. Yang is spare in his use of alphagraphic language: in the six pictures of the fight, only one alphagraphic sentence appears in one dialog box: "But on second thought, he decided that perhaps saying *one word* would make him feel better" (16, italics in the original). He then says, "DIE" out loud (16), while the words "SMAK!" and "KRASH!" appear alphagraphically, embedded within the pictures themselves (17). Although the Monkey King feels temporarily gratified by his display of power, this portion of the story ends with him feeling rejected and alone. Yang relies on the reader's cognitive memory of facial gesture to convey the Monkey King's sadness.[1]

The Monkey King is creative in the way it brings together multicultural scripts that are accessible to many readers. For example, the script of the Monkey King story relies on Wu Cheng'en's *Journey to the West*, which is set in the seventh century CE, but alters the script to include the Monkey King visiting the baby Jesus after his birth. The story of the lonely second-generation Chinese-American boy Jin combines at least two scripts: Jin gains a friend, only to lose the friend in a love triangle. The most complex of *The Monkey King*'s three subplots involves the way that Jin has sold his soul to transform himself into the blond American boy named Danny. Haunting his conscience is his embarrassing (and stereotypical) cousin Chin-Kee. The character Chin-Kee plays like a character out of a situation comedy — and indeed, Yang relies on readers' stereotypical knowledge about sit coms when he frames his pictures with applause ("CLAP CLAP CLAP CLAP CLAP CLAP CLAP CLAP CLAP") and laugh tracks ("HA HA HA HA HA HA HA") (109, 110). This is an intricate device, meant to trigger readers' understanding that several of these scenes are purportedly funny — even though they rely on such cringe-inducing images as a slant-eyed, buck-toothed, queue-wearing Chinaman carrying Chinese takeout boxes as his luggage, while he exclaims with glee, "HARRO AMELLICA!" (48). These images should trigger some level of discomfort for any reader trained to understand that cultural stereotypes are offensive, but stereotypes reside within cognition as part of our stereotypical knowledge for a reason: cultural stereotypes involve thinking in patterns, not thinking in discrete and discerning individualized moments. Moreover, cultural stereotypes depend on an absence of the emotion empathy, as Danny's inability to empathize with Chin-Kee clearly illustrates.

Indeed, Bettina Kümmerling-Meibauer identifies empathy as necessary to mature "emotional competence" (2012: 130). Kümmerling-Meibauer argues that YA novelists stimulate the reader's empathy through at least two narrative strategies: foregrounding and enhancement of awareness.

---

1. For more on human gesture, especially facial gesture, in visual narrative, see Nodelman, *Words about Pictures* (1988: 101–124) and Nikolajeva, "Reading other people's minds through word and image" (2012: 273–291).

> Foregrounding refers to those literary passages and elements that are clearly marked by the author (for example: code switching, unusual lexicon, neologisms, irony, different points of view, change of typography, contradictory assertions) in order to emphasize certain emotional conditions, while enhancement of awareness applies to literary strategies, such as overstatement, enrichment and repetition, which draw the reader's attention to the text's seminal passages and assertions. (2012: 131)

Yang relies on both foregrounding and enhancement of awareness to create the stereotyped character Chin-Kee.

Cultural stereotypes are a specific type of stereotypical knowledge, which may confuse the issue here because we so frequently refer to racism with the shorthand term "stereotype." And yet, by highlighting the failure of empathy and the stereotypical thinking involved in cultural stereotypes, Yang ultimately creates the type of cognitive dissonance from which a perspective critical of these cultural stereotypes can emerge. By the end of the novel, readers have been trained to recognize that this type of short-hand knowledge and a concomitant failure of empathy lead to prejudice, discrimination, and racism. They have also come to understand how three seemingly unrelated scripts are indeed one: Jin learns from the father of the best friend he has betrayed in the love triangle that his transformation into Danny is only a self-deception. That boy's father is the Monkey King himself, who has been posing as the Chinese cousin Chin-Kee. He teaches Jin self-acceptance when he says, "I would have saved myself from *five hundred years' imprisonment* beneath a mountain of rock had I only realized how *good* it is to be a *monkey*" (223, italics in the original). The story certainly contains disturbing implications about the essentialism of race, because at the end of the day, no one can escape their inherent identity — in this case, as either a monkey or an Asian-American.[2] Yang can only tell this intricate story with such simplicity, however, because of the way he relies on readers' stereotypical knowledge to inform and complete the stories' scripts — both graphically and alphagraphically — by relying on readers' awareness and their memories.

Memory, perception, emotion and Margaret Mahy's *Memory*

While cognitive narratologist Herman defines "mind" as a matter of the interplay among "memory, perception, emotion," he also acknowledges that storytelling

---

2. This idea was first suggested to me by Susan L. Stewart and was later reinforced by a conference paper given by Mike Cadden (2012), "But you are still a monkey: *American Born Chinese* and racial justice."

depends on all three of these cognitive processes (2007:312). Perhaps no adolescent novel does a better job of delineating storytelling's dependency upon memory, perception, and emotion than Margaret Mahy's *Memory* (1987). In the opening chapter, a protest about Maori land rights turns violent, evoking how New Zealand has lost its memory about the rights of that nation's First Peoples. The plot then centers around two specific people who are struggling with their own faulty memories: an elderly woman with severe memory loss and nineteen-year-old Jonny, who is grieving the fifth anniversary of his twin sister's death. He is haunted by memories of the day she fell off a cliff to die on the rocks below. Early in the story, for example, he notices of his own cognition, "Memory had flashed at him, but its sudden pulse, densely packed with information, had gone right through him, taking everything with it into darkness on the other side" (Mahy 2002:41). As he drunkenly tries to find his old friend Bonny, who was the only person aside from himself to witness his sister's death, he accidentally ends up at the house next-door to Bonny, where a woman named Sophie lives. She has no memory at all because it seems likely that she has Alzheimer's. When Jonny recovers from his hangover and blackout enough to realize that he has stumbled into the shadow world of Sophie's lost memory, "He did not know whether to be dismayed or grateful that his memory, like that of an erratic computer, had swallowed whole great pieces of itself" (62). Indeed, he has been drinking to forget what he remembers about watching his sister die: "His head, overloaded with memories, had been naturally drawn to a memory vacuum" (64). But as much as he is tortured by his own memories, watching Sophie, he can't help wondering if it's better never to have lived "than to wind up with broken memories," living in abjection, as Sophie does (201). In a moment when he fears for her well-being, he imagines "her lying at the foot of her stairs with the very last of her memory seeping out through the crack in her skull, barely staining the wood as it soaked away for ever. There wouldn't be much mess, there was so little memory left in there" (129). Sophie can tell him nothing about her past because she no longer remembers her own story. Jonny finds her tragedy more haunting than his own. Without memory, people have no stories.

Underscoring the cognitive nature of memory — and its relationship to the significance of memory in the functioning of a computer — Jonny notices that a computer company named *Cognito Systems* stands close to Sophie's house (40, italics in the original). Blending the idea of "cognition" and the idea of being "incognito" — which, in some ways, seems to be an accurate description of the identity loss involved in Alzheimer's — the computer company evokes both cognitive science's older metaphor of the brain as a computer and the importance of memory in cognition. Jonny contemplates "what would happen if he went into *Cognito Systems* and tried to order a new memory for Sophie.... Though memories were often regarded as careful files in a catalogue, Jonny now believed they could just as easily be wild stories, always in the process of being revised, updated, or having different endings written on to them" (206). As Jonny reconciles himself to his own memories, he understands that memory can be a shifting and unstable cognitive process.

Perception, too, is problematized in *Memory* as a function of storytelling. In the five years since his sister's death, Jonny has begun to delude himself that he actually pushed his sister off the cliff because she was taunting him. Her last words were, "You'll never catch up with me," and after she fell, their friend Bonny told Jonny to climb back to where she was standing, above a DANGER sign that the twins had been intentionally ignoring (196). Jonny has put these two perceptions together — of his sister's last words and Bonny's insistence that he move to where she was standing — to convince himself that Bonny must have told him to lie about where he was because she saw him push his sister. Jonny does not trust his own perceptions — and he has sought Bonny out five years later to confirm which of his two perceptions is right: either he pushed his sister to her death or he did not. "I could remember not doing it," he tells Bonny, "but I could remember doing it, too" (259). Bonny confirms that the girl "tripped. She tripped and fell" (259). But Jonny asks, "Once you start thinking something like that … how do you stop? It makes itself real" (259). He tells Bonny that the false memory, "seemed truer than a lot of other things that really were true" (270). Memory and perception — and misperceptions and false memories — become inseparable in his narrative about his own past. Jonny begins to think of the false memory as a "parasitic dream feeding on other guilty dreams" (270). Only once he separates real memories from false memories can he begin to heal and outgrow the intense emotionality of his grief (270).

Emotionology is the "system of emotion terms and concepts that people deploy rhetorically in discourse to construct their own as well as other minds," according to Herman (2007: 321–322). All cultures and subcultures create an emotionology — that is, a set of discourses by which we can talk about our brains' emotions and understand each other's emotions, as well (2007: 322). Bonny understands the emotionology of grief; she understands that Jonny is grieving; and she also understands why he is heightening his own grief with a false sense of responsibility. In contrast to Jonny, Sophie — who has lost her memory — has faltering perceptions and a limited range of emotions. She is either happy and content or frustrated and irritated. Her emotional register is limited because she no longer has memories that guide her in her culture's emotionology. Although she is still instinctively kind, she seems to have lost her empathy; that is, she does not always seem to register that Jonny has his own thoughts and emotions and perceptions and memories. She assumes that they share exactly the same limited memories she has. Although emotions are perceived on an individual level, we recognize them and name them in a communal way, according to the discourses in which our culture has immersed us.

Moreover, our perception of emotion depends on Theory of Mind, which is the ability to understand that other people have emotions, too (Preemack & Woodruff 1978: 109–110). Clearly, Sophie no longer has Theory of Mind. Lisa Zunshine asserts that Theory of Mind "makes literature as we know it possible" because reading fiction requires us "to invest the flimsy verbal constructions that we generously call 'characters' with a potential for a variety of thoughts, feelings, and desires and then to look for the 'cues' that would allow us to guess at their feelings and thus predict their actions" (2006: 10). Maria Nikolajeva argues that multi-media texts "can potentially teach even very young children to read other people's minds" (2012: 289), while Kümmerling-Meibauer asserts that YA novels trigger Theory of Mind in that they "stimulate readers to reflect upon the protagonists' emotional development and to transfer this learning process to their everyday life experiences" (2012: 138). Mahy's characters Sophie and Jonny further illustrate this point: Jonny's focalization of Sophie's inability to feel empathy reinforces what the reader knows about the importance of empathy in creating human communities.

Cognitive scientists recognize that knowledge has a communal nature. Influenced by Vygotsky's (1933) recognition that knowledge is socially-rooted, cognitive narratologists acknowledge that story, too, has what they call a *distributed* quality. As Herman observes,

> Minds are spread out among participants in discourse, their speech acts, and the objects in their material environment. From this perspective, cognition should be viewed as a supra- or transindividual activity distributed across groups functioning in specific contexts, rather than as a wholly internal process unfolding within the minds of solitary, autonomous, and de-situated cognizers.... Stories are often about shared or collaborative cognitive processes. (2007: 319)

At the root of Sophie's tragedy is the way that her loss of memory has made her unable to participate in the communal process of storytelling. She repeats stock phrases over and over, as if they are the closest she can come to remembering scripts. She tells Jonny numerous times that she remembers "just the way" he likes his tea (e. g. Mahy 2002: 53) and that it's better to tidy up the dishes before bed and that her late husband was "one of nature's gentlemen" (e.g. 120). Her memories are incomplete, and so are her scripts.

Echoing the issue of memory in this novel is the concept of muscle memory. Jonny and his twin sister were the two members of a successful tap-dancing act before her death, and Jonny still loves to tap dance. Jonny remembers how bullies had made him dance in his childhood. His "feet danced automatically at the memory of it, for they had a twitchy sub-memory of their own" (101). He also smiles with "conditioned reflex," because of his mother's frequent admonition that he smile (235), and when he confronts one of his childhood bullies as an adult, he again experiences muscle memory. "As he smiled back he felt a twitch of old, left-over terror, as people who have lost a leg are said to be able to feel the itching of toes they no longer have. But it didn't last. The memory of Nev was more frightening than the real man" (141). In one of the final scenes in the book, Bonny and Sophie watch Jonny dance, his muscle memory fully engaged and his false memories fully exorcised. Bonny and Sophie "watched him change into a surreal man whose feet stuttered like typewriters, though the story they wrote down vanished as soon as it was told. It was too shy a story — too full of contradictions which cancelled each other out — to stand being put into words" (265). The metaphor is embodied and complex. Jonny's feet have muscle memory — just as his brain muscles store memories — that enable him to tell a story. And reclaiming accurate memories has allowed him to heal, grow, and mature enough to tell himself a new life story. But although cognitive memories aid in storytelling, muscle memory is not given to the creation of a story that lasts. Muscle memory lives only in the moment, although a typewritten narrative has the possibility of enduring much longer.

Memory plays a major role in narrative. At the most basic level, without memory, we cannot remember what happened at the beginning of a story or keep the characters straight. Moreover, narrative relies on our memories of stereotypical knowledge stored cognitively as scripts. Narrative memory requires us both to have stereotypical knowledge stored in our brains and also to have a trigger that evokes that memory: "recall is a joint product of the interaction between general knowledge structures or expectancies and input information" or stimuli (Norenzayan et al 2006: 533). Thus, according to cognitive psychologists, "a narrative cannot be transmitted and achieve cultural success unless it stands the test of memory" (Norenzayan et al 2006: 531–532). Scripts, of course, reside entirely in the memory — and without that memory of scripts, stereotypical knowledge, and communal emotionology, we would be able neither to predict nor focus on the many scripts of growth in adolescent literature.

Causality, scripts, and *Thirteen Reasons Why*

Jay Asher's *Thirteen Reasons Why* is also clearly predicated on the idea of scripts — even though that is not a term Asher uses. The novel includes two narrators: Clay and Hannah. Clay listens to — and comments on — the thirteen tapes Hannah Baker has made to explain her reasons for committing suicide. Both Clay and Hannah are first-person narrators, but Hannah's voice in its tape-recorded form is the more aural and recursive one, since other characters can listen to her voice repeating the same information every time one of her tapes replays. Clay talks out loud to her voice on the tapes, but the conversation is not dialogic because Hannah can no longer answer him. Each of her thirteen reasons for killing herself involves a narrative, usually motivated by the eleven people she identifies on the tape as having affected her emotions negatively. Most of these narratives involve her embodiment, particularly in the ways she feels objectified as a female. The tapes also rely on dynamic repertoires as stereotypical knowledge patterns; that is, each of the thirteen reasons relies on one or more scripts that are culturally familiar to readers who are familiar with middle-class, suburban, Westernized high schools.

Issues of how adolescents experience embodiment in high school are central to the thirteen scripts that inform *Thirteen Reasons Why*. The first tape Hannah narrates — that is, the first script — involves a character named Justin and a variation on the "first kiss" script: Justin kisses her but then spreads rumors that she is a slut. Other tapes include the scripts of a slap that is motivated by female vs. female jealousy, a rape narrative, and a peeping Tom narrative. Moreover, another character writes a "Who's Hot/Who's Not" list and gives her the "Best Ass in the Freshman Class" award — which leads other males to feel that they have permission to objectify Hannah's body in such ways as slapping her ass or voyeuristically watching her through her bedroom window (Asher 2007: 39–40). With every chapter, Hannah narrates how that chapter's script-and-variation occurs because the specific details of her narrative alter slightly from the standard script about embodiment that high school readers have likely internalized. For example, the girl who has slapped her over female vs. female jealousy is the girl who gets date raped — while she is drunk — at a party. The script of the drunk-girl-getting-raped is also a fairly standard (and very embodied) script. What alters the script here is the fact that Hannah and the drunk girl's boyfriend (who has also been the first boy to kiss Hannah) stand by, knowing that Jessica is getting raped. They do nothing about it, which adds to Hannah's sense that her life is futile.

Each chapter is identified with one character and a standard script that plays a clear cognitive function meant to trigger the reader's conceptual domain of a certain emotion or moral dilemma. The story, however, avoids the totality of clichés that thirteen scripts could lead to by providing a variation on the standard script in each case. While I have identified only one or two conceptual domains per script, others could also be identified. When the narrator herself analyzes the emotionology involved in the script, I have quoted her words. (See Table 1).

Table 1 demonstrates Asher's reliance on stereotypical knowledge and the emotionology of high school. These scripts can be as simple as "first kiss" or as elaborate as "what happens when a girl gets in a hot tub with a known rapist." Asher, like all authors, employs scripts to trigger the reader's specific neurological responses, usually in the affective domain. For example, when one boy steals

Table 1.

Character	Script	Variation	Conceptual domain
1. Justin Foley	First kiss	He spreads rumor that Hannah is a "slut"	"Betrayal" (13) and rejection
2. Alex Standall	"Who's Hot/Who's Not" list (Hannah has "best ass")	Objectification of Hannah's body by other males	"Revenge" (40) and anger
3. Jessica Davis	Named "Worst Ass in the Freshman Class"	She slaps Hannah and ends friendship	Jealousy
4. Tyler Down	Peeping Tom	Hannah loses sense of security at home	Invasion of privacy
5. Courtney Crimsen	Helping catch Peeping Tom	Courtney lies to others, claiming that Hannah owns many sex toys	"Pettiness" (145)
6. Marcus Cooley	Taking advantage of a perceived "slut"	Hannah knocks him onto the floor	"Distrust" (145)
7. Zach Dempsey	Stealing someone else's rights (in this case, a bag filled with affirmations)	Hannah has been asking for help but cannot receive it because of this theft	Resentment leads a male to isolate a female
8. Ryan Shaver	Stealing someone else's intellectual property; the school editor steals Hannah's poetry	Hannah's poem gets analyzed in English classes at the high school	Betrayal of trust and invasion of privacy
9. Clay Jensen (who is the narrator)	Boy loves girl; girl loves boy	Hannah still plans to kill herself	Apology and sense of guilt for committing suicide
10. Justin Foley	Refusing to get involved (while girl gets raped)	Hannah also refuses to get involved; Bryce rapes Jessica	Watching evil without stopping it
11. Jenny Kurtz	Careless teenaged driving	Jenny knocks over a STOP sign in her car; another teenager dies because it is missing.	Avoiding responsibility
12. Bryce Walker	Sex In A Hot-tub	Despite knowing he has raped Jessica, Hannah allows the act	Abdicating personal power
13. Mr. Porter	Asking the school guidance counselor for help	He tells her to "move on"	Irresponsible insensitivity

a school mailbox designed to help students receive hand-written notes of positive reinforcement, Hannah feels a combination of emotions, including anger and disbelief, but the reader is encouraged to feel frustrated, wondering why Hannah has not confronted the boy. When Hannah has sex with someone she knows is a rapist, she is feeling resignation at the inevitability of her situation, but the reader is being invited to feel anger in protest of her self-imposed helplessness.

The range of emotions may differ between the character and readers' responses — especially because each reader's experiences and memories are personalized. But the concept of scripts is important to youth literature because so many scripts are based on stereotypical knowledge, including cultural stereotypes. For instance, few high school students are unaware of such cultural phenomenon as the objectification of the female body and date rape — both of which empower males at the expense of females. Most high school readers have internalized those stereotypical actions in their cognition as a script or set of scripts that contribute to the larger cultural narrative of differential power between the genders, but how the reader responds depends on his or her experiences.[3] Asher relies on narratives that objectify the female body with at least two purposes: to inspire the reader's anger and to instruct male and female readers about how to reject this type of sexism.

Not surprisingly, Asher embeds many embodied metaphors into the scripts he uses in *Thirteen Reasons Why*. For example, Hannah feels like the many people who have been examining her ass and assuming she is a slut are dissecting her life. Asher thus maps "dissection" onto "futility." Mapping "dissection" onto the affective domain "futility" requires the reader's cognitive action — but the metaphor is employed with repetition to ensure the cognitive mapping process can occur. For instance, when the school's newspaper editor steals one of her poems and publishes it anonymously, the English teacher allows students to "dissect" the poem in class (189). "So," Hannah asks, "did your teachers dissect me properly?" (191). The poem includes lines about opening a body to look inside of it:

> *Take away*
> *this mask of flesh and bone and*
> *see me*
> *for my soul*
>
> *alone* (191)

Hannah does not want to be dissected for her body parts; she wants people to see her "soul." She feels as if she is "breaking" (211), and she describes her "tumbling

---

3. I decided to quit teaching Laurie Halse Anderson's *Speak* (1999), for example, after witnessing the extreme emotional responses of two female students in the classroom who later self-identified as rape victims.

heart" (100). When her suicide is announced at school, one of the cheerleaders is dissecting an earthworm, "scalpel in hand, an earthworm sliced down the middle and pinned open before her" (133). This is the same cheerleader who has run over a STOP sign — which leads to a fatal accident in which a senior at their high school is killed. On the tenth tape, Hannah accuses this cheerleader of both negligence and avoiding responsibility in that death — and her own. These metaphors of being dissected — and disembodied — underscore Hannah's script about her own death. She feels that her body and therefore her life have no possible teleology other than immediate death. The dissection is complete, too, because Hannah's voice now exists as a disembodied echo in Clay's cognitive process: "her voice will never leave my head," he asserts (3).

The embodied metaphors in *Thirteen Reasons Why* intertwine with a variety of scripts to establish Hannah's growing belief that suicide is her only option. For example, she describes "her heart and her trust" as being in the "process of collapsing" (159); "[a]nd that collapse created a vacuum in my chest. Like every nerve in my body was withering in, pulling away from my fingers and toes. Pulling back and disappearing" (160). In terms of a script, she is not growing; she is "withering." On the final tape, she feels entirely "lost" and "empty" (271). The latter phrase echoes the embodied metaphors demonstrated by theorists of the *Bildungsroman* that depict the human brain as a container and knowledge or emotion as the contents that fill the container. But Asher twists this metaphor, representing Hannah's failure to grow as a script of being *emptied* by life, rather than *filled* by it.

Asher also reverses the usual depiction of growth as a journey in depicting Hannah as "lost." In many adolescent novels, the embodied metaphor GROWTH IS A JOURNEY itself becomes a script; the pattern ranges from *Adventures of Huckleberry Finn* to the latest coming-of-age road trip movie. In a typical version of the script, an adolescent experiences a crisis and either undertakes a journey to escape the crisis or to find a way to overcome it. Either way, by the end of the novel, the teenager has both journeyed and grown. But in this case, Hannah feels that she can no longer follow the appropriate path of GROWTH IS A JOURNEY. For example, her guidance counselor, failing to observe her depression, suggests that she should "move on," as if she can simply journey past the emotional pain she is feeling (278). Asher includes several variations of the GROWTH IS A JOURNEY metaphorical script in two pages that repeatedly employ the concept of the journey: the counselor tells her to "move on"; Hannah rephrases the counselor's words, asking if he thinks she should "move beyond" these events and then stating that she should "get on" with her life (278–279). The guidance counselor is "letting me go," she says in a final moment of despair (279). Eight times, then, the guidance counselor and Hannah talk about life as an embodied journey, although the guidance counselor cannot understand that Hannah is refusing to continue this journey.

The character Clay, however, follows the more traditional script of the journey as growth. Indeed, in the first chapter, Clay fears the journey onto the curving sidewalk that leads to his school; the fear of this journey is reaffirmed at the end of the novel — but he nonetheless follows this path that he dreads (3, 284). During Clay's quest to find out what has happened to Hannah, he follows a map she has given him, and he both walks and drives throughout their town as he seeks more knowledge. He also grows to be more sensitive to other people's needs. Although his quirky classmate Skye makes him uncomfortable and he is "relieved" not to talk to her mid-way through the novel, once he recognizes her withdrawn behavior as potentially suicidal, he consciously befriends her in the final chapter of the novel (105). Clay's journey is thus a fairly standard *bildungsroman* construction about psychological maturation following the path of a journey, but Hannah's journey — or failure to journey — is chilling because the reader knows from the beginning that the path she is following does not end in growth but in death.

Asher succumbs to some fairly obvious didacticism about suicide — after all, few YA authors can write about teen suicide without including messages about the moral responsibility of everyone involved, including the suicidal person. One of Clay's friends acknowledges, "We're all to blame.... [a]t least a little" (233), and Clay is later grateful that this friend "understands what I'm listening to, what I'm going through" (239), although he knows that many people will be "angry at Hannah for killing herself and blaming everyone else" (280). The students at the school discuss a list of warning signs about suicide as a thinly veiled means of helping the reader understand the embodied nature of suicidal thoughts: the text identifies sudden changes in appearance or giving away personal possessions, for instance, as possible scripts for suicidal tendencies. Hannah even professes her belief that "some people are just preconditioned to think about [suicide] more than others," positioning suicidal tendencies as a neurological — rather than a social — response to life's difficulties (253). Given that most of the reasons Hannah kills herself involve how people have objectified her body in response to her sexuality, Asher is clearly providing teenaged readers with an alternative mapping of gendered objectification: don't do it. Or protest when it happens to you. Or someone else. Ideologically, Asher wants readers to understand that objectification *is* a series of scripts that influence stereotyped behavior; objectification is a construct, not an unavoidable biological imperative.

Thirteen Reasons Why requires the reader to identify "connection" as this text's metaphor for combining the thirteen scripts into one narrative. Hannah narrates on one tape, "And the closer we get to the end, the more connections I'm discovering. Deep connections. Some that I've told you about, linking one story to the next" (177). Here "connections" are tied to causality; Hannah understands that one series of cause and effect has precipitated subsequent series of causes and effects. She narrates, "this is one tight, well-connected, emotional ball I'm constructing here" (183), and she tells Justin on the final tape, "I circled your name first, Justin. And I drew a line from you to Alex. I circled Alex and drew a line to Jessica, bypassing names that didn't connect.... My anger and frustration with all of you turned to tears and then back to anger and hate every time I found a new connection" (217). Hannah describes time as "a string connecting all of your stories," with the party being "the point where everything knots up.... getting more and more tangled, dragging the rest of your stories into it" (239). This metaphor of connection and causality implies something about how stories work cognitively. Through Hannah, the narrative instructs readers that it is their job, as readers, to rely on their own memories to cognitively connect and untangle the knots — that is, to combine the metaphors and scripts, the causality and the emotionology — that work together in any story. In other words, *Thirteen Reasons Why* demonstrates how *all* narratives function: novels are always a series of interconnected scripts that require the reader to remember and make connections to complete the text's meaning.

Hannah even comments on the inferential "gaps" that those who listen to her tape must complete:

> Yes, there are some major gaps in my story. Some parts I just couldn't figure out how to tell. Or couldn't bring myself to say out loud. Events I haven't come to grips with....
> But does that diminish any of your stories?....
> No.
> Actually, it magnifies them. (201)

She is acknowledging the importance of inference in storytelling — and in literary analysis (201). For example, in an intertextual commentary on "The Red Wheelbarrow," Hannah directly explains how literary ambiguity works: "Each word, specifically chosen, could have a million different meanings. Is it a stand-in — a symbol — for another idea? Does it fit into a larger, more hidden metaphor?" (175); either way, "[i]t's up to the reader to decipher the code, or the words, based on everything they *know* about life and *emotions*" (175, italics added).[4] This text thus acknowledges how interpretive inference emerges from the reader's cognition. Hannah also comments on the narrative importance of memory as another cognitive function with significance for storytelling: "If there's one thing I've still got, it's my memory" (223). Hannah retains cognitively the ability to remember and causally connect the stories in her memory into one larger narrative; otherwise, she could not be a storyteller. Because Hannah can remember the scripts

---

4. For more on intertextuality within the context of cognitive narratology, see Herman (2002:92). For more on the acculturating function of intertextuality in children's literature, see Stephens (1992:85–86).

and connect them causally, her cognitive work parallels the reading process that requires readers of most novels to be the active agent who makes inferences and combines scripts. Thus, *Thirteen Reasons Why* foregrounds the relationship between embodiment and cognition: Hannah's story emerges from both her embodied experiences and from the embodied cognitive processes — such as inference, memory, and understanding causality — that allow her to tell her story.

Conclusion

Cognitive narratology does not privilege embodiment over discourse, but it does invite the literary critic to understand how embodiment influences discourse through conceptualizations, such as how cultural narratives about teen suicide might be represented by embodied metaphors in a YA novel. Mark Turner notes, "[t]he cognitive study of art, language, and literature is concerned with patterns of thought and patterns of expression and the nature of their relationship" (2002:9). A cognitive narratology of adolescent literature therefore investigates embodied *patterns of thought* (or *domains*) as elaborated *patterns of expression* (or *scripts*) that exist in the discursive construct that is adolescence. Readers must rely on those cognitive functions — such as memory, perception, and emotion — to analyze causality in every story; and all of these cognitive functions work together to communicate about emotionology and the communal nature of storytelling.

Perhaps the focus in adolescent fiction on growth represents cultural fears of what happens when we stop growing taller and start aging into ever-more limited embodiment. When we are children, our embodied growth represents privilege to us, but in adolescence, embodiment becomes more problematic. We can't always control our bodies: our acne, our budding breasts, our erections, our menstruation. Thus, in adolescent literature, growth is represented in far more complex terms than it typically is in children's fiction. Authors may remember their embodied adolescent growth as complex and often negative and thus represent that growth within the discourse of their stories using semantic features that trigger adolescent readers, who are themselves experiencing growth that is at times less than pleasant, to respond cognitively based on their embodied dynamic repertoires and the scripts they have experienced as embodied beings.

But not all protagonists in adolescent literature grow into the next phase of life: Hannah Baker dies. So does the first-person narrator of Libba Bray's *Going Bovine* (2009). And that phenomenon isn't new, either. Alice dies in *Go Ask Alice* (Anonymous, 1971); Adam Farmer can't grow, but must bicycle eternally in circles in Robert Cormier's *I am the Cheese* (1977). In one sense, authors who defy the traditional narrative pattern of adolescent fiction are manipulating the script of the maturing adolescent to new and unusual effect, and in another, they are demonstrating the biophysical reality that embodied beings die — even sometimes when they are very young. It is in examining the patterns of those novels that violate the scripts of growth in adolescent literature that the blended relationship in adolescent literature between script and metaphor becomes most clear. In much YA fiction, embodied metaphors *are* the script. That is, growth — especially psychological growth — is the norm, although authors rely on an infinite variety of embodied metaphors, such as the journey or voyage, to depict that growth. Adolescent literature depends on these embodied metaphors to depict growth so often that one of the frequent assumptions readers bring to the genre is their belief that protagonists will arrive successfully at their metaphorical destination and grow, not die. The frequency with which metaphors of embodied growth are employed in the genre reinforces readers' expectations that the predominant script of any novel with an adolescent protagonist will include growth. Although authors can rewrite the script with a protagonist who dies, they still cannot escape the overpowering concept in adolescent literature that adolescent embodiment equals a script of psychological growth. Thus, adolescent literature participates in an ongoing reinforcement of social norms that growth is expected of all adolescents. As Stephens observes, scripts are "vital cognitive instruments" that "prove to be widely powerful strategies for investing normative cultural ideas" (2011: 34).

Cognitive narratology offers literary criticism more complex ways to examine growth in children's and adolescent literature than either narrative theory or genre theory alone have previously offered the field. Just as adolescents do not grow in a one-size-fits-all pattern, many narratives written for young adults defy the predictable pattern of the *bildungsroman*-influenced novel about a maturing teenager. We can trace these differences — and similarities — by examining the way narratives rely on our cognitive processes, such as memory, perception, inference, understanding causality, and emotions, to encode our physical and cognitive experiences of growth as stereotypical knowledge and/or scripts that subsequently emerge in adolescent literature.

Ultimately, growth provides the dominant pattern in adolescent literature because it is a phenomenon we know within our very embodiment. Our internalized knowledge of neuro-circuitry thus plays a major role in concepts of narrative growth. If our minds script what our bodies know, it seems inevitable that psychological growth would become the predominant model in literature written for people experiencing the greatest biophysical growth of their lives.

CHAPTER 3

Blending and cultural narratives

As I hope has become clear from the previous two chapters, the study of adolescent literature shares with cognitive narratology a focus on the intersection between physical embodiment and cultural construction. That is, childhood and adolescence are biologically-influenced stages of life that are nonetheless also structured by cultural constructions via the mechanism of language. To deny the biological processes involved in growth would be absurd. And even worse, to focus solely on those biological features of development would be to essentialize the human body, reducing it only to its anatomy. The field of adolescent literature therefore shares with cognitive linguistics an acknowledgement that biological and cultural factors both affect growth within a life stage such as adolescence.

The interrelationship between embodiment and cultural construction can be exemplified by examining, for example, the way every culture treats the embodied infant differently, with varying rituals and ways of dressing the baby, with differing ways of managing the baby's feeding and waste, with myriad ways to protect the newborn and nurture it. The same is true of the adolescent body. Although adolescence is defined in many cultures by the onset of a biological phenomenon, puberty, how adolescents are treated in any given culture is entirely a matter of social construction. Just as every culture constructs infancy differently, so too does every culture construct adolescence differently — including those historical cultures that did not even recognize adolescence as a legitimate life stage, such that pubescent children are or were sometimes plunged at young ages into work and/or marriage. Adolescence is defined solely by neither biology nor social construction; it is defined by both. In particular, adolescence is defined by how a culture *blends* its conceptualizations of puberty and post-pubertal embodiment, the process of living in the teenaged years, and the transition from childhood to adulthood. This chapter, then, explores the relationship between blending and the creation of cultural narratives, with particular attention paid to the role scripts and embodied metaphors play in the creation of these cultural narratives. Novels under analysis as examples include Angela Johnson's *a cool moonlight* (2003), Monica Hughes' *Keeper of the Isis Light* (1980), Neal Shusterman's *Unwind* (2007), and Meme McDonald and Boori Monty Pryor's *Njunjul the Sun* (2002).

Blending

Blending is a cognitive process that occurs within the brain, residing in a neuro-physiological process that is largely influenced by cultural factors that serve as the stimuli triggering the blend. The idea of adolescence is therefore a blend of many concepts that include, at a minimum, the following: biological concepts of puberty; social constructions of adolescence; religious and social rites of passage (such as bar mitzvahs or acquiring driver's licenses); economic factors that define the adolescent's ability to work or not; educational constructs of adolescent learning styles that include, in many European and/or Anglophone countries, middle school and high school models; and psychological concepts of cognitive capacity, such as Piaget's belief that the ability to understand "formal operations" (or abstract thought) marks the beginning of adolescence. The concept of adolescence is inevitably itself a blend.

According to Mark Turner, "conceptual blending is the mental operation of combining two mental packets of meaning — two schematic frames of knowledge or two scenarios, for example — selectively and under constraints to create a third mental packet of meaning that has new, emergent meaning" (2002: 10). Blending is a cognitive process; the embodied brain is required to process the blend (Turner 2002: 15). Our brains create blends both consciously and unconsciously in every moment, whether we are awake or sleeping. Blending, also referred to as "conceptual integration," is:

> … a general cognitive operation on a par with analogy, recursion, mental modeling, conceptual categorization, and framing. It serves a variety of cognitive purposes. It is dynamic, supple, and active in the moment of thinking. It yields products that frequently become entrenched in conceptual structure and grammar, and it often performs new work on its previously entrenched products as inputs. (Fauconnier & Turner 2002: 133)

In their work together, Fauconnier and Turner emphasize the following qualities of the blend: the blend is not inherent in either of the two or more concepts from which it emerges (42); blending happens unconsciously and without effort (44); and blending is a cognitive concept on which humans depend in every interaction, although they rarely recognize the process at work (56–57). Because our every thought process includes some form of conceptual integration or mapping, we are frequently unaware that we are engaged in the process of blending (Fauconnier & Turner 1998: 133).

Most significant, for the purposes of adolescent literature, "[b]uilding the blend requires composition, completion, and elaboration" (Turner 2002: 11). In other words, blending in literature occurs because of the author's composition of the text, the adolescent reader's cognitive act of reading, and that reader's imaginative process of elaborating the blend into a new meaning. In an argument that is surely also true for adolescent literature, Turner argues that blending "is a mainstay of children's literature" (2002: 12). Turner uses Crockett Johnson's *Harold and the Purple Crayon* to illustrate his point:

> Harold uses his purple crayon to draw, and whatever he draws is real. His world is a blend of spatial reality and its representation. In the blend the representation is fused with what it represents.... Child Harold's blended world has new kinds of causality and event shapes that are unavailable from either the domain of drawing or the domain of spatial living. (12)

Turner argues that human's "central" cognitive capacity is this "advanced ability for conceptual integration," noting that blending involves embodiment, language, and culture (2002: 16). We cannot study blending with discourse alone; nor can we study blending if we ignore socio-historical context. But perhaps most important, we cannot study blending, either, if we ignore embodiment altogether. In adolescent literature, blending is particularly implicated in the relationship between embodied metaphors and cultural narratives of growth.

Monika Fludernik describes blending this way: "Blending consists in fusing two scenarios together and thus creating new meaning effects.... In particular, ... blending theory aims at combining metaphor and narrative under one cognitive umbrella. Metaphor and narrative have been regarded as constitutive nonscientific modes of human cognition," but they are "like Saussure's signifier and signified: through blending, narrative approaches a situation in which one scenario merges with another, while in metaphor (generally acknowledged as a case of blending) the superimposition of two scenarios evokes narrative sequences" (2010: 926). Metaphor and scripts both involve blending; that is, they are cognitive actions that require the reader to combine two concepts or two processes to create a new meaning.

Blending in *a cool moonlight*

Angela Johnson's *a cool moonlight* demonstrates how cognitive integration of embodied metaphors and scripts occurs in adolescent literature. In this novel, African-American author Angela Johnson depicts the coming of age of a young girl, Lila, who has a fatal disease: xeroderma pigmentosum. "xp," as she calls it, is "because of my chromosomes. they can't protect me from the sun. i could be burnt and even go blind if the sun gets to me" (2003: 8).[1] As some sort of compensation for

---

1. The text of *a cool moonlight* relies only on lower-case letters; no word in the book is capitalized, although I have taken the liberty here of capitalizing the characters' names.

living her whole life either indoors or during the night-time, Lila has two friends — Elizabeth and Alyssa — who appear and play with her only at night. They wear fairy wings and are presented ambiguously as either imaginary friends or guardian angels. That is, they follow either the script of imaginary friends, in which a child imagines friends the child outgrows when s/he no longer needs them, or Elizabeth and Alyssa follow the script of guardian angels, who protect children sometimes from death and sometimes during their process of dying. Elizabeth's and Alyssa's presence in the story is never independently confirmed by any other character; that is, no character other than Lila expresses consciousness of these characters. Nonetheless, Lila asserts that her wing-wearing friends "[know] all the things that i need to know about the night. how to run in the night, find flowers in the night, and to listen in the night to everything that most people call quiet" (6). In Lila's case, her skin condition may well be an embodied metaphor. That is, although the race of her family is textually ambiguous, xp may well be a metaphor for race in this novel.[2] Racists, after all, justify their behavior on the condition of the perceived color of the "other's" skin; it is the primary factor by which racists in the Americas have for centuries justified lynchings and murders and slavery and the life-shortening conditions of enforced poverty. Certainly racism has killed more Americans than xp has. Because of her skin, Lila, too, cannot live in the world as the equal of those who define her world's norms — and her skin pigmentation (or lack thereof) is slowly killing her, just as racism has killed millions of Americans. She will not outgrow xp; indeed, she may never even reach adulthood at all. In being both a literal disease and an embodied metaphor for racism, xp serves as a cognitive blend in *a cool moonlight*.

Lila longs to have a day in the sun, and she plans throughout the novel to spend a milestone of her growth — her birthday — outdoors during the day. Readers understand that she is living in denial and that such a day would kill her. She hides her plans from her overprotective family, although Elizabeth and Alyssa help her gather articles for her "sun bag" to help her. The objects in the bag are metaphors for what Lila desires, what she lacks in her life, which is primarily sunshine. The objects all glow or glitter — except for "two *golden* feathers that are so small, so soft that they have to be from fairy wings" (127, italics added). These sun-evoking objects are also blends that require the reader to connect each physical object with Lila's emotional yearning for the sun. As Lila slowly accepts the condition of her skin, however, she eventually abandons her friends — whether they are being scripted as imaginary or angels. She is following the script of adolescent growth:

---

2. Virginia Hamilton's *Sweet Whispers, Brother Rush* (1982) is another YA novel in which a skin disease — porphyria — serves as a metaphor for racism as an insidious social disease by which the dominant culture justifies its actions based on the condition of some people's skin.

she can leave behind her imaginary/angel friends because she no longer needs them.

Lila's family then holds a birthday party for her at night. They decorate the backyard in twinkling lights — but magically, hundreds and thousands of fireflies show up on this August night in Ohio to help Lila celebrate her special coming-of-age party. Lila extends her arms, and the fireflies start to land on her, blinking and twinkling: "everybody stands there with their mouths wide open.... i'm the moon girl with fireflies. i'm all lit up" (130). She closes her eyes and starts to twirl, and the fireflies — magically, impossibly — continue to cling to her arms, lighting her up and transforming her into someone with glowing skin. The blend is, like xp, both literal and metaphorical because she has become radiant on both a literal and a metaphorical level.

As the novel ends, Lila decides that she doesn't need to be a "sun goddess" because "there's nothing wrong with moon girls" (133). This brush with magic demonstrates to Lila that she can exist — she can *be* — in the world in a different ontological space than the one she has formerly inhabited. She can refuse to think of her disease as a disability; she accepts herself with a new embodied metaphor. No longer longing to be a "sun goddess," she is happy to be a "moon girl." Johnson's use of metaphor problematizes race by showing how a girl can transform her own script to become someone who no longer feels limited by the embodied condition of her skin. The metaphorical message to all readers is a very direct: no child should ever be limited by the condition of her skin. Johnson leaves to the reader the task of uncoding the complicated blend these embodied metaphors and scripts create. But readers thinking about the symbolic value of xp in this book are performing a cognitive act of blending, as is the case when any reader contemplates symbolic value in any literature. Significantly, within adolescent literature, this cognitive act of interpreting embodied metaphors almost always interacts with the narrative's scripts to advance the novel's ideological purpose. Ideology functions on so many complex levels that it is always implicated in the cognitive process of blending.

Cultural narratives as cognitive blends

Acknowledging the relationship between biology and culture, cognitive narratology focuses on how narratives rely on embodied cognitive acts — such as language use, memory, perception, and imaginative production — as they are structured by specific cultural contexts. For example, cognitive narratologist Lisa Zunshine (2002) analyzes Anna Laetitia Barbauld's *Hymns in Prose for Children* (1781) as a text in which children are socialized into an eighteenth-century theological belief: i.e., that children are born with the inherent ability to pray. The text's socialization process relies on mapping a system of metaphors that requires the reader to adapt one conceptual domain to another (Zunshine 2002:130). If domain-specific conceptual categories are the internalized codes in our brains by which we identify objects in terms of their function, then all birds are birds (even if one is purple or another has only one leg), and "water" can be a drink or a stream or rain or an ocean or a puddle. Our brains thus understand the domain-specific category "bird" as more particularized than the category "water." Zunshine demonstrates how Barbauld manipulates several different conceptual domains to influence the reader's cognition toward a specific goal that is at once pedagogical and ideological: in Barbauld's *Hymns* birds and streams pray to God, even though praying belongs to a different domain-specific category than either birds or streams. The child reader must cognitively fuse these two categories (praying and birds or streams) in order to internalize the theological belief — the ideology — that all things are made to praise God. Zunshine argues that "as an effort to influence human beings, ideology will always be attuned to the intricacies of human cognition" (2002:126).

This ideological act, in which blends create new domains specifically aimed at manipulating a reader's belief system, involve what cognitive narratology refers to as *cultural narratives*. Cultural narratives have been called by many names: master narratives, metanarratives, dominant cultural ideologies, or even stereotypes; Zunshine herself refers to them as "cultural representations" (2002:126). In his Introduction to *The Postmodern Condition*, Lyotard provides one definition of the metanarrative: "if a metanarrative implying a philosophy of history is used to legitimate knowledge, questions are raised concerning the validity of the institutions governing the social bond: these must be legitimated as well. Thus justice is consigned to the grand narrative in the same way as truth" (1984:xxiv). In this construction, cultural narratives rely on historical understandings of culture to legitimize contemporary attitudes towards that culture. Additionally, Stephens and McCallum refer to metanarratives as "a global or totalizing cultural narrative schema which orders and explains knowledge and experience" (1998:6). Within cognitive narratology, *cultural narratives* refer to the widely-held belief systems that require a minimum of two cognitive acts to be sustained: the memory of stored stereotypical knowledge and a triggering cultural context. Cultural narratives "tap into certain cognitive contingencies that arise from the constant interplay between the human brain and its environment" (Zunshine 2002:126). We cannot learn to be patriotic or practice a certain form of spirituality — nor do we learn to become sexist or racist — unless we have had our cognition shaped by repeated cultural influences that our brain stores, for efficiency's sake, as stereotypical knowledge. Cultural narratives, then, are our cognitively-stored and culturally reinforced scripts about status, power, and constructed social roles.

For example, Monica Hughes' *Keeper of the Isis Light* explores how damaging three specific cultural narratives are: narratives of colonization, narratives of lookism, and narratives of racism. Cultural narratives of sexism are implicated in these processes, as well. The protagonist, Olwen Pendennis is the Keeper of the Isis Light, something of a lighthouse for space ships, on the planet Isis. She was born on Isis — so she is metaphorically an indigenous person — but her Earth-born parents died when she was young, leaving her in the keeping of a sentient robot called, simply, Guardian. Olwen thinks of Isis as "mine and it can never harm me in any way," demonstrating her colonialist attitudes toward the land (Hughes 2000: 88). She later repeats the statement with emphasis: "Isis is mine. Mine" — as if anyone can own an entire planet (125). When new colonists arrive from Earth, Olwen loses her unique status of being in control of the planet; she thinks of their presence as an "invasion," even though the settlers are initially peaceful (84). Guardian tells her he is worried about the germs these Earthlings carry, so he will build her a "protective suit" (31), which Olwen says makes them sound "as if they were diseased or something. Dangerous" (31). They are, indeed, both diseased and dangerous, just as European settlers in the Americas were, because they are infected with destructive notions of colonial power, race, and stereotypes of beauty. Olwen almost immediately recognizes that without the mask that Guardian has given her, "she would be completely vulnerable" in the face of the new colonists' tribalism (56).

When she first makes friends with one of the teenaged colonists, Mark, he finds it surprising that she's never looked in a mirror (62). She asks Guardian why they've never had one, and she asks him if she is beautiful. Guardian — who alone can see what lies below her mask — answers, "*I* think so" (66, italics in the original). Later, Mark mentally compares Olwen to an Andean Indian who has grown "acclimatized to high altitudes after centuries of living there"; he himself is like the "conquering Spaniards" who "were able to survive" (89). But because the wives of the Spaniards could not acclimate, they did not "bear healthy children, and so in the long run the Indians won" (89). Mark has established the significance of physical appearance and of acclimation — and thinks of the latter as a matter of "winning" over indigenous peoples.

The reader — and Olwen — eventually learn that her Guardian has genetically modified her body to withstand the radiation and inhospitable living conditions of Isis. Her skin is thicker; she has an extra eyelid; she has an elongated ribcage and widened nostrils to help her process more air; her hands have been strengthened and now include claws, and her skin is a bronze shade of green. Olwen thanks Guardian for giving her "freedom" on Isis, which she equates with "happiness" (138), but she eventually comes to understand that the new colonists consider her ugly. Indeed, once Mark sees her face, he feels "irrational horror" and can only think of her as an "alien species," even though they are both human (100, 213). The embodied metaphor of the Other as alien is blended with a script of fearing — and needing to destroy — the alien Other.

Not only is Mark enacting lookist cultural narratives; he is the person who determines the nature of his relationship with Olwen and what level of intimacy they will share. He holds all the power in their relationship. Once he rejects Olwen, they can never be equals. The gendered pattern of Mark setting the terms of their relationship is replicated in Olwen's relationship with the Captain in charge of bringing the group to Isis. He tells her that *he* is now in charge of Isis, echoing her own ridiculous notions of colonial power — and emphasizing the cultural norm that men should be in charge. The omnipotent Guardian, too, is coded male because even though robots are not sexed biologically, humans almost always configure them as gendered.

Ultimately, *The Keeper of the Isis Light* underscores the tenacity of the "epistemology of the visual," as Robyn Wiegman identifies racism and gender (1995: 8). We humans make snap judgments about race and gender based on what we see, what we perceive, about another person's race and gender. Although both race and gender are socially constructed and are not defined solely in terms of the visual, the epistemology of the visual surfaces the reality that what we see leads to our cognitive categorization of people by race and gender. In other words, our perceptions lead to a cognitive categorization that, in time, can become racist and/or sexist. Before Mark sees Olwen's face in *Keeper of the Isis Light*, he does not think he can love her: "Love?…. I've never even really *seen* her, he told himself angrily" (92, italics in the original). Olwen feels the same thing. "I want Mark to see *me*, to know *me*, not a plastic imitation," she says in a phrase that quite clearly links the visual to epistemology (103, italics in the original). Later, Olwen concludes that the settlers know only what they see: "They think that because you're ugly you must be dangerous" (160). She admonishes the settlers for killing her pet because they do not know what type of animal it is: "*He couldn't help looking the way he did*, you know" (173, italics in the original). Hughes understands that lookism — which is inherently linked to racism and sexism — is an epistemology of the visual.

The Keeper of the Isis Light thus blends lookism with racism and colonialism. If we do not perceive the Other as different — in this case, as alien — we cannot convince ourselves that we have the right to dominate the Other. The same is true of sexism. *The Keeper of the Isis Light* is very direct about problematic cultural narratives and how frequently they rely on cognitive blending that is too often visual. No cultural narrative exists as a single, unified cognitive thought. They always involve blends based on the knowledge that repetitions of experience have stored in our memories as stereotypical knowledge. And when the blend involves the belief that one group has the right to dominate another, stereotypical knowledge collapses into destructive stereotypes.

Cultural narratives and embodied metaphors in Shusterman's *Unwind*

Neal Shusterman's *Unwind* appears to rely on competing ideologies, emphasized by the novel's use of embodied metaphors and cultural narratives. The novel depends on two dominant and opposing cultural narratives, stated here in their extreme versions: the sectarian argument that bases "pro-life" arguments in ideas of the sanctity of human life (because even the fetus is made in the image of God, *Imago Dei*), and the secular "pro-choice" argument of Naturalism that there is nothing beyond life other than Nature itself. Shusterman maps two competing networks of metaphors onto these cultural narratives: mechanical metaphors correspond to the pro-choice cultural narrative and organic metaphors correspond to the pro-life cultural narrative.

Embedded in *Unwind*'s metaphors is an inquiry into the neurological nature of sentience through which Shusterman invites adolescent readers to consider whether the human soul can be defined entirely in terms of self-awareness. The text also appears to be taking a neutral stance on competing cultural narratives about abortion, but an examination of how these narratives are employed reveals Shusterman's ideological orientation.

Set in a dystopic future following culture wars that have turned into literal wars, *Unwind* describes a world in which abortion is both illegal and never practiced — because when children turn sixteen, their parents are legally allowed to have them "Unwound." The narrative is focalized by three characters: Risa and Connor, who are runaways, and Lev, whom Connor has kidnapped as a hostage, but who becomes sympathetic to Risa and Connor's cause. Risa and Connor and Lev have all been designated to be Unwinds. An "Unwind" is an adolescent whose entire body (or at least 99.44% of it) will be vivisected during a two-hour surgery so that the individual body parts can be given as tissue and organ donations to people who need transplants.

The allusion to an Ivory soap advertisement implies that the Unwinding process is, like the soap, "99.44% pure." Unwinding exists as a cultural practice that has emerged as a compromise between the "Army of Life" and the "Army of Choice"; the resulting Bill of Life "was supposed to protect the sanctity of life. Instead it just made life cheap" (Shusterman 2007: 53). In other words, "Both sides lost" (181). Risa asks "[w]as it worse … to have tens of thousands of babies that no one wanted, or to silently make them go away before they were even born?" (115). Then the text raises the stakes even higher, asking about the nature of the human soul, "What happens to your soul when you get unwound?" (171). In other words, what happens when a body is still 99.44% alive but its organs and tissue and blood and limbs are all living in other bodies? Does the soul live or die?

Unwind explores several explanations of the human soul, but the two that create the greatest tension in the narrative reflect the dialectic between a sectarian cultural narrative involving the sanctity of life and a secular cultural narrative of Naturalism. At least one character in the book reflects the view that the body of an Unwind is mechanistic, meant to service others, and "never had a soul to begin with" (172); that is, this character argues that the body of Unwinds exists only for mechanical purposes, because she believes that these people never can or will participate in any transcendent spiritual experience. The narrative's opposing definition of the soul argues that the soul of each Unwind lives on — either parasitically or symbiotically — in every part of the Unwound body that has been transplanted into other bodies so that the "divided spirits could rest, knowing that their living flesh was spread around the world, saving lives, making other people whole" (68). This latter view reflects the twenty-first century sectarian cultural narrative in the U.S. that all human life has sanctity at all moments. Shusterman thus engages adolescents in controversial — and sometimes irresolvable — cultural debates, and he relies on two recurring sets of metaphors to exemplify these debates. Both sets of metaphors are mapped onto the human body: one set of metaphors depicts the body as a machine meant to be sacrificed; the other relies on animal and plant metaphors to emphasize the organic (and presumably sacred) nature of embodiment.

Two characters exemplify the position that all embodied life is sacred: one boy, named Cy, has received the transplanted right temporal lobe of an Unwind whose inarticulate memories haunt Cy and lead him to uncontrollable behaviors, such as kleptomania. Another character, Humphrey Dunfee — whom the text identifies overtly as a metaphor for Humpty Dumpty (106) — has been Unwound by parents who have later turned remorseful and gathered together all the many people who were recipients of their son's body parts. Hundreds of people gather at a party the Dunfees hold for those to whom their son's life has been donated — and by the end of the party, all of the pieces of Humphrey converge into one unified consciousness that "coalesces into a single conversation" (334). Shusterman makes clear that the most important thing about a soul is its sentience. As one of the focalizers decides in a moment of crisis, "Whether or not souls exist Connor doesn't know. But consciousness *does* exist — that's something he knows for sure" (172, italics in the original). Later, he tells a group of escaped Unwinds, "I don't know what happens to our consciousness when we're unwound.... I don't even know when that consciousness starts. But I do know this.... We have a right to our lives!.... We have a right to choose what happens to our bodies!.... We deserve a world where both those things are possible — and it's our job to help make that world" (333). Here, Shusterman has sidestepped the issue of defining a human soul by focusing instead on the easier and more cognitive issue of consciousness. Nonetheless, the tension between human sentience and perceptions of body parts as insentient recurs throughout the narrative. Our legs, for example, don't appear to have sentience — but we know that our legs, like our hands, have muscle memory. The text seems to speculate that neurological function connects all parts of our bodies to our sentience — and possibly our souls. This exploration of neurology, brain function, and sentience places the novel squarely within the interests of cognitive narratology.

The two sets of competing metaphors about the nature of humanity on which Shusterman relies are not unlike the two ways cognitive science has historically viewed the brain: in one set of metaphors, *Unwind* metaphorizes the human body as technological, like a computer; in the second, it is organic and therefore of greater intrinsic value. The whole concept of being "unwound" is based on a metaphorical mapping of the human body as mechanistic, as a clock or timepiece that can be turned back, as if that body has never existed. Other mappings of technological metaphors onto embodiment in *Unwind* include how one girl refers to her own pregnancy as a matter of being "uploaded" (65) and the textual fact that all Unwinds are "government property" (57). Another example involves Connor, who has such severe impulse control behaviors that his parents have signed the orders for his Unwind. He thinks of his impulsivity as "a dangerous mental short circuit"; he can "feel when his brain started to fry" (62). He blames himself for his "short-circuit stupidity" (64). His father has even asked him, "Why do you have to get wound so tight?" (94). Connor is a "loose cannon" (212). Once the runaway Unwinds find shelter at a junkyard for old airplanes, they find themselves "scanned like groceries at a checkout counter. Scanned and processed" (182). Moreover, abandoned airplanes line the grounds "like crop lines, a harvest of abandoned technology" (197). The Unwinds, too, are abandoned — and according to many of these metaphors, they have no more worth to their society than the parts that comprise a junked airplane. In these metaphors, the living beings become technology and technology becomes organic, as if the airplanes — instead of body parts — could be harvested like wheat.

Another of the focalizers, Lev, eventually turns himself into a terrorist — called a "Clapper" — whose blood has been infused with an inflammable toxin that makes him able to blow himself (and others) up just by clapping his hands together in an act of random "chaos" meant only to wreak havoc (230). Metaphors that depict his body in mechanical terms foreshadow how he will transform his embodiment into a bomb. For instance, before he has become a Clapper, Lev tries to walk away from police officers who are looking for Unwinds "like he's crossing a minefield" (60). Later, he worries his heart will "explode" in his chest, "threatening to detonate" at any second (76, 77). His memories are like "a ticking time bomb in his head" (130). Lev is motivated to join the Clappers because his anger is "like the deadly charge lurking in a downed power line" (230). His heart has "hardened" so much that he "wishes it could be hard enough to be diamond instead of crumbling jade" (281). When he gives in to his feelings, they arrive "in a sonic boom" (329). More than any character in the novel, Lev's embodiment is transformed — not just metaphorically but also literally — from the organic to the technological.

Cy, the character whose right temporal lobe causes him to have a split personality, however, blends both technological and organic metaphors. He feels like there is "oil and water in this brain of mine" (184) and that his "mind will spill out of his ears and down the drains of the streets" (185); the patch job in his brain is "like puttin' spackle over a hole in a wall" (126). But Lev tries to give Cy hope using metaphors of living beings, comparing his friend to a "salmon swimming upstream" — even though both boys know that sometimes a bear is waiting to eat the salmon at the end of the journey (184). In a metaphor about ghosts — who are neither organic nor inorganic — Cy claims that the Unwind whose brain he shares is "like those ghosts that don't know they're dead" (140). Nevertheless, once Cy confronts the grief and remorse of the Unwind who "donated" his temporal lobe, Cy's metaphors return to the technological. His "entire brain seizes. He's frozen in a total system lockup" (190–191). Eventually, Cy recovers — and joins the protest movement against Unwinding, even testifying about the atrocity of the process to Congress.

But meanwhile, Connor and Roland demonstrate *Unwind*'s blending of animal and plant metaphors to convey the cultural narrative that embodiment is ethically complex. As Zunshine argues, humans have a tendency to view "natural kinds, such as animals and plants" in terms of anthropomorphized qualities and human-made artifacts in terms of their "function" is a result of the cognitive process of domain-specific cognitive adaptations (2002: 129–130). Following this pattern, *Unwind* uses these metaphors to interrogate whether all life is sacred simply because it *is* life. The domain-specific categories of "plants" or "animals" are, Zunshine would argue, a cognitive shorthand process of storing information in categories so that the brain can quickly access entire domain-specific categories of experienced memories (2002: 130). Thus, when Shusterman uses plant or animal metaphors to describe embodiment, he is asking his reader to map (quickly) an entire domain of the reader's experience — plants or animals — onto the value of human life. For example, Roland — the power-hungry antagonist with whom Connor fights for dominance throughout the narrative — has a shark tattooed on his arm, in the text's most obvious and overplayed embodied metaphor. "Sharks," the text asserts, "have a deadly form of claustrophobia. It's not so much a fear of enclosed spaces as it is an inability to exist in them…. [B]ig sharks don't last long in captivity" (100). That Roland is a shark-who-cannot-be-contained emphasizes the tension between his embodied power and the limitations placed on him by that body effectively being imprisoned by the designation "Unwind." Readers know what a shark is, and they can quickly map the embodied shark on Roland's arm onto the shark-like nature of his personality. But Roland is a sociopathic bully. Does he deserve to live — or is he a shark who deserves to die?

Evoking the standard metaphor of growth as cultivation, the botanical metaphors in *Unwind* are plentiful. Connor changes from being a "bad seed" (71) to someone with growing thoughts: a "seed" that is "planted in Connor's mind" finds "fertile ground" — even if those thoughts aren't an accurate assessment of his situation (207). Readers map "seed" and "fertility" onto the concept that Connor is growing, just as they know Connor is a trouble-maker when he thinks of himself early in the novel as a "coyote" (10) or when he thinks that he is so far into the doghouse that his name might as well be "Fido" (66). Later, he describes his impulsivity as feeling "like I've got ants crawling inside my brain" (145). Readers can map the crawling, tickling feeling of an ant into an itch in the brain and understand how uncontrollable Connor's urges are. The domain-specific categories of plant and animal thereby correlate with complex questions about the sanctity of Connor's life. The metaphors used early in the novel of canines and ants imply that Connor's life is troubled and perhaps not sacred, while the later metaphors of growing plants indicate his life is fertile and worth saving. But both sets of terms are blends that involve Connor's embodiment: he is growing, despite the ant-like itch in his cognition.

Connor's growth requires him to go "beyond his first thought, and [process] his second thought" (59). One adult asks him to write a letter about how he feels, so he writes to his parents about his sense of betrayal that they have decided to have him Unwound. He cries, certain that the intense pain he is feeling will "kill him right here, right now" (110), and in the aftermath of his tears, while he is holding a friend's baby so she can write her own letter, Connor thinks, "if his soul had a form, this is what it would be. A baby sleeping in his arms" (112). The soul is tender, vulnerable, embodied — and alive — in this metaphor. As Connor grows to appreciate his own consciousness and his ability to rely on reason in his decision-making, that is, once Connor learns some measure of self-control over his impulses, the metaphors that describe him emphasize his ability to assume agency as a living being. For example, the authority figure who runs the sanctuary in which he hides — ironically called "the Graveyard" in an embodied metaphor that foreshadows the fate of the Unwinds — tells Connor to become the person who will "ferret out the wolf in the herd" (218), and another Unwind calls him a "busy little worker bee" (220). When Connor feels futility, however, he feels "like a part of himself has already been cut out and taken to market" (302). Connor is no longer the coyote-like predator he once was, although he recognizes that being an Unwind makes him little more than a calf being led to slaughter. Shusterman uses several conceptual domains here (canines, graveyards, stockyards) as cognitive shorthand that adolescent readers can readily access in their own cognitive process of reading.

Eventually, Connor and Risa and Lev end up at a "harvest camp," where organic metaphors are mapped onto a domain of suffocation because the workers at the camp participate so consistently in the cultural narrative that the Unwinds have functionality but no souls. The adolescents are at the camp to be Unwound, their body parts "harvested," as if these teenagers were crops. Workers there wear Hawaiian shirts — and one counselor's shirt is covered with so many "leaves and pink flowers" that Risa would like "to attack her with a weed whacker" (268). In contrast to the strangling plant imagery of the harvesters, Risa is assigned to play the piano to entertain other Unwinds; the metaphors emphasize her humanity: she "plays her heart out" (276), playing the "pulse-pounding sound track of the damned" (285). She is not a crop to be harvested precisely because she has a beating heart. Even more disturbing then these metaphors, however, are those used when another character undergoes the surgery to become Unwound. The surgeons wear "scrubs the color of a happy-face" (288). Medical personnel replace his blood with a fluorescent green "oxygen solution" — which is the color of mechanistic "anti-freeze" but which also emphasizes that he is entering a vegetative state (290). The yellow-clad doctors lean around his body as it is getting dismembered on the table, "like flower petals closing in" (291). As his brain is dismembered, "memories bloom, then they're gone" (292). That same day, Lev and another group of Unwinds take a nature walk in the harvest camp compound. They find a tree onto which various employees of the camp have had branches "grafted" from their "favorite trees" to the trunk of the tree, so that one "branch sprouts pink cherry blossoms, and this one fills with huge sycamore leaves. This one fills with purple jacaranda flowers, and this one grows heavy with peaches" (295). No one can remember what type of tree it was originally, although the employees call it the "tree of life" (295). Adolescent readers are invited to map the concept of "harvesting" onto "embodiment" so that Shusterman can make an ideological point about the horror of viewing humans only as body parts to be harvested and grafted onto people more deserving than society deems the Unwinds.

Hands — both the hands of Clappers and the detached hands of donors — provide another type of embodied metaphor mapped onto unusual cognitive domains in *Unwind*. The first adult who helps Connor, for example, has a transplanted arm and hand that has been "grafted on at the elbow" (13). The fingers have "muscle memory" that allow him to shuffle cards one-handed and perform various card tricks (14). The relationship between transplanted body parts and neurological sentience are thus established early in the narrative. Soon after, Risa's first piano teacher tells her "I see those hands playing in Carnegie Hall," which seems like a compliment until she realizes that, as an Unwind, the hands may well play there without her (21). The teacher is being literal, not metonymic. Additionally, when Risa first meets Connor and he touches her, he agrees to her demands, including "[h]ands off" (46). Later, when an entire neighborhood participates in infanticide, Connor believes they all "had a hand in killing it" (75). These hands are all, of course, dismembered hands in a commentary on the neurological connectedness of all body parts. Eventually in the text, however, hands become less about dismemberment and more about empowerment. For example, readers learn that Humphrey Dunfee's hand was scarred while he was trout-fishing as a nine-year-old — which another character, who has part of Humphrey's brain remembers with excitement. Symbolically, when Connor receives a grafted right arm — one ominously tattooed with a shark on it — the hand no longer perpetrates Roland's violence. Connor touches Risa gently on the face with that hand. "It holds no fear for her now, because the shark has been tamed by the soul of a boy. No — the soul of a man" (322). The cognitive domain "hand" has been mapped onto the domain "soul" in an ideological statement about the value of all human life. And Connor, clearly, has participated in the script of adolescent growth.

In another example of the relationship between embodied metaphor, script, and cultural narrative, once Lev becomes a Clapper, his hands exude metaphorical ambiguity. His hands are explosive devices but are still able to save friends from a burning building and tie tourniquets in an emergency. He needs to save these friends because other Clappers have triggered a conflagration at the harvest camp by clapping their hands and detonating the explosive fluid their blood now contains. Lev, too, is supposed to continue his acts of terrorism, clapping his hands and adding to the destruction. But in that moment he stares impotently instead at his hands: "They look like stigmata, the nail wounds in the hands of Christ" because he is, after all, this story's sacrificial lamb, *Agnus Dei* (310). Always the most Christian (and Christ-like) character in the novel, Lev has been clothed in white as a child, until his parents donate him as a "Tithe" to the Unwinding process. In the moment he rejects his role as terrorist, he looks at his hands, and the text repeats in an almost Trinitarian litany: "He holds his hands up before him. He holds his hands up before him. He holds his hands up before him. And he cannot bring them together" — because, no matter how angry he is, "a *stronger* part of him" rejects both violence and the "lies" that have led him to acts of terrorism (310, 304). Ultimately, Lev is imprisoned with his "hands lashed to a crossbeam" so he cannot clap them; he acknowledges his posture is one of crucifixion (323). But his former pastor speaks to him about the difference between faith and conviction, and Lev begins to feel hope again: "All his life there was only one thing Lev was allowed to believe. It had surrounded him, cocooned him, constricted him with the same stifling softness as the layers of insulation around him now. For the first time in his life, Lev feels those bonds around his soul begin to loosen" (329). The metaphors "cocoon" and "constrict" represent the organic metaphors of agency and limitation that demonstrate how human embodiment is both empowering and disempowering; he is "cocooned" like a butterfly, but "constricted" in the way that a boa constrictor might eat its prey. Most important, like Connor, Lev has acknowledged the script that his actions have consequences — and that he has "put a face on unwinding" so that the public can no longer pretend that it is an act of benevolence and charity (327). He has become the iconic embodiment of Unwinding and also its sacrificial lamb. By fusing these metaphors of dismemberment and Christ-like embodiment, the text has blended competing cultural narratives of the body as simultaneously sacrificial and sacred.[3]

The final section of *Unwind* is "Part Seven: Consciousness." It opens with a quotation from Albert Einstein about how each human "experiences himself, his thoughts and feelings, as something separated from the rest — a kind of optical delusion of his consciousness" (315). Einstein identifies this delusion as a "prison" that can only be overcome if people broaden "our circles of compassion to embrace all living creatures and the whole of nature in its beauty" (315). More than any other metaphor, this mapping of imprisonment onto awareness of embodiment illustrates the text's ideological investment in teaching readers to value life. As the novel ends, Connor and Risa join forces to help other Unwinds escape, while they also work covertly to undermine the system of Unwinding. An adult who has helped them escape has told them, "people aren't all good, and people aren't all bad. We move in and out of darkness and light all of our lives. Right now, I'm pleased to be in the light" (111). Connor himself thinks he has become a better person once he has internalized Risa's voice of reason in his own cognition: "I'm a better person because you're in my head" (204). He tells the new Unwinds who arrive at their refuge, "We will *think* before we act" (333). Shusterman invites adolescents to value their cognitive abilities — but only inasmuch as they are also embodied abilities. Shusterman depicts the horror of adults dismembering adolescent bodies as a way to incorporate disobedient bodies into the body politic.[4] This metaphor of dismembering — disassembling, dismantling, dissecting — demonstrates the lie of the Cartesian split, that legacy of the Enlightenment which leaves us believing what Einstein calls the "delusion of consciousness." The

---

3. For more on the child as sacrificial in *Unwind*, see Stewart (2013), "A New Holocaust: The Consumable Youth of Neal Shusterman's *Unwind*."

4. For more on the body politic as it has been historically recognized and repressed, see Foucault, *Discipline and Punish*: "One would be concerned with the 'body politic,' as a set of material elements and techniques that serve as weapons, relays, communication routes and supports for the power and knowledge relations that invest human bodies and subjugate them by turning them into objects of knowledge" (1995:28).

adolescent characters in *Unwind* grow in their respect for their own sentience —
and the reader is left with the hope that the society itself will learn to understand
the problem with any cultural narrative that does *not* allow each adolescent to
grow to adulthood in an "undivided" state. Nevertheless, Shusterman maps this
valuation of embodiment onto the cultural narrative of valuing life. Thus, the book
is ultimately far more pro-life than pro-choice, even though the text appears initially to try to present all sides of the debate fairly. The blending of the embodied
metaphors, however, ultimately reveals the specific cultural narrative in which
Unwind is participating.

Primary and complex metaphors, blending, and cultural narratives in *Njunjul the Sun*

Lakoff and Johnson distinguish the "primary metaphor" from the "complex metaphor." According to Lakoff and Johnson, "Each primary metaphor has a minimal
structure and arises naturally, automatically, and unconsciously through everyday
experiences by means of conflation, during which cross-domain associations are
formed" (1999:46). A common primary metaphor is one that I have mentioned
before: the idea that THE BODY IS A CONTAINER. As Lakoff and Johnson explain,
"We are physical beings, bounded and set off from the rest of the world by the
surface of our skins, and we experience the rest of the world as outside us. Each
of us is a container, with a bounding surface and an in-out orientation" (1980:29).
Meme McDonald and Boori Monty Pryor's *Njunjul the Sun* relies frequently on
this primary metaphor; that is, the Australian aboriginal teenager Njunjul experiences his own body as a container when he says things like, "I'm listening up fully,
wanting more" (McDonald & Pryor 2002:122) or "Every bit of me is aching on the
way home. 'Cept my heart. It's full as" (136). He also experiences other people's
bodies as containers, as he demonstrates when he talks, literally, about his uncle
and him filling their bodies with food, even though his uncle is metaphorically full
from working hard: "Uncle and I tuck *in*…. Uncle reckons he's really *stuffed* from
a hard day's work" (103, italics added). Racist whites are also containers — and
predatory ones at that: "They'll eat you up. 'Specially you being black" (16).

Repeatedly, Njunjul expresses his emotions in terms of the container schema.
After his bus ride from the reserve to Sydney, he awakens in the morning at his
aunt and uncle's house, "belly *full*, brain whizzing, heart *bursting*" (48, italics added). The container of his body is both literally full with food and metaphorically
full of emotion. Moreover, he thinks of homesickness as an internalized feeling in
his belly: he equates homesickness with "deadweight feeling in m'belly" (68), and
he thinks of pain as something that enters his body from the outside to the inside:

"That pain soaks into you like rain, through your clothes, into your skin" (19). He also experiences love as something that can be put in and out of a container: "You gotta put something in before you get something out" (60). Later, after he has sex with a neighbor, he describes his feelings of satisfaction as if his body is a container, acknowledging that he has been sated by both sex and lemon meringue pie. He then shifts the metaphor to his hands, describing being overwhelmed as having a handful of problems : "what I got has both m'hands full, like fully" (104). In yet another instance of a body part becoming a container, his uncle describes deafness as having an ear that is an empty container: "'You don't listen, we got a name we call you. Binna-gurri. Binna, this one here,' Uncle's pulling his ear, 'means ear. Gurri means nothing *in* there. We call this boy that don't listen, Binna-gurri, deaf'" (144, italics added). The ear, the hands, the heart, and the skin are all containers in *Njunjul the Sun* — and that notion of the container as "empty" or "full" is directly linked to cultural narratives about whether or not the racial other is "empty" or "full" — and therefore worthwhile.

It is important to note that Njunjul himself evaluates his container-body not only in terms of eating and feeling and hearing but also in terms of expelling waste. As he rides the bus on his journey to Sydney, he finds himself needing to defecate: "I been busting since the sun went down," but he cannot use the bus's toilet because he can't help thinking about his excrement, no longer filling his body but instead filling the waste tank on the bus: "For the rest of the trip your goona following you, sitting up in that cubicle beside you there, travelling un-deterred, 'under-turd'!" (25). The bus, instead of his body, would carry his waste — although he himself almost immediately describes himself as Australia's waste, thinking of himself as "Garbage dumped on the edge of town" (27).[5] In this formulation of the container schema, it is better to be the container holding the waste than to be the waste itself. When he later thinks of himself as empowered, he imagines that he "can fly overhead and crap on everyone" (64).

On a less scatological level, Njunjul also experiences despair and other emotions as emptiness, as if the container of his body — especially his heart — has been emptied: "I'm sinking into that feeling. That lost feeling.... I've got none of m'own language. Not just that language from way back, from the old people. But the language of me now, from the inside" (110–111). Devoid of language, he feels empty. Later, he adds: "I'm not feeling nothing. I'm thinking I might have died already, on the inside" (116). Eventually, Njunjul's primary metaphor — that his body is a container — shifts to a more complex metaphor: that his body is a container that can be divided, cut into pieces and hurt. He describes himself as "a mess

---

5. For more on abjection as it leads to the "clean and proper social body" in adolescent literature, see Coats, *Looking Glasses and Neverlands* (2004:139).

of broken pieces" (26), and his uncle reinforces the idea, using a metaphor of food being pulverized for consumption to describe native culture. He says his culture has been "abused, cut up, sliced and diced every which way" (124). At home in the north of Australia, the container of Njunjul's body is shattered by white people; in Sydney, black people create the fragmentation: "Up home I get busted up by whitefullas for being black. Down here I get busted up by blackfullas cause they think I'm trying to be white. I'm wondering what the hell is me" (88). Either way, he fears he does not know what the inside of the container contains: he does not know who his internalized self is. "I'm trying to find that warrior *in* me to stand up and be counted" (18, italics added).

At the beginning of the novel, Njunjul feels empty because he can no longer hear the internalized voice of his ancestral spirits, a green tree frog whose voice guides him. She is internalized within him entirely as if his body is a container that holds her. As he begins to hear her voice again, he thinks, "my girragundji's voice back with me [...] unafraid [...] talking to me [...] telling me things" (34). She is "that voice inside me" that helps him express an understanding that he has internalized his culture with his embodiment, a cultural narrative that his aunt re-inforces (157). Njunjul's aunt tells him, "There's good and bad in any place, *in* any-one, good and bad *in* all cultures…. No colour of your skin gonna change what's *in* your heart" (29, italics added). This is the lesson that his aunt and uncle have been trying to teach him: that he must embrace both the inside and the outside of his container-as-body. He must accept his internalized culture *and* the externalized marker of his race, his skin color. And cultures themselves serve as containers, too, in Aunty Em's above-cited metaphor.

Njunjul begins to dance native dances with his uncle at various schools in Sydney, and the experience helps him learn to respect himself. "Something's flut-tering *inside* me. I'm struggling with the words, tough as shrugging off a cocoon," he says, as he asks his uncle to take him with him to dance at a school (130, italics added). After the dance, Njunjul thinks, "I'm sorting through the treasures I got in my heart. All the things the kids were asking…. They've given me back a part of myself" (148). His fragmented container is becoming whole again. Even more important, he recognizes that his self has been internalized within his body as container all along: "That fulla Njunjul's been there for me all along, like fully. Only me. I've not been seeing that. Now I gotta be there for him. I'm feeling that warrior sun come to me" (159). Two words are repeated throughout *Njunjul the Sun* that reinforce this idea of the body as being an empty or full container. First, Njunjul uses the term "fully" when he means "completely," as the above quotation demonstrates. Second, Njunjul refers to people as either "blackfullas" or "whitefullas." The term "fulla" has absolutely nothing to do with fullness; it is simply a slang version of the word "fellow." Nonetheless, it still creates a visual repetition of the morpheme "full," which the reader may or may not cognitively link to fullness, depending on the reader's own cultural conceptualizations.

According to Lakoff and Johnson:

> Each complex metaphor is in turn built up out of primary metaphors, and each primary metaphor is embodied in three ways: (1) It is embodied through bodily experience in the world, which pairs sensorimotor experience with subjective experience. (2) The source-domain logic arises from the inferential structure of the sensorimotor system. And (3) it is instantiated neurally in the synaptic weights associated with neural connections. (1999: 73)

Njunjul describes himself containing emotions because he has experienced his body as a container. He has conflated physical fullness (or emptiness) with emotional fullness (or emptiness) in a sensorimotor experience that depends on and influences his subjective experience. He is unconscious of the fact that he has created this source-domain logic; he makes these comparisons effortlessly. Nonetheless, his conceptualizations are inseparable from his embodiment.

The primary metaphor THE BODY IS A CONTAINER combines with another primary metaphor, CHANGE IS MOTION, to create a complex metaphor that Njunjul's body is a living container on a journey: THE BODY-AS-CONTAINER JOURNEYS THROUGH LIFE. Lakoff and Johnson distinguish primary from complex metaphor as a function of the concept of blending: "Complex metaphors are formed by conceptual blending" (1999: 46). Through the blended creation of complex metaphor, *Njunjul the Sun* demonstrates two things: that coming-of-age scripts rely on blending and that these blends contribute to the perpetuation of cultural narratives.

Njunjul is self-consciously on a physical journey that he understands cognitively to be a metaphorical journey of growth. Earlier in the novel, he describes himself, "heading straight out of town" (11), but he feels fragmented, "like half of me got left behind" (13). He acknowledges the metaphorical possibilities of his bus ride: "We could be going nowhere. Or could be heading into outer space, to the stars and back. Or locked in a time-capsule buried deep in the earth. Or heading backwards at full speed. Or just going round and round in our own heads" (17). His body as container feels "beaten and hopeless before I even get started" (18); he fears that he is "in no-man's land" (18). He sees himself as "an alien space traveller. Maybe that's what you look like when the main part of you is still way back down the highway" (25), and he philosophically agrees with his Aunty Milly, who tells him, "Sometimes you gotta go away from where you wanna be, just so you can get strong enough to go back there" (41). When he arrives at his aunt and uncle's, he narrates that "I can feel I'm starting my journey right here in the kitchen, wiping dishes with m'uncle" (47), although he can acknowledge that "I'm still travelling, not arrived nowhere.... Half of me is back there in those broken up pieces" (83).

He feels fragmented because part of his body as container has not traveled with him: the part of his emotions that feel as if they have remained at home with his family.

In an almost clichéd moment that relies on the script of sexual initiation to indicate coming of age, he thinks, "There is no way back to that boy I was.... Before it was a big dark hall, me moving around by touch, bumping into things. Now I've woken up and I'm somewhere I never been before" (97–98). He begins to realize, however, that he is lost in his girlfriend's world of self-pity and paternalism, and he begins to renavigate his journey when his girragundji tells him, "It's only you can save you" (128). He decides to take "[t]he next step" (129). A friend acknowledges the emotional difficulty of Njunjul's situation, relying on the script of the journey: "I can see in your eyes you been to some of those dark places I been.... You might look shy, but inside there you've had to fight to stay alive" (135). His uncle does the same thing, when he takes Njunjul to dance for the first time. The uncle hands him a traditional outfit to wear: "'That there,' he's pointing at the scrap of material in my hand, 'that's your real ticket. That's what'll get you on that bus ride, the most important one. The one that takes you back to yourself'" (138). As Njunjul dances, he describes how his people sketch butterflies on their thighs because: "[w]hen we dance we shake our legs like imbala, the butterfly" (139). Njunjul recognizes the metaphor because he himself has killed a literal butterfly, trying to help it out of its journey from the cocoon. "He needed that struggle to make him strong enough to live. I didn't know that then" (139). Ultimately, his own strength helps him arrive at the only possible destination: an internal valorization of his own identity. When he's dancing, he feels that "[t]hose imbala wings carry me back home" (145).

Njunjul the Sun is hardly original in its reliance on a coming-of-age script that evokes the *Bildungsroman*. A rural boy leaves his home to journey to the city, feels emotionally bereft once there, falls into idleness, has a sexual relationship that is both exalting and debasing, and redeems himself through work — in this case, demonstrating native dances at local schools.[6] As in any traditional *Bildungsroman*, he redeems himself through a work ethic that allows him to embrace his own identity. In this case, *Njunjul* seems to demonstrate a disappointing adherence to the Protestant work ethic and the Anglophone tradition of the *Bildungsroman*, which both posit work and self-acceptance as necessary to spiritual healing. Nevertheless, *Njunjul* problematizes the scripts of race by interrogating how race is socially constructed in terms of embodiment. "My skin don't fit me no more" (20), Njunjul thinks, justifying his reasons for leaving the reserve. He has been beaten by police officers, solely because he was the only blackfulla walking by a school that has been

---

6. This is a paraphrase of Jerome Buckley's definition of the standard Anglo-American *Bildungsroman* pattern (1974: 18–23).

vandalized. Afterwards, "I pissed blood for days. Don't know which hurt the most. M'kidneys or m'heart. They both been bleeding" (23). As in the earlier instances of embodied metaphors of the body as container, Njunjul creates a blend in which he conceptualizes bleeding in both literal and metaphorical terms.

In Sydney, confronted with an African-American who uses the term "nigger" freely, Njunjul admires the man's self-confidence in embodied terms: "He's turning that 'nigger' word right round and sitting on its head" (55). He also meets some Maori and admires their body art: "I spent too long with my tattoos on the inside.... Maybe that's why I can't understand that voice inside me no more. I gotta get it out. Make a sign. Tattoo my frog to the outside, on my shoulder or over m'heart" (109). When he's worrying about his cultural identity, he uses an embodied metaphor: "I'm wondering how deep that black goes" (138). And when a child at one of the schools where he dances asks him, "How long you been black?", Njunjul replies, "I reckon I was born black.... but ... I reckon it's taken me a long while, maybe right up till now, to know that" (147). In *Njunjul the Sun*, race is both cultural construction and visceral embodiment; Njunjul must successfully complete his journey in order to recognize that he has internalized his culture into his body as container in a spectacular blending of embodied metaphors and scripts. He thinks, "No difference in here, but. In me. Inside of me, I come a long way to be back where I was.... No Murri-fulla me, no this-fulla me, no that-fulla me [...] Just *me*. The fulla inside that's got no shape or size or colour. Just is" (118–119).

Njunjul's uncle and the adult friends he plays with self-consciously blend basketball and surviving racism in another complex metaphor that demonstrates the interplay between conceptualization and cultural narratives. His uncle tells him, "Basketball is life" (48), and another friend refers to basketball as "[t]his game of life" (60). Basketball helps Njunjul redefine his sense of identity: "I am whoever I wanna be, I'm telling m'self. I can be that tall I gotta duck when I walk under that net. I can be see-through like the wind. I can be the ball, or the endless ocean" (64). Moreover, his uncle tells him he must repeat traditional stories, learning them almost like muscle memory, in the same way that basketball players drill the same routine over and over to learn specific basketball shots (93). The adult basketball players give it to Njunjul "tough, man, because out in the world there you gonna need to know you can take it tough and still get up and play the game.... They're *watching* out for you" (135, italics added). His uncle tells him something that strikes the book's most false note: "We're all equal when it comes to going for the ball or the finish line. It's only the best wins, no matter about colour" (136). The cultural narrative that "the best are all equal" does not really resonate in a book that demonstrates the pervasiveness of racism this directly.

Njunjul the Sun relies on primary metaphors of the body as container and complex metaphors of life as a journey and life as a basketball game in blendings that articulate multiple cultural narratives about race, aboriginal culture, and colonialism. The text critiques the following Euro-Australian cultural narratives about indigenous peoples: they need protection (10), are thieves (12), and vandals (21). A white racist Njunjul meets during his bus journey tells the boy, "You bastards aren't that easy to get rid of" (17) and "You can hit, you lot" (17). The racist goes on to say, "You buggers are hopeless, you know that?…. "Money, booze, jobs […] You can't handle any of it. Always goin' walkabout" (18). Even worse, Njunjul's (white) girlfriend claims the same victim status that she assigns to Njunjul: "you and I have a lot in common…. We've got no one to love us. No one wants us, you and me, do they?" (99). He disagrees internally, thinking of his large and loving extended family, but she still insists, "We're both outcasts" (101). Continuing the journey metaphor, she thinks he's "walking naked in a world that's done me wrong" (110), a feeling that he succumbs to for a time. "Who am I kidding, I can be anything, anyone, anytime? As if! I'm a blackfulla. I can only be what other people expect me to be" (64). Eventually, Njunjul rejects both the cultural narratives of white racists and his girlfriend, but he is nonetheless forced to listen to these views. As his uncle observes, "For blackfulla's [sic] the insults start the minute you turn on the TV or pick up the newspaper or look at a carton of milk" (121). Njunjul understands that cultural narratives of race are complex. He says of his girlfriend, "I'm feeling real black and she's looking real white and that means we live on different planets. Other times, all that colour stuff don't matter. We have that same way of thinking and feeling no matter if we're black or blue or green" (79).

Part of Njunjul's sense of fragmentation resides in his ability to perceive that his culture itself has been shattered. "Now I'm wishing I had my language. Mine got taken away, but Aunty Milly told me stories of how our old people got punished for speaking their language. That was in the concentration camps, the reserves they hunted us mob into when them migaloos wanted our land. If the old people did their dances, sung their songs, spoke their language, they were locked up, heads shaved, punished real bad" (63). And Njunjul's uncle articulates how indigenous people experience white colonization in terms of a series of scripts: "We have to cop your mob telling us mob what we think, feel, care about, want to have on our toast […] what colour we like our knickers" (122). He concludes with a cultural narrative shared by indigenous peoples in the book: "Being black *is* being political! We don't have a choice" (122). Later, the uncle tells Njunjul that only by reclaiming their identity as the Bummah Murri can their people begin to heal. But he also identifies the need for the people who have wounded them to heal, too: "For healing, we need whitefullas to hear about our culture. We need whitefullas to heal first so that we can heal. We gotta keep these stories going if we gonna keep ourselves alive" (151). White people — not indigenous peoples — are responsible for racism, so they must be involved in changing the cultural narrative.

Conclusion

All cultural narratives rely on conceptual blends, and all cultural narratives that involve racism rely on embodied metaphors. As cognitive linguistics acknowledges, our embodied perceptions and experiences lead us to create language that, in turn, reinforces those perceptions and experiences. Although this process is largely unconscious, the creation of cultural narratives is nonetheless dependent upon the blending of complex metaphors and scripts. And these metaphors and scripts create cognitive structures that are powerful because "[a]nything that we rely on constantly, unconsciously, and automatically is so much part of us that it cannot be easily resisted, in large measure because it is barely even noticed" (Lakoff & Turner 1989:63). The internalization of these cultural narratives all too often occurs during childhood and adolescence, and so adolescent literature frequently relies on the script of an adolescent acknowledging or even outgrowing racism as a sign of growth.

As I have shown in previous chapters, growth in adolescent literature is expressed both through embodied metaphors and through scripts of growth. Perhaps one way to summarize the common growth script in adolescent literature is as follows: an adolescent experiences a crisis, learns something about how to deal with that crisis, and grows as a result. As a general rule, the adolescent character's growth involves embodied cognition: the teenager grows psychologically by relying on such embodied acts of cognition as perception, memory, and emotion. I am struck, however, by the predominance of the cultural narrative in adolescent literature that teenagers *must* grow. Teenagers such as Dallas in *The Outsiders* (Hinton, 1967) or Beth in *Little Women* (Alcott, 1968) or Alice in *Go Ask Alice* (Anonymous, 1971) who cannot achieve the maturity it would take to face adulthood die. And teenagers in formulaic series fiction, of course, frequently do not grow, for the reasons I have previously cited Nikolajeva as having analyzed (2002:65). As I mentioned in Chapter 2, in novels that question the script of growth, such as *Going Bovine* or *I Am the Cheese*, the protagonist's growth is not a given. But with these exceptions, growth is such a frequently employed script in adolescent literature that I submit it has taken on the role of being a cultural narrative: teenagers are required to grow.[7] Indeed, that cultural narrative extends well beyond the discourse of fiction, for teenaged readers — like teenaged protagonists — grow, perhaps inevitably, perhaps because of cultural expectations, perhaps both. Nonetheless, growth as a cultural narrative is a norm of adolescence.

---

7. For more on the paradox of adolescent literature teaching adolescents to outgrow adolescence, see Trites, *Disturbing the Universe* (2000:79–83).

David Herman writes about cultural narratives as scripts that indoctrinate youth into specific ideologies:

> [T]he genre is so designed as to establish and inculcate particular world models (for example, those associated with delaying gratification or resisting the gratu-itous fabrication of monsters). This genre's primary function is not to problema-tize a world that readers only think they know, but rather to help them acquire more strategies for getting to know it. Far from presuming the script expertise supporting more elaborate narrative experiments, children's fictions consolidate and reinforce the scripts on which narrative competence itself depends. Such fic-tions teach reading by teaching scripts. (2002:111)

While I personally disagree with Herman's tendency to attribute only a didactic function to literature for youth, as he does when he implies that the purpose of such fiction is to teach reading, I agree that cognitive narratology contains a perspective that is fundamental to the study of (children's and) adolescent literature, which is this: cognitive narratology "investigate[s] how narratives, through their forms as well as their themes, work to privilege some world models over others" (Herman 2002:113). Adolescent literature privileges what could be called one influential *world model* (or, as I prefer to call it, a *cultural narrative*): the model of requisite adolescent growth. If we take for granted the patterns of growth in adolescent fic-tion, and especially if we do not interrogate the embodied metaphors that inform our understanding of this narrative pattern, we risk overlooking how profoundly embodied adolescent fiction tends to be and how significantly this embodiment might shape readers' cultural narratives about growth, both their own and others'.

CHAPTER 4

A case study

Cultural narratives and the "Pixar Maturity Formula"

I would like now to provide a case study of one cultural narrative that involves and affects cognitive conceptualizations of growth: the cultural narrative that assumes women are more mature than men. This insidious cultural narrative has an ancient history that reaches back at least as far as the loyal Penelope in *The Odyssey*, but it is promulgated extensively by mass marketed media produced in Hollywood. This cultural narrative ties into at least three conceptualizations that are salient to a cognitive study of growth in adolescent literature. First, the cultural narrative that women are more mature than men is predicated on the false assumption that women will always-already mature as a result of their ostensibly maternal nature. That is, since girls will presumably become mothers and care-givers, they are supposed to somehow automatically — almost magically — mature in order to nurture others. Second, if nurturance provides girls with an automatic route to their maturation, this cultural narrative falsely implies that females really have only one path to maturity: the predetermined path to parenthood. Third, this cultural narrative insinuates that male growth is more varied and interesting and thus deserves more attention and praise than female growth.

To be clear, many contemporary authors for young adults avoid this trap and treat male and female growth with equal parts of sophistication and respect. But films for the young have lagged behind published narratives — and Pixar Animation Studios is among the worst of the purveyors of this damaging cultural narrative.[1] The fourteen Pixar feature-length films that are marketed predominantly to preadolescents and adolescents as of this writing thus serve as a case study of how one cultural narrative — "women are more mature than men" — persists and in turn contributes to the perpetuation of such additional cultural narratives as sexism, ageism, and reverse discrimination. In particular, those films that were written for and marketed more directly to teenagers than children are the most pertinent to a study on growth in adolescence: they include *Up* (Docter 2009),

---

1. For an overview of recent theoretical approaches to children's films, see Kümmerling-Meibauer (2013).

Toy Story 3 (Unkrich 2010), *Brave* (Andrews & Chapman 2012), and *Monsters University* (Scanlon 2013).

In this chapter, I will explore the Pixar maturity formula as a cognitive script that enables the cultural narrative that women are more mature than men. This exploration involves investigating pertinent definitions of maturity in both the fields of psychology and literary criticism, leading eventually to an interrogation of Heidegger's philosophical inquiry into the relationship between maturation and the knowledge of mortality.[2] Such cognitive processes as understanding causality, Theory of Mind, and separation anxiety also contribute to this investigation. My goal is to use Pixar as a case study, but the films under investigation raise the following questions: how do we define maturity? What does maturity look like in popular culture? Whose maturity do we value? And how does the repetition of a cultural narrative cognitively reinforce stereotypes?

Because media marketed to children and teenagers in the U.S. is usually produced by firms invested in earning a profit, media for youth often relies on widely-accepted cultural narratives, such as sexism, that don't challenge the status quo. Pixar movies provide a test case of how one company is, as Zunshine would have it, "attuned to the intricacies of human cognition" in their ideological "effort to influence human beings" (2002: 126). Herein, I am concerned with the cultural narrative I identified in the last chapter: the "world model" of growth. Even more specifically, I am concerned about cultural narratives that define boys' growth as more necessary and/or important than girls'.

Two recent studies document what many of us have known for a long time: males outnumber females in films marketed to the young by a considerable margin. Stacy L. Smith and Crystal Allene Cook quantified the 101 top-grossing G-rated movies from 1990–2005, and determined that only 28% of characters with speaking lines are females (n.d.: 12). Subsequently, Smith and Choueiti determined that "2.42 males are depicted for every 1 female" in the 122 children's movies released from 2006–2009 (n.d.: 1); moreover, the females in these films are far more likely than males to be depicted in terms of lookism, with slender waists, large chests, and attractive faces (S.L. Smith n.d.: 1–3).

When I raise this type of concern in public, at least one enthusiastic person assures me that Pixar is the exception to the rule because every Pixar movie contains at least one strong female character — which is true. My goal in this chapter, however, is to problematize the cognitive complexity of gender and maturation in Pixar's film. When every film contains only one female character who is scripted as

---

2. It is to be noted that neither the author nor the editors of this series subscribe to or advocate Heidegger's reprehensible fascist politics, although the philosophy articulated in his *Being and Time* offers some insights into one perspective on maturation.

strong — and when that one female character must always make up for the incompetence of multiple male characters — a strange script of reverse sexism emerges. Pixar's male characters are often depicted as flawed but still lovable, so female characters carry the burden of saving these men from themselves. Although this seems at first glance to be a positive side effect of feminism, the script isn't really progress. Pixar's sexism isn't based solely in the "girls are always helpless" thinking that informs so many Disney princess movies; instead their sexism emerges from the complicated interplay between gender stereotypes and social expectations placed on children as they mature. Thus, in this chapter I analyze the gendered ways of thinking about maturity that prevent Pixar from producing feminist texts.[3]

Maturity and causality

Virtually every Pixar movie, even those marketed to younger children, has at least one mature character who serves as the foil for the protagonist, such as Little Bo Peep in *Toy Story* (Lasseter 1995) or Mrs. Incredible in *The Incredibles* (Bird 2004). Pixar's conceptualization of "maturity," however, bears examination. Mature Pixar characters are responsible, caring, and able to analyze the relationship between actions and their consequences. That is, Pixar characters who have undergone growth to become mature understand cause and effect, although their immature counterparts may not.

Both psychologists and literary theorists associate maturity with self-actualization and social responsibility. For both groups of scholars, maturity is a function of cognitive activity. For example, Abraham Maslow (1943) describes maturity in terms of self-actualization; George Vaillant defines maturity in terms of voluntary coping mechanisms (seeking social support and conscious cognitive strategies) and involuntary coping mechanisms, a.k.a. "adaptive defense" or "healthy denial" (such as "humor, altruism, sublimation, anticipation, and suppression") (2000:91). Laura Berk notes the importance of "resiliency" in emerging adulthood; resiliency

---

3. Certainly, I'm not the only person to observe Pixar's sexism. Newspapers and blogs have commented on the phenomenon for years. Cole Abaius (2009) of *Film School Rejects* observes: "Even in the animated animal world, the protagonists are all male. The rats, the clown fishes, the cowboy and spaceman toys. The former superheroes, the cars and the ants. There have been some strong female characters, but they have never been the main focus of the story." Jen Chaney (2007) of *The Washington Post* asks, "Are the Pixar movies an animated Boys Town?" Linda Holmes (2009) of NPR wrote Pixar a letter asking them to "please" make at least one movie about "a girl who isn't a princess." Michael Hanscom (2006), perhaps Pixar's most persistent critic, writes that "Pixar is definitely a 'boy's club,' in everything from their choice of subjects to the characters in the film."

includes problem-solving, coping with stress, and "the capacity to overcome challenge and adversity" (2010: 354, 466). Similarly, literary theorists typically invoke, as Jerome Buckley does in defining the *Bildungsroman*, the mature character's ability to work and to love productively as measures of fitting into society as an adult (1974: 23). Elizabeth Abel, Marianne Hirsch, and Elizabeth Langland note that for female characters, "inner concentration" and the ability to achieve intimacy with others are marks of maturity (1983: 8, 11). According to Robin MacKenzie, "the traditional conception of maturity" depicts "the accent on inner calm and certainty; the importance of self-acceptance, reconciliation with oneself (seen as a major moral victory); the supplementary goal of social utility, participation in community and society" (2007: 352). Especially for female characters, maturity is depicted as a cognitive self-awareness. Thus, literary theorists and psychologists alike define social awareness and self-awareness as aspects of cognitive maturity, although neither psychologists nor literary theorists pay much attention to understanding cause and effect as a function of maturity.

Instead, cognitive psychologists theorize that typically-developing children begin to understand cause and effect by the time they are approximately two years of age, and they have a firm grasp of cause and effect relationships by the time they are approximately seven years old (Piaget & Inhelder 1969: 109–113; Berk 1991: 360) . Thus, understanding cause and effect is a function of early childhood, not later maturation.

Why then does Pixar correlate the cognitive ability to understand cause and effect with increased maturity? I suspect they do so largely because their immature characters' initial inability to prejudge the consequences of their own actions creates both plot conflict and humor. For example, the car Lightning McQueen in *Cars* (Lasseter 2006) is too impatient to change his tires when he clearly needs to, so he loses the first big race he is in. Similarly, *Toy Story*'s Woody the Cowboy thinks that if he can only get rid of the new toy, Buzz Lightyear, the other toys will respect him again — without recognizing that the community will turn on Woody if they think he has hurt Buzz. The events caused by these characters' failure to intuit how other people will act create both conflicts from which the characters grow and the type of humor that is predicated on a sense of superiority.

Another way to put this would be to note that characters like Woody do not have an adequately developed Theory of Mind. Nikolajeva argues that "the knowledge and understanding of other people's minds are essential social skills" (2012: 274), and as I mentioned in Chapter 2, Kümmerling-Meibauer defines empathy in terms of "emotional competence" (2011: 130). The ability to predict other people's actions and feel empathy for their feelings are thus key skills in emotional maturity — and they are skills that Pixar routinely depicts males as lacking. Even the youngest children feel smarter than Lightning McQueen and Woody when they fail to predict how other people will perceive their actions. But the cultural repetition of the immature character who cannot anticipate causality or other people's feelings participates in two disturbing cultural narratives: the myth that males are inherently insensitive, and the joke that they are funny when they are stupid.

Pixar's immature, insensitive, conflict-ridden, funny characters, however, are easily contrasted to Pixar's mature characters, who are usually female. The mature female Pixar character typically serves as a foil to at least one immature male. I call this "the Pixar maturity formula," and the script became apparent as early as Pixar's first feature-length film *Toy Story* — which was admittedly, marketed more to children than adolescents. Nonetheless, virtually all of the toys in Andy's bedroom are male and emotionally immature: Woody, Buzz Lightyear, Hamm the Pig, Mr. Potato Head, Rex the Dinosaur, and Slinky Dog. The only exception is Bo-Peep, whom the Pixar website describes this way: "she has her hands full being the voice of reason for her cowboy, Sheriff Woody, and the rest of the gang" (Pixar n.d.). In other words, Pixar itself identifies Bo-Peep as "the voice of reason" — and she clearly has her hands full because she is the only reasonably mature character in the movie. Aside from Bo-Peep, the only other female characters are Andy's mother, whose face is never shown, the annoying little sister of the evil boy next door, and Andy's baby sister, whom the toys call "Princess Drool." The standard Pixar maturity formula thus follows this script: a mature female, who is coded as an adult, accepts responsibility for herself and for others. Even in the beginning of the movie, she can intuit how other people will react by anticipating their feelings and the relationship between cause and effect, and, as I will demonstrate in my analysis of two Pixar films marketed directly to adolescents, *Up* and *Toy Story 3*, she has a higher cognitive facility than the male characters around her do because she can accept death and control her sexuality.

The Pixar maturity formula

The major protagonists of thirteen Pixar films are male — with the exception of Jessie in *Toy Story 2* (Lasseter 1999) and *Toy Story 3*. But on the credits, Jessie receives third billing in both *Toy Story 2* and *Toy Story 3*, reinforcing cultural narratives that males matter more than females. I reserve a special place for Pixar's one exception to this rule, *Brave*, in my conclusion. Moreover, all of the male Pixar protagonists grow because they *need* to grow: Nemo grows in *Finding Nemo* (Stanton 2003); Mr. Incredible grows; Buzz and Woody grow. Pixar clearly assumes that children are interested in — and perhaps even inspired by — stories about other people's growth, reinforcing my belief that growth is a pervasive cognitive script.

Disney has a long tradition of appealing to a dual audience.[4] In Disney's major releases, the story frequently includes adults who need to grow as much as adolescents do in a clear bid to pull parents into theatres along with their children. Mr. Banks established the model for adult maturation in *Mary Poppins* (Stevenson 1964), which was Disney's first commercially successful use of the adult-growth pattern. Indeed, Mr. Banks grows more than both his children put together. Following this fifty-year-old script of including adult male growth as a subplot of children's movies, Pixar makes their films and markets them to a dual audience of both children and adults, which may explain why the protagonists in Disney and Pixar movies are so often adults.

This may also be why, even though some Pixar protagonists are coded to look like adults, they don't *act* like adults. The main characters in all three *Toy Story* films, *Cars* and *Cars 2* (Lasseter 2011), *Ratatouille* (Bird 2007) *WALL·E* (Stanton 2008), and *Monsters University* are physically coded as being older than children, although they either are or act like young men. (Indeed, *Monsters University* is so attenuated to the ways that young men bond and so sexist in the ways that it follows the hackneyed script of the bromance that it deserves no further attention than this one sentence.)[5] More interestingly, in WALL·E's case the robot is at least 700 years old, indicating that he's far from being the age of a child. The protagonists of *The Incredibles*, *Monsters, Inc.* (Docter 2001), and *Up* are actually adult men. Carl in *Up*, for example, is even labeled "elderly" by his young side-kick, Russell.[6]

The Pixar maturity formula is a script that appears in most of these films. For example, Mrs. Incredible is both the most mature character and the only character in another Pixar movie marketed to adolescents, *The Incredibles*, who seems capable of understanding the relationship between cause and effect. She may well be the most mature of all Pixar characters. Her husband, Mr. Incredible, rushes off in a scripted mid-life-crisis-induced urge to save the world without thinking through the negative consequences of his actions. His children, of course, ignore their mother's injunction to keep themselves safe and also rush off to save their

---

4. Barbara Wall refers to texts that address both a child and an adult audience as "dual address" (1991: 36) to a "dual audience" (1991: 22).

5. A "bromance" is a homosocial and/or homoerotic story about male bonding between two male friends. These buddies, who are close enough emotionally to be, effectively, brothers follow a script that parallels the heterosexist script for a romance — hence the term "bromance." Original coinage attributed to Chris Cote in 1999 (TransWorld Surf). See also ("bromance," n. 2013).

6. Ian Wojcik-Andrews writes about "Kid Quests," his term for children's movies that pair children and adults who share quests (2013: 61–74).

parents — leading to more unintended consequences. The antagonist, Syndrome, shares the same male inability to perceive the relationship between cause and effect.

The other two adult females in *The Incredibles* are Mirage, something of a *femme fatale* who needs to grow before she can see the error of her ways, and Edna Mode, the temperamental, histrionic, and irascible fashion designer whose voice is that of a man — specifically, Brad Bird, author and director of *The Incredibles*. She is utterly fabulous — and ultimately little more than a caricature of Hollywood costume designer Edith Head. Moreover, Edna's desexualization is supposed to be part of what makes her funny, but she enacts a cultural narrative with damaging implications for cross-gendered and trans-gendered people.

Ratatouille is another Pixar film marketed to children, adolescents, and adults. The protagonist is a young adult male, and the film is set in a male-dominated environment — the kitchen of a haute cuisine restaurant in Paris — so all of the main and supporting characters except one are male. The kitchen's *rôtisseur*, Collette, is Pixar's first obvious attempt at creating a feminist character. She is active; she is strong; she is competitive; she is generous; she is, indeed, a well-rounded character who appears to be defying stereotypical scripts. She says things like:

> haute cuisine is an antiquated hierarchy built upon rules written by stupid old men, rules designed to make it impossible for women to enter this world…. I am the toughest cook in this kitchen. I worked too hard for too long to get here and I am not going to jeopardize it for some stupid garbage boy who got lucky. (Bird 2007)

But Collette is also the only significant female character in the movie — so of course, she is also the only mature character. (Oddly enough, although the movie has hundreds of rats, all of them are male. How are these rats procreating so prolifically if every single one of them is a male?) In any event, Collette bears the responsibility for representing all women and all mature adults. The burden is so great for one animated character to bear that she never fully gains traction as a completely likeable character, which plays into cultural narratives that "strong women are strident and often unlikable."

A few characters complicate concepts of maturity in Pixar films, but they do so in problematic ways. The Prospector in *Toy Story 2* initially appears to be that film's mature character — but he proves to be the bad guy. In *Finding Nemo*, because the mother is eaten by a barracuda relatively early in the movie, the closest thing to a helpful or mature adult is a turtle, Crush, who talks like an adolescent, but proves to be wise because he is 150 years old. He's generous and a good role-model, but Pixar nonetheless still depicts him as an adolescent male, implying that it is impossible for males to be truly mature, especially if they like to have fun.

As I have already mentioned, WALL·E is even older than Crush, although the robot is as gendered as the turtle. Robots can't procreate, so why do they need to be gendered in the first place? WALL·E's love interest, Eve, is nothing but a flying robotic uterus. (She is designed to open herself up and store life forms inside her body so as to nurture them in a conceptual blend that merges technology and biology.) The closest thing the film *WALL·E* has to a grown-up is Captain McCrae, whose ship has been orbiting the earth for centuries while all the humans grow increasingly fat and lazy from living in centuries of microgravity. Like all males in Pixar movies, however, McCrae needs to grow into his maturity. He is initially as inept as everyone else aboard the starship Axiom and only later grows into a semblance of the maturity that real leadership requires.

Mature characters in Pixar films, then, are usually scripted as female and as adults. The scripting depends greatly on cognitive functioning, such as understanding causality and empathy — which females are scripted to do almost automatically and males are scripted as needing to learn. The Pixar maturity formula emerges from cognitively gendered conceptualizations and contributes directly to widespread cultural narratives about female maturity and male immaturity.

Up and Being-towards-death

More than any Pixar movie, *Up* problematizes not only maturation but also maturity. The plot is shaped entirely by a competition between two elderly men hoping to achieve something significant that will help them deal with their individual fear of their mortality. Despite his highly problematic politics, Heidegger's work in *Being and Time* has some pertinence to the study of growth and maturation — especially in the context of men approaching their deaths. According to Heidegger, we are all always dying, which involves understanding ourselves as Being-in-time; in other words, we live constantly aware of death as the opposite of life: "The 'end' of Being-in-the-world is death" (2008: H234).[7] That said, in Heideggerian terms, the ability to mature is inherent in life, and human maturity depends on a cognitive awareness of temporality and sentience (one's own and others'), of care and concern, and of the limitations of being, as being is constrained by death. All maturation then is implicated in Being-towards-death, according to Heideggerian philosophy.

---

7. According to Heidegger, "This end, which belongs to the potentiality-for-Being — that is to say, to existence — limits and determines in every case whatever totality is possible for Dasein" (2008: H234).

But people who fear death, living in constant anxiety about it, lack the maturity that comes from understanding Being-in-Time: "[a]nxiety in the face of death must not be confused with fear in the face of one's demise" (Heidegger 2008: H251). Being-towards-death is not the same thing as fearing death, which Carl and Charles Muntz clearly do in *Up*. They fear death so thoroughly that they go to great lengths to compensate for their fears. The only human mature enough to face death with acceptance in *Up* is, of course, an adult woman. Carl's wife, Ellie, exemplifies Being-towards-death in conceptualized maturity; the two men demonstrate their fear, denial, and resultant immaturity.

The movie opens when Ellie and Carl are children who yearn to have an adventure like their hero, Charles Muntz, who assures them, "Adventure is out there!" (Docter 2009). Although Ellie can talk while she is a little girl, in the montage of scripts that follows depicting their adult life — their marriage, Carl working as a balloon vendor, their shared disappointment in not having children, their love despite life's disappointments — Ellie has no voice. Ten minutes and 47 seconds into the movie, Ellie is dead, and no other female character speaks in the entire movie, except a female cop whose lines last about eleven seconds. Ellie has spoken for a total of 3 minutes and 50 seconds. During the almost four minutes she has a voice; Carl doesn't. He says only "well," and "wow," with one "*gasp*" in between (Docter 2009). As a child, then, Ellie is already more mature and articulate than Carl, so she must be silenced and effaced in the main plot of the movie so that he may grow to her level of maturity.

After Ellie dies, Carl still loves the house he has shared with Ellie so much that he inflates a mass of balloons and floats his house away from the construction surrounding him and the threat of being moved to a nursing home. Metaphorically, the floating house is the container that protects Carl's body and serves to keep Ellie's protective spirit close to him. But Explorer Scout Russell has intrusively stowed away in the escaping house because he wants to earn his "Assisting the Elderly" badge. Carl doesn't want the boy's assistance; he wants to fulfill his childhood promise to Ellie to go to Paradise Falls, South America. Coincidentally enough, without any navigational tools or maps, the house lands right across the plateau from Paradise Falls.

Near Paradise Falls, Russell discovers a marvelous bird, whom he assumes, of course, is a male. Carl assumes the bird is male, too. The audience assumes the bird is male. Everyone always assumes Disney animals are male, unless they are specifically told otherwise. Russell names the bird "Kevin," and even when they discover she is a mother, they keep calling her by the patriarchal and colonialist name the two males have imposed on her.

And then the competition between males begins in a fairly predictable script. It would seem that Charles Muntz has been seeking that exact same bird — Kevin

— for decades, to prove to the scientific society that stripped him of his reputation that this large bird is not mythical. In the many decades he has spent living in South America, Muntz hasn't caught a single bird, although he has managed to create a servant class for himself out of dogs by inventing collars that allow them to talk. Those collars aren't anywhere near as miraculous as the fact that the movie has as many dogs as *Ratatouille* has rats — and not one of those dogs is female. Again, I ask, how are they procreating? How can a whole species be born and mature and procreate without females? Another obvious cultural narrative is being reinforced here: males matter more than females.

In any event, both of the old men in *Up* are chasing their fear of death. Muntz wants to return with the bird so he can return to glory before he dies; Carl wants to have an adventure before he dies. Carl is granted his wish largely because (to give him credit), he does grow. He learns to help others and accept help from them. Before he meets Russell and Kevin, he has only ever interacted with or depended on Ellie. Carl is rewarded because he grows; Muntz is defeated because he cannot. But because they are men, not women, the plot is predicated on the cultural narrative of their need to grow.

In the final scene, Carl fills in as Russell's father at his Scouting award ceremony — and Russell's mother, like every other female in the last 77 minutes of the movie, does not speak. As it happens, plots about male growth account for approximately 85% of the movie's length. Male growth is clearly more interesting than female growth in Pixar's *Up*.

Toy Story 3, separation anxiety, and control

If *Up* preys on people's fear of death, *Toy Story 3* preys on a variety of different types of separation anxiety. *Toy Story 3* relies on blended cultural narratives to achieve the effect of depicting the separation necessary to maturation in terms of separation anxiety: the audience must understand the back story of the previous *Toy Story* movies, and they must understand the cultural narrative in which American parents have trouble letting their children mature and become independent. Indeed, Pixar marketed the movie to the young adults, now heading to college themselves, who had grown up watching *Toy Story* fifteen years earlier. It is thus among the most adolescent of Pixar's films.

Woody and the gang fear separation from their father-figure, Andy, because he is now old enough to head to college — like many of the young adults who had watched *Toy Story* as three-year-olds and *Toy Story 3* as eighteen-year-olds. Andy's mother also expresses her separation anxiety in both the opening and closing scenes of the movie, reflecting the growing trend of hovering "helicopter parents" who have even more anxiety about being separated from their kids than the kids have about being separated from their parents. Moreover, when Andy decides to take Woody to college but leave his other toys behind, Woody faces another type of separation anxiety: fear of being removed from his community of friends. One of those friends, Jessie the Cowgirl, already has a long-established separation anxiety because the little girl who used to own her abandoned her years ago. When Andy's toys get donated to a childcare center, they meet a strawberry-scented teddy bear, Lots-o'-Huggin' Bear, who tyrannically rules the daycare center because he was so scarred when his owner abandoned him. Eventually, the toys escape the daycare center (and the city dump) and return to Andy, who gives them to a young friend, Bonnie, whom he trusts will play nicely with his toys. The final scene in which Andy and Bonnie play together with the toys is supposed to mark two rites of passage: the toys' transition to a new owner and Andy's transition into adulthood. Children — and adults — are meant to be reassured that transitions are normal and maturation will turn out all right, despite everyone's normal separation anxieties.

But who really needs to hear those cultural narratives the most? Young adults headed to college? Parents sending their children to college? Baby Boomers and Gen X-ers grieving transitions in their world caused by global warming and weather disasters, terrorism, deep recession, and demographic shifts? The movie is as YA as any movie Pixar has released except *Monsters University*. But in *Toy Story 3*, viewers receive a burden linked to maturation, one that implies that as part of their maturity, they will be responsible for the elderly, the broken, and the disposable — even though those previous generations failed to care for themselves or their world.

Several subplots of this film combine to create a guilt-laden cultural narrative: that the young are responsible for ensuring a safe future for their elders. This involves the gendered nurturing implicated in the Pixar maturity formula. Of the thirty toys who are characters in *Toy Story 3*, twenty-three are male or coded male, including the male big baby-doll. And although Woody and Buzz have grown more mature, women characters are this movie's most efficient problem-solvers. Andy's mother still has no name, and she is anxious about his leaving, but she is a mature adult — and the movie includes no other adult male human who has speaking lines. As for the female toys: Jessie and Mrs. Potato Head are as anxious as ever, and Bo-Peep is gone. Her role as the "voice of reason" proves to have been made obsolete by Barbie's increased maturity. Woody also meets a toy named Dolly, however, who immediately solves whatever problem is set before her. She is one of Bonnie's toys, and she is the only functionally mature character of that group of toys. Although Barbie weeps hysterically in the first part of the movie, only too grateful to be rescued by a Ken doll at the daycare center, she grows very quickly. She moves with Ken into his Dream House (which is, technically, a Barbie Dream House), and tries to do his bidding — but alas, she is forced by the Pixar maturity formula into a level of maturity that Ken will never achieve. Barbie helps thwart the tyranny of the dictator Lots-o'-Huggin' Bear, and in her moment of glory, she paraphrases the Declaration of Independence, insisting, "Authority should derive from the consent of the governed, not from the threat of force!" (Unkrich 2010). Here is true maturity: she is a female standing up to an abusive male, spouting rhetoric with which both American liberals and conservatives can agree.

Interestingly enough, Barbie is embodied in very sexual ways. That is, *Toy Story 3* represents Pixar's first foray into a genuine exploration of sexuality as a component of maturation. Certainly, Mr. and Mrs. Incredible kiss, as do Collette and Linguini in *Ratatouille*. Mirage is flirtatious in *The Incredibles*; so are *Cars'* Sally the Porsche and *Toy Story 2*'s Bo-Peep and Jessie. But none of those characters are as sexualized as a Barbie doll — and Pixar always ensures that these flirtatious female characters are unthreatening and effectively chaste. If Mrs. Incredible is having sex, well, that's OK; she is married after all. But most characters in the Pixar maturity formula are desexualized or flirtatious virgins. Barbie, then, would seem to be a potential anomaly, but Pixar handles Barbie's inherent promiscuity deftly by transforming Ken into a eunuch (which Ken dolls are, after all). He is obsessed with clothing and therefore unthreatening because his highest priority is his wardrobe. He is, at best, desexualized and immature, or — at worst — a mean-spirited example of homophobia as a cultural narrative. This, then, is the final piece of the Pixar maturity formula: females are mature when they can accept and control their sexuality. Buzz Lightyear can barely control his sexual energy when he is set in his Spanish-speaking mode — surely one of the most racist stereotypes yet to escape from the Pixar studio. But he is at his most immature when he can't control his libido; Jessie is no better when she eggs the behavior on. The mature body recognizes the power of sexuality and controls itself — and only women are capable of this type of sexual self-control in Pixar movies. Not all females do control themselves sexually, as Jessie demonstrates, but she is not coded as a full-grown adult woman, either. She is, after all, a "cow*girl*." Ancient scripts about females being responsible for controlling human sexuality are reinforced throughout these films in a 1950s "it's the girl's job to say no" sort of cultural narrative. This, of course, also ties into ancient cultural narratives that link maturity to reproduction and maternity.

Barbie's self-control and maturity in the face of tyranny demonstrate the second layer of adult ideology that *Toy Story 3* imposes on youth. Fears about consumption and planned obsolescence seep between the cracks of this sterile, middle-class environment. Moreover, although a few children in the daycare center are people of color, most are white. Andy and his family, Bonnie and her family, and the family that abandoned Lots-o' are all white. They all live in single-family homes, untouched by recession. Poverty doesn't exist, and the only contact the film has with working class humans involves the guys who drive the garbage trucks in town. All of this middle-classedness leads to a great deal of disposable income, and the toys become the metaphor for this disposability. As they are sent to the dump, each scene grows more intense. The dump is the blatant metaphor for a level of conspicuous consumption that is meant to be unconscionable in a recession economy. The viewer is inundated first with piles and then with mountains of waste that humans have generated — with a clear message that young people will have to clean this mess up someday, even though they are responsible for neither the mess nor the recession that makes all this waste so obviously wrong. Raising the stakes on the psycho-drama of waste, Pixar works Being-towards-death into their environmental scare tactic. As Buzz, Jessie, Woody and their six friends slide slowly into the raging fire of a trash incinerator, they gaze with sad acceptance at one another, clasp hands, and grimly face death together. This is Buzz Lightyear's moment of greatest maturity, for it is he who calmly communicates to Jessie — and she then to all the other toys but Woody — the certainty of their death as individuals and as a community.

They are saved, of course, by a *deus ex machina*. Literally, the "little green men" space alien toys operate a mechanical junkyard claw and pull the toys out of the jaws of hell. Thus, Pixar gets to have it both ways: the characters acknowledge their Being-towards-death (in ways far healthier than *Up* does), but the toys still don't need to die in order to accomplish this script of maturation.

They can't die, of course, because this is a G-rated movie and such movies do not allow for a holocaust of nine beloved characters. Even more important, however, these toys insist that they must live in order to take care of Andy. "We are his *toys*," Woody says as an invocation of their sacred responsibility to take care of their parent-figure, Andy (Unkrich 2010). People, like toys, will inevitably grow older and broken. Children who do not take care of their toys, like toys who do not take care of their owners, are meant to feel guilty for their negligence. Of all the separation anxieties that saturate this film, the fear of the child no longer taking care of the elderly is the most pervasive. *Toy Story 3* saddles the young with responsibility for the aging population as effectively as *Up* does. Part of maturation is and should be accepting care for the elderly — but when the older generation has been as profligate as the generation that has generated as much trash as *Toy Story 3* depicts, something in the equation seems flawed. Why should young people have to assume responsibility for a generation that has shirked theirs?

In sum: according to *Toy Story 3*, adolescents are responsible for the environment, for standing up to unjust tyranny, and for calming their elders' fears of becoming obsolete. These cultural narratives about responsibility, however, are mixed because, at the end of the day, only women are truly mature in this film. Various male characters grow into maturity, and Woody even achieves maturity by the very end of *Toy Story 3*, but these male characters either achieve their maturity late or do not sustain it for long. Thus, *Toy Story 3* and *Up* both hold adolescents responsible for adults' future, despite teenagers' lack of economic, political, or social power. Only adult women in Pixar films can sustain maturity, which they do in largely cognitive terms: by accepting social- and self-responsibility, by anticipating the relationship between cause and effect, by resiliency in the face of problem-solving, and most important, by accepting death and controlling their sexuality. That is, their embodiment as sexualized-but-dying organisms is fully integrated with their cognition. In giving women so much responsibility for being self-aware while they save men from themselves, the Pixar maturity formula absolves males of sustained maturity.

Conclusion

With the film *Brave*, Pixar demonstrates that the studio is aware of the inherent sexism in the Pixar maturity formula. Although all the males in *Brave* are grossly immature, for the first time, the film depicts two flawed female characters who both need to grow: a mother and her adolescent daughter, Merida. Merida rejects the scripted narrative of the marriage plot, although she falls prey to another script that is overused in Hollywood: the teenaged daughter's Freudian conflict with her mother.[8] Merida wishes her mother would change, and change the mother does: into a bear. Queen Elinor thus serves as a blended conceptual metaphor who, quite literally, enacts the script of the "Mama Grizzly." Indeed, that metaphor is so literal here as to be a laughable cliché — but at least, for the first time, Pixar has created a film that manages to avoid the Pixar maturity formula. Unsurprisingly, the film was not an immediate financial success in grossing only $66.7 million in its first weekend, as compared to *Toy Story 3*'s $110.3 million first weekend take and *Up*'s $72 million, adjusted for inflation (Dennis 2012). Merida's maturation, however, revolves solely around two axis: her mother and marriage. While the adolescent protagonist wins the right to decide who she will marry, or even if she will marry, the plot rests on a blend of the marriage plot and the mother/daughter plot.[9] In other words, although immature males in Pixar movies face a variety of different

---

8. For more on mother/daughter conflicts in literature for youth, see Trites, *Waking Sleeping Beauty* (1997: 100–121).

9. Although the term "marriage plot" is a conventional term in Anglophone literary criticism, see Marianne Hirsch, *The Mother/Daughter Plot*, for more on both the marriage plot and the

types of conflict, the one girl who needs to mature faces the only two standard crises that have faced adolescent girls since Persephone had to decide between Demeter and Hades. Is it any wonder that adolescents raised on a steady diet of Pixar's cultural narratives might well conclude that boys' growth is, indeed, more interesting than girls'?

Ultimately, my concern about the Pixar maturity formula stems from the cultural narrative, the world message, being conveyed to adolescents. Young people — especially adolescent girls — are given the message that their growth is not very interesting, but it is nonetheless their job to improve the world. This formula also implies a cultural narrative that it is normal for adult males to be immature and that it is abnormal for adult women to have the same daily incompetencies, fears of death, and libidinal drives that men have. That combination creates gendered cultural narratives about maturity that are unbalanced and unsustainable. For example, not only do these movies imply that only women can be truly competent adults, but they also imply that the drive for competence can lead those women to over-functioning perfectionism, as is the case with Colette, with Andy's mother, and with Queen Elinor. The films also imply that males are rarely capable of overcoming their narcissism long enough to mature significantly, as is the case with Buzz Lightyear. And *Up* implies that only women are self-actualized enough to accept death. Moreover, these cultural narratives are as insulting to men as they are to women.

Early feminism called for females to be depicted as something more than just passive, house-bound girls. Pixar has clearly responded with smart, strong women like Mrs. Incredible, Collette in *Ratatouille*, and Barbie in *Toy Story 3*. But the response has been a limited one. It's as if Pixar believes that in depicting one strong woman per film, the studio has fulfilled all moral obligations to portray other females in a ratio that equals the depiction of male characters. Simply focusing on one mature female, however, is still tokenism, even if that character is the strongest character in the film. Even worse, if that one woman is invariably the only mature character, audiences experience cultural affirmation of male immaturity, replicating the cultural narrative that women are more mature than men. The repetition of information creates stereotypical knowledge — here, as a maturity formula that privileges only male growth — and reinforces stereotyped scripts.

What then are the cognitive effects on adolescents and preadolescents? How do these films affect the self-perceptions of young adults? And how do they affect the way that girls and boys think differently about maturation? Given the frequency with which the cultural narrative "women are more mature than men"

---

mother/daughter plot (1989: 10–11). For more on the myth of Persephone influencing narrative structure in children's literature, see Blackford (2012: 1–20).

is repeated, it seems possible that viewers of both genders might well internalize gendered and self-fulfilling conceptualizations of maturation from the sheer volume of repetition.

Feminists — like Marxists, post-colonialists, race theorists, Queer theorists, and all scholars of alterity and otherness — have identified damaging cultural narratives and their ideological implications for decades. Cultural narratives enscript cognitive conceptualizations, entailing them in ways that prevent people from considering alternative cultural narratives. How many times, for example, does an adolescent need to watch films in which females are the only mature characters before s/he concludes that women in all walks of life are, indeed, more mature than men? The enscripting process of the cultural narrative thus limits conceptualization, usually because enscripting works unconsciously. Cognitive psychologists believe stereotyping to be a categorization that is "automatically activated upon perception of a category member" (Lepore & Brown 1997:275), and they believe the process is a largely subconscious one (Oliner 2000).[10] However, one example of a shifting cultural narrative demonstrates that it is possible to alter the entailments of cultural narratives: changing attitudes toward gay marriage in the U.S. in the last decade exemplify how cultural narratives can be re-enscripted. That said, cultural narratives about gender and race (and most forms of otherness) are enscripted so frequently and so early in the lives of children and adolescents, through books, films, television, the media, parenting, schools, and religion, that sexism and racism are deeply embedded in the cognition of many, many people.

Male immaturity has been a source of comedy from ancient times to Homer Simpson. Pixar is not alone in relying on scripts of male incompetence for humor. They are, however, deluding themselves if they believe their efforts to date are feminist. Instead, they are perpetuating sexist norms as pervasive cognitive categorizations that emerge from embodiment and reside in both conscious and unconscious conceptualizations of growth to reinforce ancient stereotypes.

---

10. For more on cognition and stereotyping, see Bodenhausen and Macrae (1998) and Macrae, Bodenhausen, and Milne (1995). In addition, although Lawrence Hirschfeld (1996) employs questionable research methods in his experimental design, he does outline the cognitive dimensions of racism as an effect of human categorization in *Race in the Making: Cognition, Culture, and the Child's Construction of Human Kinds*.

CHAPTER 5

Epistemology, ontology, and the philosophy of experientialism

As well as exploring such cognitive issues as embodied metaphors, scripts, and cultural narratives, theorists informed by cognitive linguistics are concerned with epistemology, ontology, and consciousness in the effort to understand not only how the brain works, but also to engage philosophically with how we *know* and what we do with knowledge. Lakoff and Johnson refer to their philosophy as "experientialism," arguing that "[o]ur experience of the world is not separate from our conceptualization of the world. Indeed, ... the same hidden mechanisms that characterize our conscious system of concepts also play a central role in creating our experience.... [T]here is an extensive and important overlap between those mechanisms that shape our concepts and those that shape our experience" (1999: 509). In other words, the ways that we experience, categorize, and conceptualize ideas, such as growth, are inseparable from our philosophical understandings of those concepts.

Lakoff and Johnson first articulate their theory of experientialist philosophy in *Metaphors We Live By*:

> We reject the objectivist view that there is absolute and unconditional truth without adopting the subjectivist alternative of truth as obtainable only through the imagination, unconstrained by external circumstances.... An experientialist approach ... allows us to bridge the gap between the objectivist and subjectivist myths about impartiality and the possibility of being fair and objective.... This does not mean that there are no truths; it means only that truth is relative to our conceptual system, which is grounded in, and constantly tested by, our experiences and those of other members of our culture in our daily interactions with other people and with our physical and cultural environments. (1980: 192–193)

Lakoff and Johnson reject all notions of the Cartesian split between body and mind because — as they put it — "the mind is inherently embodied, reason is shaped by the body" (1999: 5). They argue that philosophical questions emerge from three things: "a reason shaped by the body, a cognitive unconscious to which we have no direct access, and metaphorical thought of which we are largely unaware" (1999: 7). These three components of cognitive linguistics — embodied reason, an inaccessible unconscious that shapes that reason, and metaphorical thinking, which is also implicated in our conscious and unconscious reasoning — help me analyze growth in terms of such fundamental philosophical concepts in adolescent literature as ontology and epistemology. The novels in David Almond's Skellig sequence, *Skellig* (1998) and *My Name is Mina* (2010), as well as Walter Mosley's *47* (2005) and Sherman Alexie's *Absolutely True Diary of a Part-Time Indian* (2007), demonstrate the relationship between maturation and experientialist philosophy in adolescent literature. Philosophy, as inflected by cognitive linguistics, provides one avenue for exploring how literary characters experience growth both ontologically, in terms of their being, and epistemologically, in terms of how they know.

For example, in David Almond's *My Name is Mina*, Mina philosophically asks a conceptual question, "Is there a God? Was there ever emptiness?" (2010: 16). *My Name is Mina* is the prequel to Almond's *Skellig*, in which Mina tells her friend Michael, "Sometimes we have to accept that there are things we can't know.... Sometimes we think we should be able to know everything. But we can't. We have to allow ourselves to see what there is to see, and we have to imagine" (1999: 140). Mina and Michael fundamentally question what it means to be and what it means to know. They also worry whether they should help someone who might be homeless when their parents don't even know what they are up to, a situation that creates a recurring ethical tension throughout *Skellig* about what these children value and how much responsibility they bear for others. Their growth, then, involves a considerable amount of philosophical conceptualization.

Skellig and *My Name is Mina* demonstrate how significant both embodied reason and the relationship between the cognitive unconscious and metaphorical thought are to adolescent literature. Walter Mosely's *47* and Sherman Alexie's *The Absolutely True Diary of a Part-Time Indian*, on the other hand, problematize the relationships between epistemology, ontology, and categorization — in this case, specifically the construction of race as a cognitive concept. This chapter will thus proceed in two sections: in the first section I will analyze embodied cognition in *Skellig* and *My Name is Mina*; that is, I will examine how the protagonists' maturation engages what Lakoff and Johnson would describe as "reason shaped by the body," eventually demonstrating how Almond employs metaphorical thought to interrogate complex philosophical questions about being, knowing, and values. In the second section, I will discuss racial construction as an epistemological and ontological issue integrally connected with maturation, concluding with a commentary on the relationship between cognitive linguistics and philosophy in the context of adolescent literature.

Embodied reason in David Almond's novels

At the beginning of Almond's novel *Skellig*, Michael finds in the garage of his new home a man he initially assumes is homeless but who proves to be a creature that may perhaps be an angel, or a new phase in evolutionary history, or something else altogether. Michael nonetheless understands the creature, Skellig, and his ontological status entirely in terms of embodiment, as does the only friend to whom the boy shows Skellig, Mina (the girl next door). Michael establishes a set of epistemological questions when he relies on his perceptions to question how he has gained knowledge about Skellig; that is, the text makes clear that he knows what he knows by emphasizing how he gains knowledge through his five senses. For example, he knows Skellig has wings because he first feels them on Skellig's back, "[l]ike thin arms, folded up. Springy and flexible," and because he sees them with his own eyes (Almond 1999: 30). Indeed, Michael's first perception of Skellig relies on vision, "that's when I saw him" (8), and he subsequently doubts his own perception, thinking later that night, "I'd never seen him at all. That had all been part of a dream" (10). Skellig later underscores how significant vision perception is to Michael when the man asks the boy sarcastically, "Had a good look?…. What are you looking at, eh?" (30). That last question is, indeed, the text's pivotal ontological question: what *is* Michael looking at? Skellig is remarkable, with fingers and knuckles "twisted and swollen" by arthritis, "hundreds of tiny creases and cracks all over his pale face" (29). Skellig tells Michael that "Arthur Itis…. is the one that's ruining me bones. Turns you to stone, then crumbles you away" (31). Readers might well wonder if Michael has simply found an old gargoyle in the garage and is imagining it into being.

Michael invites Mina to meet Skellig. The initial scene that involves the three of them serves the almost mechanical purpose in the text of assuring the reader that Michael is neither imagining nor inventing this creature; Skellig has an ontological reality that Mina, too, can perceive. "I'll see whatever's there," she whispers to Michael as they enter the garage, underscoring the perceptual importance of vision to her knowledge-acquisition (74). When Michael looks at Mina as she first observes Skellig, the boy emphasizes her embodiment: "I looked back at Mina's dark form looking down at us, her pale face, her mouth and eyes gaping in astonishment" (75). She also underscores the cognitive importance of perception in *My Name is Mina* when she writes in her journal: "Look at the world. Smell it, taste it, listen to it, feel it, look at it. Look at it!" (2010: 31). She is discursively portrayed as both body and mind; she is, as Lakoff and Johnson would have it, "an embodied mind" because her cognition — particularly her perception — is inevitably housed within her body (Lakoff & Johnson 1999: 37–38). Michael and Skellig, too, are embodied minds in the same sense; their minds and bodies cannot be separated. Eventually, Skellig reveals his wings, "They were twisted and uneven, they were covered in cracked and crooked feathers. They clicked and trembled as they opened. They were wider than his shoulders, higher than his head" (Almond 1999: 94). Michael touches them with his fingertips and palms and feels "the bones and sinews and muscles" that support the wings (95). When Mina asks Michael why he is touching them, Michael's answer reflects his attempt to understand how he knows what he knows about his entire world:

> "What you doing?" she whispered.
> "Making sure the world's still really there," I said. (95)

Michael and Mina nurse Skellig back to health with aspirin, cod liver oil, beer, and Chinese food. Skellig calls beer "Nectar…. the drink of the gods" (75) and Chinese food "the food of the gods" (29), implying that he may well be a fallen god himself. He is an eating, breathing, thinking being who sometimes eats live rodents and vomits pellets of their bones, just as owls do. He may be human or animal or angel, but he is an embodied, sentient being. The text gives the reader no determinant answer as to Skellig's ontological status; rather, readers are given information about his and others' perceptions, embodiment, language, and thought — and are left to draw their own conclusions. After experiencing Skellig, Michael and Mina grow to trust their own perceptions, acknowledging that what they are seeing is both real and miraculous. Readers are thus invited to conclude that acknowledging embodied perception is a key component of mature cognition.

Mina is specifically embodied as "little and she had hair as black as coal and the kind of eyes you think you can see right through" (Almond 1999: 25); she frequently sits in trees. She describes herself in *My Name Is Mina* as "very skinny and very small and she had jet-black hair and a pale face and shining eyes" (Almond 2010: 43). Her doctors believe that she should be medicated to "make her feel better," but her mother understands, "They'll stop her from feeling anything at all. She's not some kind of robot. She's a little girl that's growing up" (44). Mina's mother thus makes a direct link between the embodiment of physical growth and psychological growth. She tells her daughter that as she grows, "she'd feel stronger more often and not feel so small" (43). That is, growth involves both body and mind. This second novel is direct in discussing cognition in terms of the mind and human thought when Mina insists in her journal that her mind "is not in order. My mind is not straight lines. My mind is a clutter and a mess. It is my mind, but it is also very like other minds. And like all minds, like every mind that there has ever been and every mind that there will ever be, it is a place of wonder. !THE MIND IS A PLACE OF WONDER!" (11–12). As *My Name is Mina* draws to a close, Mina and her mother stare at the stars, and her mother tenderly cradles her daughter's head in her hands. "I can nearly hold your whole head in my hands," she tells Mina; "Your head holds all those stars, all that darkness, all these noises. It holds the universe" (282). She then rests her daughter's head against her own and says, "Two heads, two universes, interlinked" (282). Again, the text is connecting embodiment and cognition, this time with an affirmation that human society depends upon our ability to recognize each other as embodied minds that are dependent on one another. In other words, Mina's mother is teaching her daughter something about her own values: it is a good thing to recognize and appreciate that other people have their own intricate and complex thought processes. The philosophical implications are rich: our being, our ontological status, depends on our embodied minds, as does our epistemology, our ability to know what we know. But even more important, without the ability to recognize each other as embodied minds, we would not have the ability to treat each other ethically, with the values that acknowledge and respect the other. Because Mina is learning to value the complexity of other people's minds, she can accept the complexity of Skellig's when she meets him — and she values him enough to help him. Mina must, however, first grow to understand her own cognitive complexity. As Mina later writes in her journal, "Does everybody feel this excitement, this astonishment, as they grow? I close my eyes and stare into the universe inside myself" (Almond 2010: 287).

In *My Name Is Mina*, Mina writes about how she observes Michael's embodiment almost entirely in terms of action and emotion (as opposed to writing about him in terms of thinking): he "stare[s] glumly" at the yard in his new home and "kick[s] it hard" (13, 31); he bounces his ball in the yard, against the garden wall, and against the garage (262–263). "He glares at the street as if he hates it" (263). She notices his "[c]lenched fists. Hard eyes" — and she agrees with her mother that he needs a friend now that he has moved into a new neighborhood (294). The character Skellig does not appear in *My Name Is Mina*, but in *Skellig*, the mystical creature also demonstrates a relationship between embodied action and emotion. Three times, Skellig holds hands with children and dances with them in a circle in ways that enliven them: twice with Mina and Michael, once with Michael's baby sister who is dying but becomes miraculously revived by Skellig's dance. In the first dance, Skellig "seemed stronger than he'd ever been. He took my hand and Mina's hand," and the three circle in and out of light and darkness in a moonlit attic until they are whirling so fast that:

> Each face spun from shadow to light, from shadow to light, from shadow to light, and each time the faces of Mina and Skellig came into the light they were more silvery, more expressionless. Their eyes were darker, more empty, more penetrating.... It was like we had moved into each other, like we had become one thing. (Almond 1999: 119–120)

Eventually, Michael perceives "ghostly wings" growing on Mina's back (120). Skellig calls the two children "a pair of angels" and tells them that he has been healed by "the owls and the angels" (166, 120). Later, he dances with Michael's baby sister and perhaps heals her, and in his final meeting with Michael and Mina, they dance again in a circle: "We began to turn. Our hearts and breath were together. We turned and turned until the ghostly wings rose from Mina's back and mine, until we felt ourselves being raised, until we seemed to turn and dance in the empty air" (167). Although Skellig expresses few emotions other than pain and frustration early in the novel, by the time he has regained enough health to initiate action himself, his actions create emotional catharsis for those who move with him.

Michael, Mina, and Skellig all demonstrate the impossibility of the Cartesian split. That is, none of them can *know* without embodied experiences that affect their rationality and *being*. As French philosopher Maurice Merleau-Ponty writes in his refusal to accept the Cartesian split, "I'm conscious of the world through the medium of my body" (1962: 82). Sensory perceptions affect Michael's, Mina's, and Skellig's thoughts — which are clearly embodied — and the abilities and limitations of their bodies subsequently cause them to make the value judgments they do. Michael and Mina, for example, perceive Skellig's embodied suffering and consciously decide to come to his aid. As they help him heal, he heals others — including them and Michael's baby sister. Additionally, *My Name Is Mina* actively expresses how important it is for humans to recognize that we are extraordinary beings, despite the pain that surrounds us. As Mina puts it: "this horrible world is so blooming beautiful and so blooming weird that sometimes I think it'll make me faint!" (Almond 2010: 31). Mina tells Skellig he is beautiful twice (Almond 1999: 85, 94). She is acknowledging that he is beautiful because he exists as an embodied being, both viscerally and cognitively. Her growth — like Michael's — depends upon reason as an embodied faculty — and that cognitive ability to reason depends upon conceptualizations that involve ontology, epistemology, and a value system predicated on those conceptualizations.

The cognitive unconscious and metaphorical thought

Cognitive linguists explore both the *brain* and *thought* as interrelated phenomena; thinking cannot happen independently of a biologically-situated brain. They also acknowledge that most cognition is *unconscious* thought, rather than conscious. Lakoff and Johnson even assert: "It is a rule of thumb among cognitive scientists that unconscious thought is 95 percent of all thought — and that may be a serious underestimate" (1999: 13). As I have noted in Chapter 1, these cognitive linguists also argue that human thought — both conscious and unconscious — depends heavily upon categorization, which they understand as the brain's primary form of cognition. For example, when Mina divides the world into the value-driven and perhaps overlapping descriptions "blooming beautiful" and "blooming weird," she is categorizing, without even realizing that she is. Categorization, in turn, affects how our brains manage information in the form of concepts. How we know what we know depends on our ability to separate categories from each other: chair from child; anger from joy; beautiful from weird. Concepts, in turn, lead to *conceptual structures*, or conceptualizations, with which our brains can understand complicated concepts such as "emotions" as one category and "anger" or "joy" or "grief" as more specific categories within that structure — and our cognition allows us to understand that categories such as "joy" and "happiness" are more interconnected than "joy" and "anger."

Moreover, as we have seen, cognitive linguistics emphasizes how dependent upon embodiment our conceptual structures are. As I discussed in Chapter 1, at an early age, we develop the ability to create categories based on our bodies: "here" is closer to our bodies than "there"; "being full" is a concept we understand both from eating and from relying on our sense of sight and sense of touch to perceive containers being filled (Lakoff & Johnson 1980: 51; Lakoff & Johnson 1999: 31–35). Because we define concepts in terms of our bodies, we systematically create and rely on embodied metaphors.

Not unlike *Anne of Green Gables*, *Skellig* relies on the embodied metaphor that maps vision on to understanding. For example, when Michael takes Mina into the garage to be witness to the phenomenon he has found there, he tells her: "I'm worried that you won't *see* what I think I *see*" (Almond 1999: 74, italics added). On one level, Michael is worrying that Mina won't share the same visual perception that he has, but on a far more significant metaphorical level, he is worrying that Mina won't understand, that Mina won't accept that Skellig is real. Michael connects directly the concepts of "thinking" and "seeing" when he says "what I think I see" (74). Later, Mina and Michael talk to Mina's mother about various types of visions, including William Blake's. Here, too, humans structure concepts of the spiritual and mystical using an embodied metaphor of sight, *visions*. Mina's mother shows them Blake's drawings of his visions and then says, "Maybe we could all *see* such beings, if only we knew how to…. But it's enough for me to have you two angels at my table"; "Yes," she continues, "Isn't it amazing? I *see* you clearly, two angels at my table" (132, italics added). The perception of seeing and the cognitive act of understanding are structurally fused in this woman's dialogue. Moreover, characters in this novel often say, "See?" as shorthand for "do you understand?" (Almond 1999: 22, 37, 58), and on the very first page when Michael describes discovering Skellig, his narration establishes the conceptual connection between the embodied perception of seeing and the embodied concept of understanding: "I'd soon begin to *see* the truth about him, that there'd never been another creature like him in the world" (1, italics added). Michael demonstrates how embodied experience — that is, *experientialism* — structures our epistemology.

Another set of conceptual metaphors in *Skellig* and *My Name Is Mina* involves a quotation from William Blake that hangs next to Mina's bed: "How can a bird that is born for joy / Sit in a cage and sing?" (Almond 1999: 50). Mina uses the metaphor of the caged bird to explain why she does not attend school: "schools inhibit the natural curiosity, creativity, and intelligence of children. The mind needs to be opened out into the world, not shuttered down inside a gloomy classroom" (49). The metaphor is a complex one: CHILDREN ARE BIRDS is mapped onto SCHOOLS ARE CAGES, which Mina reiterates in *My Name is Mina* (Almond 2010: 18). When Mina is assigned a writing task on her school's standardized, high-stakes testing day, she stares out the window at the birds, which are free, unlike her. The head teacher stares from the hallway through the glass door of their classroom, emphasizing how caged the children are. Mina, however, has already understood language in terms of imprisonment and power, having written in her journal, "I'll try to make my words break out of the cages of sadness, and make them sing for joy" (Almond 2010: 19). She writes, "My stories were like me. They couldn't be controlled and they couldn't fit in" (15). Her teacher, whom she calls Mrs. Scullery, has told her "that I should not write anything until I had planned what I would write. What nonsense!.... Does a bird plan its song before it sings? OF COURSE IT DOES NOT! It opens its beak and it SINGS so I will SING!" (12–13). And, indeed, Mina learns that nonsensical language can help her break free from the prison cage of school. During the high-stakes test, she answers the prompt, "Write a description of a busy place," with a nonsense essay entitled "Glibbertysnark" (160–161). It opens, "In thi biginin glibbertysnark woz doon in the woositinimana. Golgy golgy golgy than, wiss wandigle," and continues to describe the glibbertysnark's adventures in a busy place (161–162). The head teacher and teacher, both unamused, fail to understand the nonsense, and so Mina's mother elects to homeschool her. Mina is "VERY VERY VERY PLEASED" that she has been "TAKEN OUT OF SCHOOL!" (163). No longer its prisoner, she sits in a tree, bird-like, observing a nest of blackbird's eggs as they first hatch and later grow to hatchlings. Her mother tells her "I can imagine you as a bird," and Mina imagines that the blackbirds think she is "some kind of weird bird" herself (80, 24). She learns about the archaeopteryx, the winged dinosaur from whom all birds evolved — and who makes a reappearance in *Skellig*. She meets the owls who live in the attic of her grandfather's house in *My Name Is Mina*, and those owls also reappear when Mina and Michael take Skellig to shelter him in that attic and the owls begin to feed him. At various points in *My Name is Mina*, she thinks about bats, goldfinches, skylarks, chickens, and starlings; references to eggs and to angels fill the pages of both books. Michael's teacher talks about Icarus and his wings melting in *Skellig*, and both children talk to their parents about whether or not shoulder blades have been left over, after evolution, from the place where wings once grew.

At one level, CHILDREN ARE BIRDS and SCHOOLS ARE CAGES operate as fairly traditional (and obvious) symbolism. The children, after all, live on the none-too-subtly named "Falconer Road." Almond extends the traditional use of bird symbolism, however, both linguistically and philosophically. Linguistically, Almond uses a cluster of words surrounding the idea of flight to evoke cognitive freedom. Mina suggests in her journal, "Sleep while you fly. Fly while you sleep" (Almond 2010: 202). She loves afternoons with her mother when "ideas grow and take flight" (87). In *Skellig*, Michael's English teacher tells him to "let your imagination fly" (155). He also dreams that his sister is a baby bird in a nest; when he is awake and she has had her recuperative surgery, he observes her arching "her back like she was about to dance or fly" (Almond 1999: 180). At one point, Mina climbs out of her tree feeling disoriented, "like I was coming out from a poem or a story, or like I was a poem or a story myself. Or like I was coming out from an egg!" (191). She believes that "words should wander and meander. They should fly like owls and flicker like bats," and some pages of her journal "will be like a sky with a single bird in it. Some will be like a sky with a swirling swarm of starlings in it. My sentences will be a clutch, a collection, a pattern, a swarm, a shoal, a mosaic. They will be a circus, a menagerie, a tree, a nest" (11). She despises people who are "bird trappers … who trap the spirit, people who cage the soul" (180). Mina also reminds the reader again that schools are "CAGES and PLACES TO BE AVOIDED!" (Almond 2010: 123).

This interconnected set of metaphors demonstrates how entailment affects conceptualization. If we think about the imagination "taking flight," we at least temporarily limit how we are thinking about imagination and so are not likely to simultaneously think about it in other terms — say, by way of contrast, thinking of imagination as spontaneous combustion or fertile soil. Since the following concepts all belong to the conceptual category of birds — flight/flying, cages/traps, emerging from eggs — these entailments work together in these two novels to link linguistically the concepts of children and freedom. Almond's use of this categorical entailment is consistent and intricate. While some readers of *Skellig* may miss the point that children need freedom, no reader of *My Name is Mina* possibly could. Mina makes the point directly in her journal: "CHILDREN HAVE TO BE LEFT ALONE SOMETIMES!…. SOMETIMES CHILDREN MUST BE LEFT ALONE TO BE STILL AND SILENT, AND TO DO" (Almond 2010: 111).

Another complex network of entailments in these two novels involves the underworld, Persephone, death, and the use of "dead" as an adjective, as in "dead easy and dead stupid" (Almond 2010:92). When Michael first hears Skellig in the garage, he hears a gentle scratching sound, and then "dead quiet" (Almond 1999:4); his baby sister's face is "dead white" before she is healed, and her hair is "dead black" (11). The use of "dead" as slang for "very" is not accidental: Mina is working through her grief that her father has died; Michael is facing his grief that his sister might die — and their experiences with Skellig seem like a brush with death. "I thought he was dead," Michael says upon first meeting Skellig (1). Furthermore, in *My Name is Mina*, Mina attempts to journey into the underworld by exploring an abandoned mine, and she thumps on the earth in the spring to awaken Persephone. When Michael suggests naming his newly healed baby sister "Persephone," his father rejects the name, and they give her instead a more consistently life-affirming name, "Joy" (Almond 1999:182). Ideas about death and the underworld intertwine to invoke ontological questions about what it means to be a living body — and the adjective "dead" itself becomes the linguistic intensifier that underscores the importance of this type of philosophical questioning. Thus, these texts explore ideas about what it means to be "dead" — as opposed to "alive" — both linguistically and philosophically. In other words, Mina and Michael are conceptualizing Heideggerian Being-towards-death as a logical stage of their maturing and embodied reason.

Both *Skellig* and *My Name is Mina* employ a network of entailments involving the metaphor THE LIVING BODY IS A CONTAINER. Mina's mother, after all, has told her that her brain "holds the universe" (Almond 2010:282); that is, Mina's brain is a *container* that holds ideas. People in the hospital "lay exhausted, *filled* with pain" (Almond 1999:66, italics added); Mina's teacher accuses her of being "*full* of nothing but stupid crackpot notions" (Almond 2010:155, italics added); Mina is happy when someone tells her to live her life well, "Live it to the *full*" (Almond 2010:72, italics added). This entailment ultimately involves various ontological and epistemological questions: What is the human body? What is thought? How are we filled with knowledge about our bodies' being? How do we think about our bodies as containers? But these uses of the words *filled* and *full* also demonstrate how linguistic entailments shape human thought. It is almost impossible *not* to think of our bodies as containers, but here, Mina's ability to conceptualize ontological status emerges from what she knows and how she knows it; her epistemology is shaped by her embodiment.

Thus, the linguistic entailments in *Skellig* and *My Name Is Mina* also serve the philosophical issues at work in these novels. Although Skellig's ontological status is never defined, the novels return time and again to questions about what defines the living human body, how things are created, what it means to live Being-towards-death, and what happens after humans die. For example, Mina observes that most household dust is actually particles of dead human skin: "lots of people's skin mingles together and dances in the light, and the skin of the living and the skin of the dead mingle together and dance in the light!" (Almond 2010:73). Moreover, she thinks of herself as a mortal container when she observes that "[t]he human body is 65 percent water. Two-thirds of me is constantly disappearing and constantly being replaced. So most of me is not me at all!" (124). Mina also wonders how new things are created. As she writes, she thinks, "Look at the way the words move across the page and *fill* the empty spaces. Did God feel like this when he started to *fill* the emptiness? Is there a God? Was there ever *emptiness*?" (15, italics added). Later in the novel, she again equates writing, language, and creative power: "Maybe writing was a bit like being God. Every word was the start of a new creation" (237). More than the other characters in these two novels, Mina puts into words the nature of what it means to create something and how we know what that feels like. Ultimately, she is questioning the ontological status of human creation.

The most basic philosophical question in both novels may be the one that Mina and Michael both ask Skellig, "What are you?" (Almond 1999:78, 167). When Michael asks the question, Skellig answers: "Something like you, something like a beast, something like a bird, something like an angel" (167). Mina speculates, however, that "the only possible angels might be us," implying the ontological sameness of angels and humans (Almond 2010:29). As for birds, they are "quite extraordinary enough without having souls" (77); "If there is a God," Mina writes, "could it be that he's chosen the birds to speak for him?" (66). She emphasizes this point in her journal: "THE VOICE OF GOD SPEAKS THROUGH THE BEAKS OF BIRDS" (66). Although Mina tells Michael in *Skellig* that her father is in heaven "watching us" (Almond 1999:50), she writes in the prequel that "I don't really believe in Heaven at all, and I don't believe in perfect angels. I think that this might be the only Heaven there can possibly be, this world we live in now, but that we haven't quite realized it yet" (Almond 2010:29). Moreover, Mina tells Michael that Blake believed souls could "leap" out of the body and back into it, relying on the container metaphor that the body is a container in which to hold the soul. Mina then defines the soul leaping out of the body-as-container using a dance metaphor: "That's what [Blake] said. The soul leaps out and then leaps back again.... It's like a dance" (Almond 1999:152). That dance, of course, is reflected in Skellig's circular dancing that seems to meld the souls of the dancers together.

Skellig and *My Name is Mina* are no more determinant about who we are as humans and how we know what we know what we know than the texts are in defining Skellig's ontological status. And yet the very asking of the questions leads to a significant set of value judgments: we may not know who we are, but we need to care for those who need us, such as Skellig and Michael's sister and the baby birds that Mina and her mother defend from a marauding cat. Both texts clearly imply that children should be given the freedom to observe life, analyze it, and decide for themselves how to live it. We may not entirely understand our own being and how we know what we know, according to these novels, but maturation requires us to understand our own values and lead ethical lives, nonetheless. Anything related to our epistemology, ontology, and values are shaped entirely by how our conceptualizations have been influenced by experience as we grow.

The ontology and epistemology of racial construction

In his preface to *The Order of Things* (1994), Foucault cites the magic realist Jorge Luis Borges, who points out in an article on analytical language that it is fundamentally impossible to categorize the universe: "obviously there is no classification of the universe that is not arbitrary and conjectural. The reason is very simple: we do not know what thing the universe is" (Borges 2000: 104). Borges cites an ancient Chinese encyclopedia that lists an incongruent series of descriptors to divide animals into such categories as "(a) belonging to the Emperor, (b) embalmed, (c) tame, (d) sucking pigs, (e) sirens," and so on (Borges, cited in Foucault 1994: xv). Foucault uses the encyclopedia to define categorization as "a table, a *tabula*, that enables thought to operate upon the entities of our world, to put them in order, to divide them into classes, to group them according to names that designate their similarities and their differences" (Foucault 1994: xvii). Foucault is preoccupied here with differences and how "since the beginning of time, language has intersected space" (1994: xvii). That is, language systems, or discourse, create epistemologies by which people order information.

Foucault does not quibble with Borges about humanity's fundamental inability to know what the universe is, but Foucault does analyze how categorization became the predominant episteme of the Classical age (1994: 57–58). That is, the scientific discourse of the Enlightenment led scholars to an epistemology of classification — the best example of which is biological taxonomy. While cognitive scientists like Lakoff and Johnson might argue that categorization is cognitively inevitable, the fact remains that it was only in the Enlightenment that categorization became a privileged form of epistemology.

Following Foucault, Cornel West documents how race, as a category of oppression, was also an outgrowth of Enlightenment thinking; he links the discursive construction of white supremacy to an epistemological shift that privileged the scientific revolution's willingness to categorize based on perceived notions of biological difference (1999: 70–75). Race, in other words, is an epistemology predicated on discourse, not biology; it was the pseudo-scientific language of racial categorization that created race. Audrey Smedley defines race itself as an epistemology:

"Race" is a shorthand term for, as well as a symbol of, a "knowledge system," a way of knowing, of perceiving, and of interpreting the world, and of rationalizing its contents (in this case, other human beings) in terms that are derived from previous cultural-historical experience and reflective contemporary social values, relationships, and conditions. Every culture has its own ways of perceiving the world; race is the kaleidoscope through which Americans have been conditioned in our culture to view other human beings. (2007: 15)

Aileen Moreton-Robinson also relies on Foucauldian logic to argue that "[w]hiteness as an epistemological *a priori* provides for a way of knowing and being that is predicated on superiority, which becomes normalised and forms part of one's taken-for-granted knowledge" (2005: 75–76).

As the epistemology of race shifted in the eighteenth century, so too did the ontological status of non-whites — but "whiteness" had to be invented as a racial category first to create the binary of "white" and "non-white" (Allen 2002: 32). As Theodore Allen observes: the concept of the "white race" was invented in the era of colonialization to justify "reduc[ing] all members of the oppressed group to one undifferentiated social status, a status beneath that of any member of any social class within the colonizing population. *This is the hallmark of racial oppression* in its colonial origins, and as it has persisted in subsequent historical contexts" (2002: 32, italics in the original). Similarly, Edward Said reminds us that the epistemology of so-called Western thinking depends on this binary discourse of the racialized other: "European culture gained in strength and identity by setting itself off against the Orient as a sort of surrogate and even underground self" (2003: 3). Please note that Foucault is himself being Orientalist when he analyzes Borges' use of the Chinese encyclopedia:

> [I]s not China precisely this privileged *site* of *space*?.... Even its writing does not reproduce the fugitive flight of the voice in horizontal lines; it erects the motionless and still-recognizable images of things themselves in vertical columns. So much so that the Chinese encyclopaedia quoted by Borges, and the taxonomy it proposes, lead to a kind of thought without space, to words and categories that lack all life and place, but are rooted in a ceremonial space, overburdened with complex figures, with tangled paths, strange places, secret passages, and unexpected communications. There would appear to be, then, at the other extremity of the earth we inhabit, a culture entirely devoted to the ordering of space, but one that does not distribute the multiplicity of existing things into any of the categories that make it possible for us to name, speak, and think. (Foucault 1994: xix, italics in the original)

In other words, Foucault, the philosopher who studies categorization in terms of an intellectual archaeology, himself succumbs to the Enlightenment-era racism that predicates superiority on superficial categories of otherness.

Ron Mallon (2006) notes that the resulting epistemological shift following post-Enlightenment thinking led to three ontological views of race, all of which depend on or negate ideas of difference. *Racialism* posits that race is inherently biological, a view that most contemporary theorists now reject. The extreme rejection of this view is *racial skepticism*, an argument that race does not exist at all, which Mallon calls "the ontological consensus," since most theorists no longer believe race is a biological category (2006: 529). Racial skeptics reject what Mallon identifies as "race talk" because they believe that any discourse acknowledging race only perpetuates cultural racism (526). Mallon defines *race talk* as "the practices of using terms like 'race,' 'white,' 'black,' 'Asian,' and 'Hispanic' (and their associated concepts) to label and differentially treat persons" (526). In between these positions of racialism and racial skepticism is *social constructionism*: "Like their skeptical opponents, racial constructionists infer from the failure of racialism that race is not a biological kind. But unlike racial skeptics, racial constructionists seek to develop an account on which race does exist but is a socially constructed kind of thing" (Mallon 2006: 534). Constructionists understand that there is nothing essential or biologically inherent in people that determines their race, but they still acknowledge that cultural forces require people to experience race as part of their identity — especially if they are labeled non-white and living in a western culture. As Charles Mills explains, "race can be ontological without being biological" (1998: xiv). Mills describes the "racial contract" as the epistemological system created by whites to justify "the differential privileging of the whites as a group with respect to the nonwhites as a group, the exploitation of their bodies, lands, and resources, and the denial of equal socioeconomic opportunities to them. All whites are *beneficiaries* of the Contract, though some whites are not *signatories* to it" (Mills 1999: 11, italics in the original). My argument is built on the premise that race is a discursive social construct, a cognitive categorization, that saturates the lives of adolescents in many Western countries, reinforcing false epistemologies of difference. Multicultural novels about maturation almost always depict the protagonist's maturation as being implicated in this categorization and its concomitant conceptualizations of race.

Like race, adolescence is also a cultural construct predicated on differential privileging of power. Unlike race, however, age does have a biological component: human development involves physiological changes from infancy to childhood and from puberty to adulthood and old age. Various theories — and cultures — rely on discourse to define this stage of life differently; prior to the twentieth century, western cultures did not even have the discourse that established adolescence as a life-stage.[1] Although the earliest theorists of adolescence defined it as a purely biological concept (just as early theorists of race did), most scholars of adolescence now understand the concept to be more influenced by discourse and cultural construction than by physiology (Mintz 2004: 196–199).[2] Maturation, of course, is no more of a binary than race is; people age across a spectrum throughout their lives. Nonetheless, adults frequently employ discourse to transform the spectrum of aging into a binary: people can be categorized as either "adult" or "non-adult." Empowerment plays perhaps the biggest role in defining this binary because adults typically have more socio-economic and political power than teenagers. Maria Nikolajeva (2009) identifies this power as *aetonormativity*: adults define norms in all cultures, so normativity is always already a function of maturity. As Nikolajeva explains, *aetonormativity* comes from the root word for "age," *aeto-* (2009: 8). The carnivalesque interrogations of power issues in children's and adolescent literature, Nikolajeva argues, help to "queer" the dynamic established by adult norms (2009: 6–10). In western cultures, it is adults, specifically white adults, who define the racial contract — and societal prescriptions demand that adolescents learn to think of themselves as racial beings. If by the time young people reach adolescence they have not begun to define themselves in terms of race and age, they are often forced to, at least within the confines of adolescent literature.

For example, a character in Walter Mosley's *47* acknowledges that the cognitive categories of race and age intersect, particularly in racism's infantilizing effects: "White peoples gots as many ages as you can count but slaves on'y gots four ages. That's babychile, boy or girl, old boy or old girl, an' dead" (2005: 1). The speaker knows that each slave's social status is reinforced by these terms, all of which are defined by white oppressors to reinforce racial difference, and all of which are predicated on the notion that whiteness is *different* (somehow) than non-whiteness — just as adulthood is *different* (somehow) than non-adulthood.

To varying degrees, *47* — much like *The Absolutely True Diary of a Part-Time Indian* — also demonstrates how authors strive to empower readers by asking them to confront racial categorization as part of their own maturation. Nevertheless, although the protagonists in both of these novels follow the *bildungsroman*-inspired trajectory of characters growing to increased maturity, the adolescent characters who grow are never permitted to grow into a maturity that precludes the existence of racism. That is, while these authors problematize race and racism, they

---

1. See Steven Mintz, *Huck's Raft* (2004). Mintz cites G. Stanley Hall's 1904 work *Adolescence* as the book that "systematized earlier ideas about youth that could be traced at least as far back as Rousseau's *Emile*" (Mintz 2004: 196).

2. See also Adams and Berzonsky (2006: xxi–xxiii) and Christenbury, Bomer, and Smagorinsky (2009: 3–10).

never confront the fact that racism is an unavoidable function of adulthood in the Americas. Indeed, as Smedley observes, "race is a pervasive element in the cognitive patterning of Western thought and experience" (2007: 1). Especially in the United States, with its horrific legacy of slavery still affecting American conceptualizations of otherness, many YA novels demonstrate how race pervades cognition. Specifically, *The Absolutely True Diary of a Part-Time Indian* and *47* show adolescents that they can outgrow the racist experiences of their adolescence, but they can never completely outgrow the cultural narratives that construct race.

Categorization, and epistemology: *The Absolutely True Diary of a Part-Time Indian*

Sherman Alexie's *The Absolutely True Diary of a Part-Time Indian* involves a Spokane Indian, Arnold Spirit, who cognitively understands race in very embodied ways: he is an artist who draws cartoons of himself, his family, and his friends that emphasize their bodies, facial features, and hair. Arnold decides to go to a white high school, twenty-two miles from his home, rather than continue to attend the poverty-stricken school on his reservation. Arnold is brutally honest about all forms of racism, which he attributes to white settlers — that is, white adults: "Of course," he says, "ever since white people showed up and brought along their Christianity and their fears of eccentricity, Indians have gradually lost all of their tolerance. Indians can be just as judgmental and hateful as any white person" (Alexie 2007: 155). He defines the ontological status of the Indian in terms of generational poverty: "My parents came from poor people who came from poor people who came from poor people, all the way back to the very first poor people" (11). He recognizes that poverty affects how people experience their world, how they know it:

> It sucks to be poor, and it sucks to feel that you somehow *deserve* to be poor. You start believing that you're poor because you're stupid and ugly. And then you start believing that you're stupid and ugly because you're Indian. And because you're Indian you start believing you're destined to be poor. It's an ugly circle and *there's nothing you can do about it.* (13, italics in the original)

Arnold recognizes that the ontological condition of poverty creates a subsequent epistemology of poverty that is linked to racism — and, in his tribe's case, to a specifically embodied phenomenon: alcoholism. Arguing against Tolstoy's assessment of unhappy families being unhappy in different ways, Junior asserts, "Well, I hate to argue with a Russian genius, but Tolstoy didn't know Indians. And he didn't know that all Indian families are unhappy for the same exact reason: the fricking booze" (200).

Racism in this novel takes a number of disturbing forms. A white man threatens Arnold and his girlfriend: "if you get my daughter pregnant, if you make some charcoal babies, I'm going to disown her" (109). Another white man exploits Native American culture by trading in beaded costumes and justifying his behavior because he "feels Indian" in his "bones": "I love Indians. I love your songs, your dances, and your souls. And I love your art. I collect Indian art" (162–163). Arnold understands him to be someone who commodifies Native American culture, making "Indians feel like insects pinned to a display board" (163). Native Americans discriminate against each other in this novel, categorizing each other as "apple[s]" for acting "red on the outside and white on the inside" (132), and Arnold feels like "like two different people inside of one body" (61). Thus, the novel uses a variety of metaphors to show how race is conceptualized as a set of ontological categories, all of which depend on concepts of superiority and inferiority.

The worst result of racism in the novel involves alcohol. According to Arnold Spirit, because Indians can no longer be nomadic, they have "forgotten that reservations were meant to be death camps" (217). They have collectively lost hope because they are trapped forever on these reservations. In the narrator's cultural critique of his tribe's ontological status, he argues that too many Native Americans console themselves with alcohol — supplied, of course, by a white culture invested in ensuring that Native American cultures remain impoverished. Five different characters in the novel die in alcohol-related deaths. Arnold's grandmother, who has never had a single drink in her life, is run over by a drunk driver, who is also Native American. Another Native American man shoots his best friend over the last drink in a wine bottle; that man later kills himself in remorse. Perhaps the most horrifying deaths occur when Arnold's sister and her husband are too drunk to realize their mobile home is on fire. As Arnold puts it: "That's really the biggest difference between Indians and white people.... All my white friends can count their deaths on one hand" (200); but Arnold has been to forty-two funerals, and "90 percent of the deaths have been because of alcohol" (200). In Alexie's cultural critique, alcohol, race, and poverty are inevitably linked — and they are the direct legacy of white exploitation of Native Americans and their lands.

This harsh realism shifts, however, after his sister's almost surreal death, at which time Arnold experiences an incident that relies on altered laws of the universe. His initial reactions to the news of her death are inappropriate: he has an erection when the guidance counselor who delivers the news hugs him, and he laughs hysterically for quite awhile after hearing what has happened. Then something fantastic occurs. "I was laughing so hard that I threw up a little bit in my mouth. I spit out a little piece of cantaloupe. Which was weird, because I don't like cantaloupe.... I couldn't remember the last time I'd eaten the evil fruit" (205). Arnold remembers that his sister loved cantaloupe — and he abruptly falls asleep and dreams about a school picnic he attended when he was a seven-year-old. During the picnic, he ate seven pieces of cantaloupe — "I'd eaten so much cantaloupe that I'd turned into a cantaloupe" (206) — and he then got stung on the face by a wasp and was hospitalized. The text leaves the regurgitated cantaloupe the day of his sister's death completely unexplained. Nothing provides for the possibility that he has vomited something "like" cantaloupe from his body; the text says simply that the character "threw up a little bit" in his mouth and then "spit[s] out a little piece of cantaloupe" (206). The text is unambiguous: Arnold has vomited a food he has not eaten in seven years. When Arnold vomits something he has not eaten since childhood he is demonstrating embodied consciousness at work. Arnold is literally abjecting his thoughts of his sister from his own body. He associates Mary with cantaloupe — and cantaloupe with the pain of having been stung by a wasp while eating cantaloupe seven years earlier — so he is metaphorically cleansing his body of both Mary and the pain of her death.

Interrogating Julia Kristeva's work in *Powers of Horror* (1982), Karen Coats demonstrates how abjection operates in adolescent literature (2004: 137–160). The "clean and proper" social body expulses the undesirable, which becomes especially compelling during adolescence because it is a stage during which the abject takes on significant psychological power in terms of "three categories of bodily abjection — oral, anal, and sexual" (Coats 2004: 143). Coats specifically connects adolescence to abjection:

> At the level of the social, we think of adolescence in terms of the way it, like abjection, breaches and challenges boundaries. It is an in-between time, a time where what we know and believe about children is challenged, and where what we hope and value about maturity is also challenged. (142)

Coats implies that adolescence is effectively a cultural categorization. Moreover, throughout *The Absolutely True Diary of a Part-Time Indian*, the issue of abjection is connected to the United States government's policy regarding Native Americans: Indians have been pushed to the social rim of "white" culture to "cleanse" the social body and make way for white settlers to own land that has previously been held communally by indigenous peoples. As Coats observes, "Throughout social history, the exclusions of peoples based on race, sexuality, and disabilities have established and bolstered both personal and national identities" (2004: 141). Alexie relies on embodied consciousness here both to protest the abjection of Indians from Euro-American culture and to depict how embodied the physical grief of this one character has subsequently become. His grief is so physical he is literally abjecting memories of his sister.

The point about the cultural abjection of Native Americans is emphasized near the end of the novel when Arnold re-narrates a story his father has told him. Turtle

Lake is unusual in its perfect roundness and its depth. No one wants to swim there because some years ago, a horse — dubbed Stupid Horse — has drowned in the lake, which has metaphorically received its name because it is shaped like a turtle. "There were all sorts of myths and legends surrounding the lake. I mean, we're Indians, and we like to make up shit about lakes" (Alexie 2007: 222). Turtle Lake is thus identified with native culture. Within a few weeks of drowning in Turtle Lake, however, Stupid Horse's carcass mysteriously washes up on the shores of Benjamin Lake, which is ten miles away. Two things are salient about Benjamin Lake. The narrator describes trees on the reservation so old that they "were alive when Benjamin Franklin was born" two pages prior to Arnold's description of Turtle Lake (220), preparing readers to associate the name "Benjamin" with the white government that has abjected Native Americans from its culture. Second, Lake Benjamin is also associated with the pervasive poverty and adult alcoholism of the reservation because the drunk hit-and-run driver who has killed Arnold's grandmother has been found "hiding out at Benjamin Lake" after the crime (157). Thus, Stupid Horse has drowned in a lake that is conceptually linked to native culture, but the horse is subsequently abjected into a lake that is conceptually linked to the corrupting influence of white culture.

After the people who have found the horse's carcass drive it to the dump and burn it, Turtle Lake itself catches fire — even though the burning horse is nowhere near the lake. Perhaps the metaphor of fire dancing on water is one of an epiphany — the narrator's sister, Mary, is, after all, buried in the Catholic cemetery. But the flames on the lake also serve metaphorically to remind the reader that "fire-water" — alcohol itself — has been the most destructive force in the novel. Eventually, almost inevitably, Stupid Horse's carcass — miraculously unaffected by the fire — washes back to Turtle Lake, where it does not rot for weeks and then abruptly decays. The skeletal remains of the horse collapse "into a pile of bones. And the water and the wind dragged them away" (224). Arnold calls the story "freaky" — but he never indicates to the reader whether the narrative of Stupid Horse is to be taken as "shit" his tribe has made up or read as mythology. Adolescent readers are left to empower themselves by deciding whether this is an Indian legend or a cultural critique of relations between the nations of the Spokane and the United States — or both. Either way, this story-within-the-story helps readers conceptualize the inevitable drag of Euro-American culture on Spokane culture and how the destructiveness of "fire-water" has harmed the Spokanes' embodiment.

Arnold's retelling of this tale happens in the context of his reunion with his best friend on the reservation, Rowdy. Arnold has been remembering both the story of Stupid Horse and the day in his childhood when he and Rowdy have climbed the tallest tree on the reservation, which proves to change Arnold's cognitive understanding of their reservation: "We could see from one end of the reservation to the other. We could see our entire world. And our entire world, at that moment, was green and golden and perfect" (226). His epistemology has shifted because he has grown: he no longer knows the world as exclusively either Spokane or not. He can perceive himself as having an ontological status that is both independent from and coincident with his race. Life on the reservation is, at times, hideously ugly, but it is also sometimes "green and golden and perfect" (226). Arnold experiences his racial status in embodied terms, but racism is inexplicable in terms of social construction and human ethics. "I used to think the world was broken down by tribes," he tells one of his teachers, "By black and white. By Indian and white. But I know that isn't true. The world is only broken into two tribes: The people who are assholes and the people who are not" (176). In *The Absolutely True Diary of a Part-Time Indian*, Alexie narrates two scripts of abjection: one involving a piece of vomited cantaloupe and the other involving Stupid Horse. These scripts serve to underscore the ultimately abject ontology of the poverty and the alcoholism that affect the daily lives of the people in Arnold's tribe. But Arnold knows he will continue to experience this poverty and alcoholism daily if he stays on the reservation — even once he has grown into adulthood. Indeed, the reader is left to infer that he will be even more racially oppressed as an adult than as a child if he succumbs to alcoholism. The ontology of adulthood here is grim. The reader may be empowered by interpreting this novel's many layers, but the text implies that Arnold can never grow out of the ontological experientialism of racism.

The ontology of racism: *47*

In few YA novels is the collision between a mythical world and the world of realism more jarring than in Mosley's *47*. The novel's setting and characterizations are so solidly based in historical realism that Mosley's use of science fiction is the type of "ontological disruption [that] serves the purpose of political and cultural disruption," as Zamora and Faris claim magic realism strives to do (1995: 3). Mosley's purpose is to disrupt the traditional slave narrative so that he can provide readers with an African-American male hero. Writing about *47*, Mosley asserts:

> For a long time I have known that many young black children find it hard to read stories about slavery because of their healthy resistance to identify with victims. My goal for this book was to create a character that rises above his role as a victim by becoming a victorious hero.
>
> To accomplish this end, I used the speculative and mythical genres to create possibility where more realistic storytelling and historical perspective might not. (Mosley, n.d.)

By inventing a hero from another world, a world where skin color doesn't matter but the fight against power-craving evil forces does, Mosley creates a role model for adolescent readers of any race. More important, he has that traveler from another planet teach the eponymous slave of the book's title, who is named only "47," how to redefine his own self-image. "Neither master nor nigger be," the alien insists repeatedly to 47.[3] And in time, bestowed with the power that comes from an alternative reality, 47 accepts his destiny to become John the Conqueror (or "High John") and thus be a role model for twenty-first century adolescent readers. Mosley clearly hopes his readers will never categorize themselves as either "nigger" or "master" — which also have clear parallels in this text with "child" and "adult" because of slavery's infantilizing effects.

Tall John — who appears to 47 as an adolescent but who is actually an adult — has searched for 47 for three thousand years, journeying through time and outer space for the specific purpose of shifting the identity of one slave: 47. 47 expresses incredulity upon meeting Tall John, but Tall John never questions his own ontological status, which leaves to readers the task of reconciling the issues of the mythic and identity in this book. From his other-worldly friend, 47 eventually learns to tell other slaves that he is "Not nigger but man" (Mosley 2005: 173), an indication that he has a perception of his ontological status that defies the discursive racism on which slavery was predicated, but significantly, he can only be empowered as a man, not as an adolescent. During a pivotal moment in the text, Tall John transforms 47 to his full-grown, adult size and grants 47 immortality. Apotheosized as John the Conqueror, then, this man-god will have a new identity and a new way of being in the world. He knows he will never be a child — or a slave — again.

Even more directly than Alexie, Mosley writes about identity in terms of categorizations that involve both epistemology and ontology: if you *know* yourself to be a "master" or "nigger," you will *be* one or the other of these things. Mosley rejects the racist discourse of the reprehensible epithet used to subjugate an entire American racial group for centuries because he understands the effect of discourse on self-perception and subsequently on *being*. 47 even refers to the way he has accepted slavery in his youth in epistemological terms: he thinks in his "*slavemind*" as a child (101), but as he grows, he realizes "that the real chains that the slave wore were the color of his skin and the defeat in his mind" (146) — something of a feint of hand that blames the victim and undercuts Mosley's empowering intentions. 47 tells Tall John, "I understand…. I ain't got no mastuh 'cause I ain't no slave" (146). But the only way that Mosley has been able to write this critique of American race relations has been to create a fantastic world in which an adult whose race

---

3. The refrain first occurs in Chapter 5 (Mosley 2005: 66).

is incomprehensible to humans can show the inhabitants of the planet Earth how outrageous and unbelievable the conceptualized categories by which they justify racism are — because those categorizations are based entirely in racist cognitive discourses. The protagonist, however, must still escape from the South and slavery, and he must spend the rest of his adult life as an immortal fighting racism. He cannot be empowered as an adolescent, and he can never escape the oppressive categorizations by which racism operates. Racism is a cognitive script controlled so well by concepts of white privilege that it becomes an unavoidable cultural narrative for both white people and people of color in many works of fiction.

Conclusion

"Slavery might be the most unbelievable part of this whole story but I assure you — it really happened," Mosley writes in the preface to *47* (2005: viii). Racism *is* unbelievable, but we can explain how it happens; we can analyze its discourses and the attendant social practices that account for the cultural narrative of racism as an adult norm that affects most adolescents in countries that have been implicated in a colonialist and/or a slave-holding past. Racism is only one of the cultural narratives that profoundly affects literary conceptualizations of growth, but studying those conceptualizations serves as an exemplar for how powerful the relationship between categorization, conceptualization, and cultural narratives can be.

47, The Absolutely True Diary of a Part-Time Indian, and *Skellig* follow a similar pattern in that they are initially about a growing adolescent, set firmly within realism, but within the realism of a microcosm that allows for a social critique of an entire system, such as family life or reservation life or plantation life. The characters in these realistic microcosms experience some form of discrimination at the hands of a dominant culture in which Euro-American adults appear to be setting all social norms. The adolescent protagonists experience devastating conflicts because of their race (or a skeletal structure that certainly serves as a metaphor for "the Other"). A fantastic event happens in the world "as we know it," and the story is narrated from the perspective of an adolescent who experiences conflict but who cannot fully reconcile him- or herself to the world in which s/he lives, so the focalizer leaves space for readers to intuit either a political and/or a cultural commentary about dominant cultural narratives in each novel.[4] As Waller argues, the inclusion of the fantastic in YA realism:

---

4. For more on magic realism, see Faris, who refers to the process of destabilizing narrative focalization as "defocalization," and she identifies it as a fundamental element of magic realism

offers a potentially ... complex matrix of representational and ideological meaning. Whereas teenage realism purports to portray teenagers and their lives *as they
really are*, fantastic realism has the potential to subvert the dominant discourses of
adolescence and offer an alternative set of ideological positions. (2009: 26, italics
in the original)

Thus, these protagonists' ways of knowing their world shift because of their dis-
ruptive encounter with the fantastic, and all of these characters end the novel with
a different sense of their ontological status. They may have learned how to respond
to discrimination, but they cannot transcend it. Readers must determine both the
relationship between each story's magic and its realism, but they are also left with
the stark reality that the ontology of otherness persists into adulthood, especially
in the case of *47* and *The Absolutely True Diary* (and similarly, *Njunjul the Sun*).
Social construction allows individuals to shift their status from being adolescents
who are discriminated against to adults better prepared to confront racism, but
race and racism remain constants in adulthood, as in adolescence.

It is specifically in this site of contestation, in this friction that forces the reader
to contemplate simultaneously both realism and the fantastic, that experientialist
philosophy empowers adolescent readers to think about the ontological and epistemological implications of race as a discursive construct. Amaryll Chanady argues that the fantastic emerged as a way for post-Enlightenment writers to critique
rationalism (1995: 132), and Rosenberg subsequently employs Perry Nodelman's
concept of the child as other to define adults as the "rationalists" under critique in
literature for youth because adults are the agents who define the culture in which
children are raised (2001: 16–17). In other words, these novels force readers into a
consciousness that adults create discursive constructs: race and racism are cognitive concepts, not unalterable reality or biological fact. Ultimately, by plunging the
reader into a collision between what can and cannot be, between what is and what
should be, these texts invite adolescent readers to question racism as a discursive
— and destructive — aetonormative conceptualization, informed by adult categorizations that continually reinforce stereotypical cultural narratives.

What then is the relationship between philosophy and cognitive linguistics —
and why does this intersection matter to adolescent literature? On the most basic
level, cognitive linguistics teaches us that human development includes the ability
to categorize, conceptualize, and create metaphorical structures that have epistemological significance in childhood. Humans' developmental ability to understand metaphor begins early in childhood. Young adult novels are one mechanism
by which adolescents experience the conflation involved in embodied metaphors,

---

(Faris 2004: 43–59). For more on fantastic realism and the YA novel (including magic realism),
see Waller (2009).

as David Almond's multiple metaphorical uses of vision, birds, and death demonstrate. Furthermore, adolescent literature also provides the opportunity for us to analyze the epistemological implications of metaphorical networks on youth, especially as these networks create entailments that influence how children and adolescents conceptualize cultural narratives, including the discursive construction of race. As Lakoff and Turner observe, "[t]o study metaphor is to be confronted with hidden aspects of one's own mind and one's own culture" (1989: 214).

Moreover, cognitive linguistics provides a middle ground between philosophical debates about empiricism and relativism. F. Elizabeth Hart (2001) writes about this debate in terms that capture the philosophical tension as it bears on epistemology. Empiricism, relying as it does on concepts of perception and scientific data, tends to valorize the primacy of ontology in affirming *being* as the central goal of knowledge. Relativism, on the other hand, relies so heavily on our understanding of humanity as culturally constructed that epistemology — that is, *knowing* — gains prominence in philosophy informed by relativism. Hart advocates a third position, through cognitive linguistics, one that prioritizes experientialism. As she demonstrates, Lakoff and Johnson argue that concepts form our experiences; that is, what we know influences our being, and our being is influenced reciprocally by how we know. Within linguistics, then, Lakoff and Johnson (1999) have tried to mediate a "third position" (Hart 2001: 320–321), in which the ontology of the rational human being co-creates the epistemology of the socially situated human being.

> We are philosophical animals. We are the only animals we know of who can ask, and sometimes even explain, why things happen the way they do.... Philosophy matters to us, therefore, primarily because it helps us to make sense of our lives and to live better lives.... Since everything we think and say and do depends on the workings of our embodied minds, cognitive science is one of our most profound resources for self-knowledge. (Lakoff & Johnson 1999: 551)

As Lakoff and Johnson also observe, in order to be articulated, all philosophy depends on metaphorical thinking: "The fact that abstract thought is mostly metaphorical means that answers to philosophical questions have always been, and always will be, mostly metaphorical" (1999: 7).

Theirs is a recognition of the relationship between body and mind, between conscious mind and unconscious brain function, and between language and perception. This "third position," as Hart calls it (2001: 320), seems to me crucial to the study of adolescent literature because childhood and adolescence are, by definition, embodied states. Although earlier metaphysicians could afford to ignore childhood as a time when humans are not yet fully rational, post-structural relativists have not necessarily been able to account for the newborn infant, born with a distinct personality but not yet exposed in meaningful ways to social construction. (Anyone who has observed personality differences in identical twins within moments of birth can testify to this phenomenon.)

Cognitive linguistics, however, provides a way to account for the child both as embodied in infancy/childhood/adolescence, while simultaneously being shaped conceptually by the ideological pressures of the world in which s/he grows. In other words, post-structuralism does not always fully account for the biological definition of infancy/childhood/adolescence; nor does essentialism or empiricism fully account for the cultural factors that define how the individual is formed by and matures as a result of social pressures. But in investigating how language shapes our concepts, and how concepts, in turn, shape the human ability to conceptualize, Lakoff and Johnson allow for the type of corporeal philosophy that Elizabeth Grosz calls for in *Volatile Bodies* when she writes:

> human bodies have irreducible neurophysiological and psychological dimensions whose relations remain unknown and ... human bodies have the wonderful ability, while striving for integration and cohesion, organic and psychic wholeness, to also provide for and indeed produce fragmentations, fracturings, dislocations that orient bodies and body parts toward other bodies and body parts. (1994:13)

Cognitive linguistics thus allows for adolescent literature to integrate the study of the body and the mind in ways that acknowledge human development, cognitive development, and philosophical inquiry.

To underscore the relevance of cognitive linguistics to the philosophical questioning that inheres within adolescent literature, I cite one of Mina's teachers, who says, "our brains make stories naturally ... they find it easy" (Almond 2010:236). In this passage, Almond openly acknowledges the cognitive function of storying. The brain is hard-wired for storytelling, so brains find it "easy." This teacher adds "that stories weren't really about words.... They were about visions. They were like dreams" (237). Almond and Mosley and Alexie engage adolescents in stories that include metaphysical and existential questions: What does it mean to *be*? What does it mean to *grow*? What does it mean to *think* and to *know*? And most important, how do we learn to enact the values that emerge from the socially constructed epistemologies that have emerged, in part, from the stories we create and those that we read? Such novels as these, then, help us understand the usefulness of experientialist philosophy to the study of maturation in adolescent literature.

CHAPTER 6

The hegemony of growth in adolescent literature

Cognitive science encompasses every aspect of the relationship between brain and thought (both conscious and unconscious thought). Cognitive linguistics focuses on the relationships between embodiment and categorization, including how language usage, such as the employment of metaphor, influences our conceptualizations and how cognition and our lived experiences lead us to understand, create, and remember scripts, blends, and cultural narratives. As I have mentioned, the language of our conceptualizations frequently relies on metaphors that limit and define how we think about certain concepts. How then do conceptualizations of growth, including metaphors of growth, affect the academic study of adolescence? What entailments and cultural narratives are attendant upon those metaphors of growth? In what ways do our expectations that the young will and must grow influence how we study the literary and the historical construct of the adolescent? How does the biological fact of growth create a metaphorical structure that defines, and even limits, epistemological approaches to the study of adolescent literature?

In this chapter, I propose to investigate growth as a metaphorical concept that has profoundly influenced the study of (child and) adolescent development, first investigating various conceptual metaphors of growth and their implications as represented by a range of philosophers and writers writing in western traditions. I then move into an analysis of growth metaphors that are specific to the study of the history of childhood and to the field of adolescent literature itself. I am intrigued by the possibility that cognitive conceptualizations about childhood influence the academic study of childhood in ways that epistemologically structure the field in terms of growth. I thus explore metaphors of growth in both the study of childhood and adolescence as a way to examine the intellectual history of maturation as a concept and to examine the relationship between maturational metaphors and cognition. In this chapter, I argue that growth, as it is conceptualized, constrains our thinking about childhood and adolescence so powerfully that growth can be said to have an almost hegemonic presence in the field. This chapter thus serves as an archaeological synthesis and meta-analysis of metaphors of growth in the academic study of childhood and adolescence rather than in fiction written for the young.

Growth: The archaeology of a metaphor

The word "growth" has many meanings because so many things grow, evolve, or develop, but I focus in this conceptual archaeology, as I have throughout this book, on those instances in which "growth" refers to maturation, rather than the frequent use of "growth" as a synonym for the word "to become." I rely on Foucault's term "archaeology" in the sense of its interrogation of metadiscourse:

> Archaeology tries to define not the thoughts, representations, images, themes, preoccupations that are concealed or revealed in discourses; but those discourses themselves, those discourses as practices obeying certain rules.... [I]ts problem is to define discourses in their specificity.... It defines types of rules for discursive practices that run through individual *oeuvres*. (1994: 138–139)

In other words, as I investigate how metaphors of growth influence scholarly conceptualizations of adolescence and adolescent literature, I am focusing more on Wordsworth's concept of the child being father to the man than on the night growing dark or the economy growing stronger.

If metaphors are a means by which we compare two things, conceptual metaphors are those in which we use two concepts in the comparison (Lakoff & Johnson 1980: 3–4). Lakoff and Johnson provide three loose categories of conceptual metaphor that prove helpful in the analysis of how scholars employ metaphors of growth. One category of conceptual metaphor, according to Lakoff and Johnson, is the "orientational metaphor," which are those metaphors that rely on concepts of spatial orientation to make a comparison (1980: 14). Thus, when we refer to a child or teenager as "growing up," we are organizing our knowledge about the many changes the child has undergone entirely around the spatial change of the child growing physically taller — that is, vertically upwards. As I've previously discussed, since the metaphor UP IS GOOD entails an upwards orientation as positive, the metaphor of "growing up" blends two concepts: psychological maturation is occurring, and upwards directionality is positive. Growth, then, often carries with it the connotation — that is, the entailment — that maturation is positive.

The emotional and cognitive changes that maturation involves also lend themselves to the second type of conceptual metaphor, which Lakoff and Johnson call "structural metaphors"; that is, they "allow us, in addition, to use one highly structured and clearly delineated concept to structure another" (1980: 61). Lakoff and Johnson offer the following examples as common structural metaphors employed in English: "LABOR IS A RESOURCE" and "TIME IS A RESOURCE" (68). In other words, "don't waste time" is a metaphor shaped by the concept that time is a resource that can be wasted.

The third category of conceptual metaphor, the "ontological metaphor," is the human tendency to categorize "things [that] are not discrete or bounded ... e.g., mountains, street corners, hedges, etc." (Lakoff & Johnson 1980: 25). Ontological metaphors involve our cognitive habit of "viewing events, activities, emotions, ideas, etc., as entities and substances" (25). Lakoff and Johnson provide two examples: INFLATION IS AN ENTITY and THE MIND IS A MACHINE (26–27). Lakoff and Johnson acknowledge that the three categories of conceptual metaphor — the orientational, the ontological, and the structural — are overlapping categories. When ontological and structural metaphors overlap, I follow Lakoff and Johnson's lead in identifying that metaphor as part of the larger group of conceptual metaphors: structural metaphors.

In the following section, I will investigate various ways that growth has historically been treated conceptually, including such structural metaphors as GROWTH IS INEVITABLE and GROWTH IS THE CHANGE FROM INNOCENCE TO WISDOM and GROWTH IS PHASED. Such concepts as "inevitability" and "learning" and "phases" themselves represent structured concepts, so when we compare growth to these concepts, we are relying on conceptual metaphors that are structural.

Because categorization is fundamental to conceptualization, I will examine in the next section how many thinkers have conceptualized growth within certain categories. My examination includes philosophers and poets, theologians and novelists. Although the works of the specific thinkers I include here span a historical trail that is 2500 years long, my intention in what follows is not to imply that these specific philosophers and writers that I quote have somehow followed a linear trajectory of intellectual growth by which they have influenced each other. Robert Nisbet thoroughly traces the metaphor of growth as it has led to interpretations of history as either linear or cyclical, "in a long succession of philosophers, historians, and social scientists in the West: among them Heraclitus, Aristotle, Polybius, Lucretius, Seneca, Florus, St. Cyprian, St. Augustine, Francis Bacon, Pascal, Fontenelle, Turgot, Hume, Condorcet, Hegel, Compte, Spencer, and … giving company to Spengler and his theory of cycles, such otherwise dissimilar figures as Toynbee, Berdyaev, Reinhold Niebuhr, Sorokin, and the late Robert H. Lowie" (1970: 19–20). I refer readers seeking a complete historiography of the metaphor of growth to Nisbet's work, since I am not arguing that these writers' and philosophers' ideas are an outgrowth of one another's works.

On the contrary, since my goal throughout this book has been to interrogate the connotation of growth as a metaphor for positive change (as words such as "development" and "evolution" may connote), I present various texts in chronological order only to demonstrate the myriad ways that growth has been conceptualized within certain categories over time. Although I have chosen in the following section to present the work of thinkers who are well-known for their metaphors of growth, innumerable others could have been included here. Those which I have included, however, demonstrate the point that metaphors for growth exist in three dominant categories, as Lakoff and Johnson (1999) would categorize conceptual metaphors: embodied concepts of growth, epistemological concepts of growth, and ontological concepts of growth. While some metaphors of growth evoke less predominant strains of conceptual thinking, such as those that involve economic or phenomenological terms, the major categories do tend to overlap since, for example, all phenomenological and cognitive experiences reside within embodiment. Nonetheless, metaphors of growth have epistemological implications for the ways that we know — or think about — growth. When we consider growth as a concept that is biophysical or epistemological or ontological, for example, we tend to limit (or entail) how we are thinking about childhood to a narrower privileging of only one aspect of human growth, such as *only* physical growth or cognitive growth or ontological status.

Growth and its historical conceptualizations

Classical literature provides more than one example in which a conceptual metaphor of physical or biological growth has led to mapping growth ontologically, as a condition of being human. For example, in *Generation of Animals*, Aristotle explores sexual reproduction — specifically, the function of semen. Aristotle provides a schema for different ways that a new thing can be generated: "it is one thing when we say that night comes from day or a man becomes man from boy, meaning that A follows B; it is another if we say that … the whole is formed from something preexisting which is only put into shape," as when a bed is made out of wood or a sculpture is made from bronze (Aristotle 2012: Book I, Part 18). He believes the third type of generation involves "contraries aris[ing] from contraries," as when "a man becomes unmusical from being musical, sick from being well" (Book I, Part 18). The fourth type of generation he classifies as being "the efficient cause," that is the "moving principle" in which what emerges has been contained all along within the original (Book I, Part 18). Aristotle then draws this conclusion: "either the semen is the material from which [the offspring] is made, or it is the first efficient cause. For assuredly it is not in the sense of A being after B"; that is, assuredly semen does not create offspring in the way that a man grows naturally and logically from a boy (Book I, Part 18). Whatever we want to conclude about the scientific accuracy or inaccuracy of Aristotle's thoughts about semen, his dismissal of "A being after B," just as "a man becomes man from boy," demonstrates something about his understanding of growth. He uses the structural metaphor of growth from boy to man to demonstrate growth in linear terms of inevitability: growth happens no matter what (as long as the child remains alive). Thus, in Aristotle's conceptualization, growth is an ontological reality in the sense that children are inevitably *being* in a state of growth. In childhood, growth is inevitable.

Ovid, too, uses inevitability as a metaphor of growth that has ontological implications when he explains how Jason reaps soldiers from dragon's teeth that have been sowed in a fertile field: "And as the infant receives the human form in the womb of the mother, and is there formed in all its parts, and comes not forth into the common air until at maturity, so when the figure of man is ripened in the bowels of the pregnant earth, it arises in the fruitful plain" (Ovid 2012: Book VII, Fable 1). Like Aristotle, Ovid depicts growth as an aspect of childhood that inherently and inevitably affects the living child's state of being. The premise of Ovid's work in *The Metamorphoses* indicates his interest in changing states, but his conceptualization of metamorphosis itself is one of neutral value: that is, the change involved in metamorphosis does not necessarily mark either an improving or a declining condition. Ovid overtly describes his intention in his own words in "The Argument" as being "to speak of forms changed into new bodies" (Book I). Thus, not all metamorphoses involve improvement because not all change represents growth (although all growth involves change). Nevertheless, Ovid relies on the same basic metaphor that Aristotle does: the child grows inevitably into a more mature form, changing as s/he does so, but Ovid complicates the understanding of growth by insisting that the ontological status entailed in the growth of the young inevitability involves change. In this regard, Ovid employs metaphors that Lakoff and Turner might perhaps identify as common in literature, since they list among their evaluation of commonly recurring literary metaphors the following: "TIME IS A CHANGER" (Lakoff & Turner 1989: 40). They also contrast the idea of "TIME IS A CHANGER" with the idea that time is a motion or a personified stalker: "TIME MOVES" and "TIME IS A PURSUER" (44, 46). In other words, the inevitability of growth is a literary metaphor that has existed since the days of Aristotle and Ovid.

About five decades later than Ovid, also writing in Greek, Paul penned the famous metaphor of growth that is found in I Corinthians of the Christian Bible's New Testament: "When I was a child, I spake as a child, I understood as a child, I thought as a child: but when I became a man, I put away childish things. For now we see through a glass, darkly; but then face to face: now I know in part; but then I shall know even as also I am known" (13:11–12).[1] Paul's structural metaphor for growth involves some of the same sense of inevitability as Aristotle's and Ovid's but it adds an additional and more epistemological concept: growth involves the movement from knowing little to knowing more and in wiser ways. In Paul's words, "childish things" entail speaking, understanding, and thinking in less mature ways than adults do — and Paul also relies on the analogy between

---

1. I rely on the King James Version (KJV) here not because it is the most definitive translation from the Greek but because it is the version that has had the most influence on literature written in English.

childhood and adulthood to explain what will happen when he experiences spiritual perfection, presumably either in death or following the apocalypse. He knows now only "in part," but "when that which is perfect is come," he will experience full and complete knowledge (I Corinthians 13:10). The spiritual implications of this passage have little relevance to the exploration of growth as a metaphor. Rather, Paul's assertion that incomplete knowledge is the provenance of childhood and wisdom the provenance of adulthood creates a structural metaphor in a different category: growth entails learning and epistemological development. The corollary creates yet another commentary on childhood: that childhood involves ignorance. For Paul, then, growth is overcoming ignorance by learning. This metaphor is effectively an epistemological one.

Ptolemy divides growth into the seven stages of man. He believes that each stage is dominated by an astronomical entity, with the moon responsible for the "quick growth and moist nature" of infancy, with Mercury governing "the intelligent and logical" cognitive faculties of the learning child from four years-old to fourteen, with Venus ruling the romantic passions from puberty to adulthood, with young manhood dominated by the Sun, which "implants in the soul at length the mastery and direction of its actions, desire for substance, glory, and position, a change from playful, ingenuous error to seriousness, decorum, and ambition" (cited in Eyben 1993: 34, 35). Ptolemy includes emotion — even passion — along with cognition in youth's development into a young adult. But if a primary goal of maturation also includes a "desire for substance, glory, and position," then economic responsibility serves as another marker of growth. The young man is he who begins to accept financial independence as an indicator of separation from his parents and who gainfully employs himself. (Women, apparently, need not concern themselves with the seven ages of *man*.) All irony aside, growth is — for both genders — a matter of increased economic productivity.

Shakespeare borrows Ptolemy's seven ages of man, emphasizing growth as an ontological process of *becoming* that is structured into phases. In *As You Like It*, Jacques utters his famous soliloquy that begins:

> All the world's a stage …
> And one man in his time plays many parts,
> His acts being seven ages. At first the infant,
> Mewling and puking in the nurse's arms.
> Then the whining schoolboy, with his satchel
> And shining morning face, creeping like snail
> Unwillingly to school. And then the lover,
> Sighing like furnace, with a woeful ballad
> Made to his mistress' eyebrow. (Shakespeare 1974: II.vii: 139–149)

In this passage, several conceptual metaphors intertwine. At the most basic level, humans are metaphorically compared to actors in Jacques' soliloquy, but more important for my purposes here, infants are depicted entirely in embodied, visceral terms, as mewling and puking, while children are depicted in epistemological terms, as boys invested in learning and knowing. (This specific line in Shakespeare's play corresponds to the sense of growth depicted by Paul and Ptolemy, that growth involves learning.) Once biophysically mature enough to grow a beard, however, young men are depicted entirely in terms of emotions, invoking Ptolemy's recognition that growth involves changing emotions. Perhaps the most bleak line of Shakespeare's extended metaphor is his acknowledging that growth leads inevitably to death:

> Last scene of all,
> That ends this strange eventful history,
> Is second childishness, and mere oblivion,
> Sans teeth, sans eyes, sans taste, sans every thing. (1974: III.2: 163–166)

Man is, in effect, Being-towards-death. But before dying, man will experience the second childhood of "oblivion" — that is, a return to an innocent state of unknowingness. Even though Shakespeare relies on a circular metaphor to evoke the return in old age to speechlessness and blindness, the metaphor is still effectively linear or perhaps a spiral. Growth moves in one direction only: people grow inevitably older and move towards their own deaths. Thus, Shakespeare relies on multiple metaphors about growth, including the following: that growth is embodied by phases; growth is ontologically inevitable and unidirectional — and it leads to death, which is both an embodied reality and an ontological status. Lakoff and Turner would identify the following basic metaphors at work here: "STATES ARE LOCATIONS," "DEATH IS A FINAL DESTINATION," "DEATH IS NIGHT," "CHANGE OF STATE IS CHANGE OF LOCATION," and "LIFE IS A PLAY" (1989: 7–8, 20).[2]

In the seventeenth-century, while attempting to disprove the theory that humans are born with an innate understanding of certain ideas or principles, John Locke (1690) argued that the adult who:

> attentively considers the state of a child at his first coming into the world, will have little reason to think him stored with plenty of ideas, that are to be the matter of his future knowledge. It is by degrees he comes to be furnished with them: and though the ideas of obvious and familiar qualities imprint themselves before the memory begins to keep a register of time or order, yet it is often so late before some unusual qualities come in the way, that there are few men that cannot recollect the beginning of their acquaintance with them. (Locke 1836: 52)

---

2. See also Lakoff and Turner (1989: 21–22).

In other words, growth involves shifting one's epistemology through learning; and growth involves memory, since long-term learning does not occur without memory. This makes growth an accretive process. Moreover, growth depends on experience: "if a child were kept in a place where he never saw any other but black and white, till he were a man, he would have no more ideas of scarlet or green, than he that from his childhood never tasted an oyster, or a pineapple, has of those particular relishes" (52–53). Locke argues by analogy throughout the essay, but one of his most frequent comparisons involves comparing the adult, who has knowledge, with the child, who has less. The chief metaphor attributed to Locke in this essay, that of the *tabula rasa*, never explicitly appears in the essay, although his conceptualization of the child as a person with a mind that is trainable because it is empty or devoid of fact portrays the child's mind as an empty container and growth as the process of filling that container. Locke's embodied metaphors conceptualize growth almost entirely in terms of epistemological development, but he contributes to this archaeology the structural conceptualization that growth is accretive.

Rousseau (1762) opens *Emile* with a metaphor comparing the growth of a child to the growth of a tree: the uneducated man would have nature stifled within him, "like a sapling chance sown in the midst of the highway, bent hither and thither and soon crushed by the passers-by" (2012: Book I). Rousseau continues to compare the growth of a child to the growth of a tree using growth as the source domain and education as the target domain:

> Plants are fashioned by cultivation, man by education. If a man were born tall and strong, his size and strength would be of no good to him till he had learnt to use them; they would even harm him by preventing others from coming to his aid; left to himself he would die of want before he knew his needs. We lament the helplessness of infancy; we fail to perceive that the race would have perished had not man begun by being a child....
>
> We are born weak, we need strength; helpless, we need aid; foolish, we need reason. All that we lack at birth, all that we need when we come to man's estate, is the gift of education. (2012: Book I)

Rousseau understands that growth involves embodied change, but he uses education as his most extensive metaphor for growth, complicating Locke's comparison of growth to the acquisition of knowledge. In Rousseau's economy, three external forces teach the child because "education comes to us from nature, from men, or from things. The inner growth of our organs and faculties is the education of nature, the use we learn to make of this growth is the education of men, what we gain by our experience of our surroundings is the education of things" (2012: Book I). If human growth requires education, then humans are also dependent on more than their own brains to grow. Growth is dependent not only on embodied experiences ("nature") and our phenomenological perception of the world ("things"), growth is also dependent on others ("men"). Rousseau's identification of the relationship between perception and growth provides an alternative explanation for growth: it is phenomenological. In Rousseau's work the source domain and the target domain shift almost commutatively: growth *is* education, but perhaps more important, education *is* growth. Rousseau's metaphors thus combine the epistemological, the phenomenological, and the embodied to create another type of metaphor for growth: the phenomenological.

Influenced by Rousseau's injunction to "[a]ddress your treatises on education to the women" because they control their children's lives emotionally and intellectually, Mary Wollstonecraft wrote *A Vindication of the Rights of Woman* (1792), in which she extends the conceptual metaphor "education is growth" to girls as well as boys (Rousseau 2012: Book I). Her chief concern resides in the way that girls are trained only "to the desire of establishing themselves, the only way women can rise in the world — by marriage" (Wollstonecraft 2002: Introduction). This educational failure, of course, leads women to be weak, since "strength of body and mind are sacrificed to libertine notions of beauty" (2002: Introduction). Moreover, this desire makes "mere animals of them, when they marry, they act as such children may be expected to act" (2002: Chapter 1). Central to Wollstonecraft's metaphor of growth is the movement from weakness to strength, which she considers in both biophysical terms and cognitive terms. As she writes, "[c]hildren, I grant, should be innocent; but when the epithet is applied to men, or women, it is but a civil term for weakness" (2002: Chapter 2). Thus, rather than extolling the cognitive virtues of innocence, Wollstonecraft deplores it as a form of weakness:

> Consequently, the most perfect education, in my opinion, is such an exercise of the understanding as is best calculated to strengthen the body and form the heart; or, in other words, to enable the individual to attain such habits of virtue as will render it independent. In fact, it is a farce to call any being virtuous whose virtues do not result from the exercise of its own reason. This was Rousseau's opinion respecting men: I extend it to women…. (2002: Chapter 2)

More than once, Wollstonecraft also uses childhood as a metaphor for women. She even points out how irrational it is for men to repress women's intellectual growth by infantilizing them: "Men, indeed, appear to me to act in a very unphilosophical manner, when they try to secure the good conduct of women by attempting to keep them always in a state of childhood" (2002: Chapter 2). Thus, Wollstonecraft's chain of conceptual metaphors follows the logic of a syllogism: childhood is innocence; innocence is weak; childhood is weak; therefore, women who act like children are also weak:

> And will moralists pretend to assert, that this is the condition in which one half of the human race should be encouraged to remain with listless inactivity and stupid acquiescence? Kind instructors! what were we created for? To remain, it may be said, innocent; they mean in a state of childhood. (2002: Chapter 4)

Wollstonecraft describes growth as a movement from weakness to strength; growth is a matter of becoming stronger in her dominant metaphor, although one suspects that she cares more about cognitive strength than biological or physical strength. In Wollstonecraft's conceptualization, growth is getting stronger.

Written in 1802 but originally published as "Moods of My Own Mind, No. 4" in the 1807 *Poems in Two Volumes*, Wordsworth's frequently anthologized "My Heart Leaps Up When I Behold a Rainbow in the Sky" contains his most famous metaphor of growth: "The Child is Father of the Man" (1807:line 7). In this ontological formulation, the man exists within the child, who will — as inevitably as A follows B — transform eventually into an adult. But the child represents both hope and joy to Wordsworth, so maturation involves a loss of these things. For example, in "Michael" he claims that "a child, more than all other gifts … / Brings hope with it, and forward-looking thoughts" (lines 146 and 148), while in his ode "Intimations of Immortality" he writes that " … the growing Boy … / Beholds the light, and whence it flows, He sees it in his joy" (1807:lines 68, 70–71). If children are born "trailing clouds of glory," then growth involves "Shades of the prison-house" that "begin to close / Upon the growing Boy" (1807:lines 64, 67–68); "Full soon thy Soul shall have her earthly freight, / And custom lie upon thee with a weight" (lines 127–128). If "[d]elight and liberty" are "the simple creed / Of Childhood, whether busy or at rest, with new-fledged hope still fluttering in his breast," then growth involves an epistemological recognition of "our mortal Nature" (lines 137–139, 147). Thus, Wordsworth exemplifies growth as both the loss of innocence and as ontologically oriented towards death:

> We will grieve not, rather find
> Strength in what remains behind;
> In the primal sympathy
> Which having been must ever be;
> In the soothing thoughts that spring
> Out of human suffering;
> In the faith that looks through death,
> In years that bring the philosophic mind. (lines 180–187)

In Wordsworth's metaphorical formulation, growth is loss: specifically, the loss of innocence.

Wordsworth invokes a cultural narrative about growth as the loss of innocence in writing about growth in ontological terms; other cultural narratives in the nineteenth century emerge from Darwin, who relies on biological metaphors to talk about evolution, and from Freud and his followers, for whom growth is largely psychological and cognitive. But something of the ontology of innocent flesh giving way to the corrupting pull of death's inevitability resurfaces in the twentieth century in Heidegger's philosophy. His metaphors bear similarity to both Shakespeare's and Wordsworth's ontological metaphors of growth. Heidegger argues that we are all always already dying, which involves an understanding of ourselves as Being-in-time; in other words, we live constantly aware of death as the opposite of life. Maturation (and death) inhere within life itself:

> When, for instance, a fruit is unripe, it "goes towards" its ripeness.... The fruit brings itself to ripeness, and such a bringing of itself is a characteristic of its Being as a fruit. Nothing imaginable … would eliminate the unripeness of the fruit, if this entity did not come to ripen *of its own accord*. (2008: H243, italics in the original)

All living things carry inherently within them, then, this unidirectional biological tendency toward growth that leads inevitably to death and the cessation of growth. According to Heidegger, growth is the path to death; growth is always already Being-towards-death.

The implications of growth metaphors

While this summary of a few metaphors about growth demonstrates varying attitudes towards childhood and adolescence, perhaps more important are the epistemological implications these conceptual metaphors create. Cognitive and embodied models of growth have, in the past, tended to emphasize the Cartesian split between body and mind, while ontological models tend to elide that split because both body and mind inhere within one's ontological status. Some of these metaphors imply that growth is inevitable, while others imply that growth always involves change, so we can conclude that conceptualizations of growth usually involve biophysically embodied change, epistemological change, and/or ontological change. Moreover, if growth inheres within all living things, and if all living things inevitably change, the final act of mutability is death, which inheres genetically within each living thing.

If those early phases of growth — for humans, infancy, childhood, and adolescence — are only temporary stages in the inexorable march to mortality, however, then youth itself is ontologically temporary — a metaphor that might seem sensible to some scholars of childhood studies, since children are only young for a short while. But this metaphor might give us pause. For example, the temporary nature of childhood makes it an easy target for dismissal, as in such formulations as "she'll outgrow her immaturity" or "it's just a phase." Negative connotations about the ontology of the childlike are made easier because that stage is "only" temporary; childhood contrasts nicely in many metaphors with the putative fixity of adulthood, when we are ostensibly "mature" and "stable." Alternatively, those metaphors of growth that focus more on the child's epistemology than on her or his ontological status imply not only that learning *affects* growth but also that learning even *effects* growth. Children grow *because* they learn, or even *only when* they learn. Whether the metaphor assumes childhood weakness and stupidity, as Wollstonecraft implies, or innocence as Wordsworth does, this model of growth values *knowledge* (or "innocence," which is the lack thereof) more than any other factor. Ultimately, various metaphors of growth imply that childhood and youth are temporary, and children and adolescents *must* learn in a model that privileges the learning mind over the biophysically evolving body.

What then are the wider implications for the way we think about childhood and adolescence? When being young is linked to changing from a state of lack of knowledge to an "evolved" state of knowledge, adulthood is privileged as the "evolved" form of the human being, although admittedly, more Romantic conceptualizations of the child as innocent have worked since the nineteenth century to deconstruct this view and posit the child as superior to the adult. Either way, however, a power imbalance occurs: one phase of life is marked superior to the other. Because childhood is transitory and adulthood lasts for most people, it is to be hoped, longer than childhood and youth, all metaphors of growth except the Romantic ones imply a relationship between "growth" and "improvement" in the experientialism of the embodied mind. Except for the Romantic viewpoint, we experience growth as learning and being *more* than when we were young, so our ability to conceptualize growth is entailed by the experiences of our embodied reason.

A historiography of growth metaphors

A historian of childhood in medieval Germany, James A. Schultz, observes that "[i]deas about childhood affect not only the way we treat children of the past: they affect the way we write the history of childhood" (1995: 2). The conceptual metaphors of growth that historians employ, like those of philosophers and poets, thus have long-term implications for the study of youth. For example, those historians who collapse metaphors of the child growing into a metaphor of how a culture or civilization grows tend to demonstrate epistemologies in which the child is depicted negatively, as powerless, immature, or unstable. Robert Nisbet identifies metaphors of growth as the central historiographical metaphor in 2,500 years of Euro-American history: "Of all metaphors in Western thought on mankind and culture, the oldest, most powerful and encompassing is the metaphor of growth" (1970: 19). Nisbet cites Oswald Spengler's *The Decline of the West* to illustrate a typical instantiation of this type of metaphor: "civilization (or mankind or society or the nation, as the case may be) 'passes through the age-phases of the individual man. It has its childhood, youth, manhood, and old age'" (Spengler, cited in Nisbet 1970: 20). The comparisons to childhood and old age are not flattering, since historians employing these metaphors tend to rely on "childhood" as a metaphor to infantilize a culture and "old age" to mark its decline.

Ella S. Armitage demonstrates this infantilization of a historical era in *The Childhood of the English Nation; or, The Beginnings of English History*. The opening sentences state the metaphor boldly:

> A Nation has a growth as truly as an individual and a nation's history should be the story of that growth, and not a mere chronicle of disjointed facts. And just as the life of an individual receives its character to a large degree from the events of its earliest years ... so the key to the history of a nation must often be sought in its earliest days....
>
> The first step in every nation's history is that by which it passes from barbarism to civilisation, from anarchy to organisation. (1885: 1)

Armitage depicts immaturity as a lack of "character," and she has no doubt about what has caused the greatest growth in the history of twelfth century England: "We may roughly describe the most striking feature of the twelfth century by saying that then people began to think" (219) — by which Armitage means, scholars and philosophers began to develop new ideas, rather than handing down only the received notions of the classical age. Armitage's extended metaphor fits squarely into the tradition of Locke's and Rousseau's metaphors for growth as epistemological: the child England cannot grow until it learns — just like the individual human child needs to learn — to think for itself.

Contemporary with Armitage's work, Edward Clodd's textbook, *The Childhood of the World: A Simple Account of Man's Origin and Early History*, relies on the same metaphor. His history intends to teach children how "different races have advanced from savagery to civilization" by tracing "the progress of man in material things" and "his mode of advance from lower to higher stages of religious belief" (1887: vi). As he puts it, "The progress of the world from its past to its present state is like the growth of each of us from childhood to manhood or womanhood," even though we can learn from history that some civilizations eventually have "decayed and died" (52). By invoking the "progress" of "material things" and "higher stages of religious belief," Clodd joins an economic model of growth with a spiritual (and racist and colonialist) one: youth is a state of material and religious poverty. Moreover, Clodd implies that cultures grow like children do — but the seeds of their own death lie within that very growth.

Even more remarkably, some fairly recent historians of childhood and youth rely on the same metaphor, that civilization — and even the field of childhood studies itself — grows, just as the young grow. In *Growing Up with the Country*, Elliott West, for example, tells us that:

> Thirty years ago, the literature in the field [of the history of childhood] was like a child — small, but growing every day. Today, it is more like an adolescent — large and gawky, full of promise, but also a little uncertain about its future. The study of western children, however, cannot even be called infantile; it is at best embryonic. (1989: xviii)

West is referencing as the field's "embryonic" point of origin that most infamous of childhood historians, Philippe Ariès — whose methodology has been scathingly critiqued for its many flaws.[3] In his 1960 *L'Enfant et la view familiale sous l'ancien règime*, Ariès depicts as infantilized a culture he (erroneously) believed did not recognize childhood. He asks the following questions, relying on a conceptual metaphor of childhood to compare the tenth century to the nineteenth: "How did we come from that ignorance of childhood to the centring [sic] of the family around the child in the nineteenth century? How far does this evolution correspond to a parallel evolution of the concept people have of the family … ?" (Ariès 1962: 10). Later, he writes, "What a long way we have come to reach this point!" — the point in question being the establishment of childhood as a time of purity and innocence (108). Ariès' reliance on orientational metaphors of distance — "how far" and "what a long way" — coupled with structural metaphors such as "evolution" indicate his interpretation of the Middle Ages as immature. That depiction belittles both the era and the subject under scrutiny: childhood.

More than any other historian, in *Growing Up in Medieval London*, Barbara Hanawalt criticizes Ariès for the paucity of evidence on which he made his sweeping claims. She is scrupulous in avoiding metaphors that depict the Medieval era as the "Dark Ages," which she demonstrates as the metaphorical "foil" by which Ariès and his followers, such as Lawrence Stone, make "our own times look good by comparison" (1993: 6). In other words, Hanawalt recognizes that Ariès' depiction of the Middle Ages as immature is a failure of metaphor. Nonetheless, Hanawalt finds herself falling prey to the same easy tendency to use words that depict historical

---

3. See Stone (1974: 28); Wilson (1980: 147); Pollock (1983: 263); Hanawalt (1993: 7–10); Schultz (1995: 2). Schultz even metaphorizes Ariès himself, turning the historian into a father who has suppressed the growth of an entire discipline: "Thus it is that the 'Father of Family History' has stunted the growth of his child" (Schultz 1995: 9).

phenomena as having biophysical properties of growth: in medieval London, "one can argue for a *growing* concern about children and adolescents" (6, italics added); our legal institutions "*grew out* of that past" (9, italics added). Social structures "evolved" (107) and "the very apparent preoccupation of books of advice, city ordinances, royal decrees, and even the language of court cases indicates a *growing* preoccupation with potential problems" of adolescence in medieval London (110, italics added). Did this preoccupation really indicate an increasing concern with the problems of youth, or did it indicate an increase in literacy and the subsequent crafting of laws that were recorded in history? In any event, Hanawalt cannot avoid using a metaphor of growth to imply that increasing attention to growing youth demonstrates a positive thing: London's "lively neighborhood concern for the welfare of children" (56). In Hanawalt's metaphor, growth is awareness — even though, in the absence of written records, she cannot really prove that medieval London was unaware of the problems of childhood and adolescence.

It is not unusual for historians to write about growth in terms of upward trajectories of growth or downward trajectories of devolution. Those — such as Armitage and Clodd and West — who write about history in terms of "development" or "evolution" from an immature civilization to a more mature one rely on scripted metaphors of growth as positive, while those concerned about decline tend focus more on the later stages of growth that invoke scripts of dissolution and death. As the title alone indicates, C. John Sommerville's *The Rise and Fall of Childhood* falls into this latter pattern:

> For the past 400 years children have enjoyed or endured increasing adult attention. That is largely because we have become more and more preoccupied with the future.... But something is happening that might change all this. After hundreds of years of economic expansion, the West now faces the possibility of long-term economic decline. All of our economic and social problems are made worse by any rise in population and by the need to sacrifice for the welfare of our children and future generations. So it is possible that we are at a turning point in the history of childhood, and that things are turning down. (1982: 9)

Given current economic conditions, Sommerville's concern in the 1980s with the global economy seem prescient, but he nonetheless couples his history of childhood with notions of social maturation and eventual decay that are reminiscent of Shakespeare, Wordsworth, and Heidegger.

Historians' ability to conceptualize historical change is entailed by the metaphors of growth on which they rely. Whether historians view "growth" as positive or negative, they position childhood within very specific conceptualizations, too. These conceptualizations of childhood have less to do with embodiment than they do with epistemology and ontology. In the formulations I have cited, childhood is either a time of ignorance that affects a status of negative social conditions, or it is a time of purity and innocence that precedes a decline into corruption. Either way, the ability to think about historical change is entailed by the concept of growth.

Growth and the historiography of literature for youth

Growth is also a prominent metaphor within the study of children's and adolescent literature, and the ways that literary critics use the term undoubtedly influences perceptions of childhood and adolescence within the field. As Seth Lerer writes in his recent history of children's literature, "Perhaps we never can escape the evolutionary metaphors that govern our literary and life histories" (2008: 173). He thus implies that growth is inescapable in our "literary histories" and "life histories" — but he does not seem to recognize that he is using the exact same metaphor to describe the history of children's literature. Peter Hunt also employs this metaphor in his history of children's literature, *An Introduction to Children's Literature*. Hunt writes about children's books during the era of 1860–1920, "In a sense, children's literature was growing up — growing away from adults" (1994: 59). Karín Lesnik-Oberstein takes a more pragmatic approach to the matter when she traces how the field emerged historically from educational goals; because of this history, she notes, some critics "ascribe powerful educational and developmental functions to a child's reading" in the ways they perceive children's books as both helping children learn about the world and "strengthening" their minds (1994: 3). Is it inevitable that scholars tracing the history of literature written for an audience of humans-who-are-growing will employ metaphors of growth?

Literary historian Hayden White would argue "no" — that there are actually four models of literary narrative that correspond loosely with Northrop Frye's Jungian analysis of genre. White describes the *emplotment* of history as the process whereby historians (and/or literary critics) transform historical fact into subjective narrative, and he identifies four patterns of emplotment: those scholars who write about the past using metaphors of pilgrimage; those who employ metaphors of evolution and growth; those who trace downward spirals or devolution (such as Gibbon's *The Decline and Fall of the Roman Empire*), and those who analyze history ironically, as bound to repeat itself in repetitive cycles.[4] White does not recognize the cognitive basis for these emplotments; instead, he identifies their existence solely as a function of textuality. White writes:

---

4. See White (1978: 12, 82–83).

> [H]istorical narratives are not only models of past events and processes, but also metaphorical statements which suggest a relation of similitude between such events and processes and the story types that we conventionally use to endow the events of our lives with culturally sanctioned meanings. Viewed in a purely formal way, a historical narrative is not only a reproduction of the events reported in it, but also a complex of symbols which gives us directions for finding an icon of the structure of those events in our literary tradition. (1978: 88)

Cognitive literary theory, however, allows us to recognize that White's term "emplotment" is a matter of script. That is, a scholar's internalized cognitive conceptualization of such scripts as evolution or devolution influences in turn how s/he conceptualizes literary history.

In this section, I would like to explore the metaphorical emplotments (that is, the scripts) that occur when literary critics write about historical changes in children's literature. I examine the way the following texts employ scripted conceptualizations of growth: Seth Lerer's *Children's Literature: A Reader's History from Aesop to Harry Potter* (2008), Beverly Lyon Clark's *Kiddie Lit: The Cultural Construction of Children's Literature in America* (2003), and Kimberley Reynolds' *Radical Children's Literature: Future Visions and Aesthetic Transformations in Juvenile Fiction* (2007). These books do not all share the same patterns of scripted emplotment, which demonstrates that our field is developing multiple strategies for self-analysis and explanation — surely one mark of the field's increasing complexity. In effect, I am analyzing these texts historiographically, for to study historiography is to study the history of historical study itself. Two noted historians, Conal Furay and Michael J. Salevouris, define historiography as "the study of the way history has been and is written — the history of historical writing.... When you study 'historiography' you do not study the events of the past directly, but the changing interpretations of those events in the works of individual historians" (1988: 223). My hope is to demonstrate historiographical diversification in our field by examining three things: 1) these sample texts' scripted emplotments, 2) their contribution to the ideologies surrounding the cultural narratives of children's and adolescent literature, and 3) their methodologies. In writing a brief historiography of growth in our field, I hope to perform the type of analysis that demonstrates how we can utilize cognitive narratology to theorize about historicism in productive ways that enrich both our scholarship and our profession. While we are sometimes governed almost blindly by our use of metaphors of growth and development when we write about the history of children's literature, I find it significant that we are not always so.

I begin with Seth Lerer's *Children's Literature* because it chronicles the longest span of history of those I'm investigating. Lerer demonstrates how Greek and Roman children's education was guided by texts written for and adapted to the use of children, tracing how the memorization and recitation considered central to education in both cultures required the existence of texts with which children could engage. Lerer notes the significance of social class in driving the educational ideologies of these cultures, and he focuses with exquisite care on Aesop's Fables and its many adaptations in later cultures. Lerer is at his strongest in tracing the genealogies involved in adaptation. For example, he notes the long-lasting hold *Robinson Crusoe* has had on the Anglophone imagination, even tracing vestiges of Crusoe in Winnie-the-Pooh's "expotition" to the north pole and his finding of footsteps — not Friday's, but his own — when he is tracking woozles. Lerer also analyzes the influences of Locke and Darwin, especially noting the impact of the latter on the colonialist literature of the British Empire.

Lerer makes clear that one of his ideological goals in writing this book is to contribute to a cultural narrative that favors preserving the book as artifact. He writes, "I argue for the continuance of books in an age marked by visual technology" (2008:16). He also claims as his ideology the following: "children's literature is not some ideal category that *a certain age may reach* and that another may miss. It is instead a kind of system, one whose social and aesthetic value is determined out of the relationships among those who make, market and read books" (7, italics added). But rather than adhering to the class-conscious ideology this proclamation implies, Lerer instead constructs a Romantic child. Lurking around every corner in his book is an innocent and educable middle-class white child with easy access to literacy — not unlike his own son, whose reading he frequently describes.

If Lerer's ideology is ultimately Romantic, then it should follow as no surprise that the forms of emplotment he most frequently employs are those of the journey and of growth. He is given to using phrases like "Puritanism was a movement for the future" (81), and "Books, like Americans, are children" (96), and "Evolution, like imagination, lets us see how things turn into other things" (186), and "Childhood and freshman year are periods of change" (208), and "The legacy of fairy-tale philology lies in the ways in which we may imagine … personal growth and linguistic change" (223), and "It is a cliché to aver that the First World War ended the childhood of the Edwardian era" (263). The rhetoric in all of these phrases includes metaphors of growth, movement, or change, so discerning readers can conclude that Lerer posits the history of children's literature as an evolutionary model and childhood as a matter of purity, innocence, and goodness.

Beverly Lyon Clark's *Kiddie Lit*, however, takes an almost diametrically opposed approach to emplotment. In Clark's model, America was once almost idyllic in "how highly the nineteenth-century elite regarded" children's literature, "compared to the twentieth-century elite" (2003:xii). Clark problematizes the tendency among scholars of cultural studies to view childhood as a "stepping-stone" to adulthood (10). She notes the particularly prominent tendency among white middle-class scholars to view childhood as something that is only a stage, something that will be left behind, and that is, therefore, unproblematic in its construction (10–12). She particularly excoriates stage theorists, whose rhetoric encourages the disparagement of "what we consider childish" (11); they are "pernicious because of the way they are inherently dismissive of childhood, the way they image childhood as something other than the ideal, something that needs to be grown out of" (11). She cites Jacqueline Rose to note that the "journey metaphor" of children being "on their way" to adulthood is a common one (Rose, cited in Clark 2003: 12). She asks what would happen if we thought of every life stage as equally valuable? "How impossible would it be for educators — whose very goal is change — … to reimagine stages and development?" (Clark 2003: 12). Thus, Clark resists the pattern of both evolution and the journey in her historical study of children's literature within the context of the American literary canon.

Curiously, however, the emplotment pattern that Clark occasionally reflects is one of devolution. Her basic premise — that children's literature was more respected by literary critics in the nineteenth-century than in subsequent centuries — is one of devolution, of downward mobility, of a fall from the garden of Eden, if you will. She tracks the "critical trajectories" (16) of such authors as Frances Hodgson Burnett and Henry James, to demonstrate James' ascension to literary heights and Burnett's descension to the depths, noting that James himself uses disparagingly such terms as "'puerile,' 'infantine,' and 'jejune' to disparage" (35). She notes that various academics write about Hawthorne's work for children "dismissively" and "[reduce]" children's literature to only a few notable authors (65). She examines how New Critics in the mid-twentieth century distinguished *The Adventures of Tom Sawyer* as a book for children to elevate *Adventures of Huckleberry Finn* as a literary book — in the process, causing *Tom Sawyer* to fall from grace — and the canon. She investigates how Alcott's various genres "bled into each other"; in the twentieth century, her books for children were removed with almost surgical precision from the canon so that she became virtually unstudied for much of the twentieth century. According to Clark, L. Frank Baum's reputation suffers because he wrote for a profit — and he wrote at a time "when children's literature was increasingly divorced from that for adults and had become, by definition, non-elite" (139). Only the MGM movie, she believes, revived *The Wizard of Oz* from the "critical black hole" into which it had "slipped" (147). Although Clark acknowledges that the "dismissiveness, condescension, and marginalization" of children's authors is now less prevalent than it once was, hers is still an emplotted trajectory of prelapsarian children's literature having fallen in disgrace from the literary heavens (125).

Clark's methodology focuses as closely on language and discourse as Lerer's does, but she takes an approach that is less philological and more archival. Clark examines the critical reviews and cultural reactions to a text more frequently than she analyzes the text itself. The combination of Clark's methodology and the emplotment of her narrative approach to children's literature reveals her ideology towards texts written for children. She believes that the genre is not best separated from texts written for older people; she believes the genre is best studied in the context of its cultural reception and therefore its cultural construction. Her ideological intent is a revisionary one: she wants to reclaim childhood and the literature of childhood as valuable life stages, worthy in their own right as the object of study. Her ability to combine her respect for childhood with her intellectual passion emerges as she quotes Walt Disney in the final sentence of *Kiddie Lit*: "What the hell's wrong with something being childish?" (Disney, cited in Clark 2003: 183). Ideologically, Clark bases her claim for the study of children's literature on her refusal to denigrate childhood as a life stage. The implication resounds with import for other aspects of childhood studies: she is one of many scholars whose literary criticism argues in favor of a cultural narrative of increased societal respect for childhood.

Kimberley Reynolds shares the same goal in *Radical Children's Literature: Future Visions and Aesthetic Transformations in Juvenile Fiction*. Reynolds' goal is to "map the way that children's literature contributes to the social and aesthetic transformation of culture by, for instance, encouraging readers to approach ideas, issues, and objects from new perspectives and so prepare the way for change" (2007: 1). She believes that children's literature occupies a "paradoxical cultural space" in being "simultaneously highly regulated and overlooked, orthodox and radical, didactic and subversive" (3).

Relying on work from a broad range of scholars, including Juliet Dusinberre, Betty Greenway, Judith Plotz, Claudia Nelson, Julia Mickenberg, and Humphrey Carpenter, Reynolds demonstrates how influential childhood reading was historically to the shaping of Modernism. Given that much of her project is dedicated to refuting Jacqueline Rose's claim that children's literature rejects Modernism, Reynold's scholarship is convincing. Indeed, whether she is writing about the way that picture and text work together to create a medium first available in children's literature that subsequently opened the way to other literatures or whether she is writing about nonsense or sexuality or self-harm, Reynolds' typical methodology is to move between scholarly studies and close textual readings to support her clearly stated ideology: she wants to "[change] the way children's literature is perceived in culture by recognising the way books — and increasingly other narrative forms — for children have fostered and embedded social, intellectual and aesthetic changes" (23). Reynolds shares with Clark — and with other notable recent literary historians who study children's literature, like Mickenberg — an ideology that seeks to change and improve the reputation of children's literature, both as texts and as a field of study. Reynolds notes:

> Children's literature is one way through which children and young people receive stories about how the world works and ways of thinking about themselves and the things they do. Texts such as these can provide new narrative strands that for some will simply be interesting, but for others may offer alternative versions of the stories they are telling themselves about themselves. (113)

Reynolds actually problematizes metaphors of growth in the study of childhood when she writes about stage theorists (70) and when she writes about the literature children are given:

> A nursery is both a place for the young and a place of development; far from necessarily languishing and becoming aesthetically inert when directed at a juvenile audience … such genres are often refreshed and developed for use in new ways.… Just as we never leave childhood behind, so the narratives ingested in childhood endure and shape adult thinking and behaviour at many levels. (19)

Rather than lapsing into some sort of child-is-father-of-the-man ideology, Reynolds very matter of factly insists that memory keeps us from ever being either the Romantic construction of the child *or* the construction of the child as somehow separate from the child we once were. The result is a sophisticated conceptual metaphor that acknowledges growth as both ontological and cognitive.

The root metaphor that most fascinates me in Reynolds' work is her use of the word "transformation," which appears in her very title. Some of the key passages from her work rely on this notion of children's literature as having transformative or liberatory or evolutionary potential. For example, she writes: "Much of the symbolic potential of childhood in culture derives from the fact that children have most of their choices before them: they represent potential" (2) and "Because writing for the young has a future orientation, there is often a freshness and urgency to the storylines of children's fictions that correspond to the fact that their target readers are generally encountering ideas and experiences for the first time" (3). She writes about adolescence as a "trajectory," and she notes that Ariès "is surely right in recognising that the first stages in human development are not just biological — not just about getting bigger and learning to function in society — they are also cultural inventions and shaped according to society's needs and sense of itself at any given moment" (70). She concludes with an analysis of the influence electronic media may be having on children's literature: " … while ideologically children's literature may be struggling to construct new visions of how society could function, aesthetic transformations are in process" (179), adding later that "a major transformation of children's literature itself is taking place in cyberspace" (180).

In other words, Reynolds is able to identify the metaphor of childhood growth as a positive historical projection while also still — as Clark does — problematizing that metaphor as culturally grounded in societal needs to believe that children can and will improve the future.

Reynolds and Clark do not espouse views of childhood that involve children trailing clouds of glory who then devolve into adulthood or else evolve into some higher being called "adults." Although both of them rely on metaphors of growth — and in Clark's case, on an emplotment of devolution — both of them base their analyses in notions of childhood as one stage of life that has as much usefulness and meaning as any other stage of life. While it is difficult to avoid metaphors of growth when writing about children, and while it can be difficult to avoid metaphors of evolution when writing about history and the passing of time, literary critics in our field, such as Clark and Reynolds, have begun to grapple with the problems created by basing models of childhood *and* models of history in metaphors of growth. These are not scholars who expect children to save the future for adults, nor do they expect adults to save children from the horrors of adulthood. Rather, they employ metaphors of growth about childhood in constructivist ways that contribute to the recognition of children's and adolescents' texts as having cultural pertinence, especially in the history of ideas and aesthetic changes over time. If the scripts (or emplotment) vary between these two authors, the cultural narratives they are advancing are not so very different in helping situate childhood on a necessary spectrum of the life span.

Children's literature criticism by Lerer, Clark, and Reynolds demonstrates that the use of metaphors influences the unavoidable use of scripts in emplotment. Those scripted emplotments, in turn, have ideological implications about how youth as a stage of life is analyzed. When scholars like Clark and Reynolds investigate and critique those metaphors in their histories, they demystify childhood and adolescence *and* adulthood, demonstrating the significance of childhood studies to all literary scholars.

Because it is such an emphasized aspect of the study of children's and adolescent fiction, I cannot help but wonder if growth has not come to occupy a privileged narratological position in children's literature (both its fiction and its literary criticism) that is hegemonic. Thinkers throughout time have described metaphors of growth in terms of the ontological, the epistemological, and the biophysically embodied; historians and literary critics have tracked "progress" and "decline" in terms of metaphors of growth that assume their readers understand both the biological and cognitive implications of human growth. Traditionally, many scholars have relied on metaphors of growth to describe historical change; most of those scholars imply something about the powerlessness of childhood when they employ those metaphors — although such noteworthy critics as Clark and Reynolds work hard to avoid the hegemony of growth as a historical script. The use of metaphors of growth to describe change should give us all pause: do those of us in childhood studies ever want to write about childhood and adolescence employing metaphors that effectively entail youth as negative, as something to be outgrown?

Afterword

As a feminist in the 1990s, I worried frequently about essentialism — meaning that I worried that it was theoretically wrong to attribute behaviors to anyone because of biological determinants, such as sex or race. I still believe that. And yet my work in cognitive narratology has helped me to see the significant ways that our culture self-replicates ideas, such as the hegemony of growth in adolescent literature, with entailed conceptual metaphors and cultural narratives that have become scripted by repetition. If all I ever read are books about growth, I train my brain to read for growth — and once my brain is trained to read for growth, I am sure to find stories about growth everywhere. If I am a creative writer, I am sure to replicate those patterns of growth as I write new stories. If I am a critic, I am sure to analyze that pattern. Ideas about growth then become an almost endless loop in adolescent literature.

We replicate scripts of growth to organize our own experiences of growth, to organize our understanding of other people's growth, and to help organize our society — because in all cultures, all embodied beings are ever-changing. The categorizations of infancy, childhood, adolescence, adulthood, and old age are pervasive cognitive phenomena in western cultures that lead, in turn, to various language structures that privilege growth. Metaphors of growth are one obvious example of our cognition structuring a concept around our embodied experiences. Scripts of growth, particularly the pattern of the *Bildungsroman*, are another example of our cognition basing its conceptualizations in embodied knowledge. My motivation for analyzing these scripts has been to ask how those conceptualizations translate into cultural narratives that privilege certain models of growth, most notably, growth as improvement, over other models of growth, such as the much less laden concept of growth as simple change.

Cognitive readings of adolescent literature — and the closely related field of children's literature — can help attenuate scholars to the intricate relationship between textuality and reception; that is, critics who are aware of the significant role cognitive conceptualization plays in reading and interpreting literature for the young have the potential to recognize how heavily dependent on the brain's forms of shorthand, such as schemas and scripts, narratives are. Moreover, cognitive readings allow us to examine the role language and conceptualization play in creating larger cultural narratives that influence the epistemology and ontology of youth.

I submit that the cultural narrative that children will and must grow influences many authors of adolescent literature, literary critics, and historians to privilege metaphors in which growth is depicted in terms that are value-positive, as opposed to employing terms that are value-neutral or value-negative. In this way, the biological fact of growth creates a metaphorical structure that can, if we are not careful, devalue youth, defining and even limiting the epistemology of childhood studies to privilege a conceptualization of growth as a hegemonic force within the field of adolescent literature.

While it is true that there is nothing inherently evil about growth because it is a fundamental factor in everyone's life, I still cannot help wondering if we are not somehow missing other ways of being, other epistemologies, that would help young readers understand literature — and life — in less goal-oriented ways. After all, in literary depictions, coming of age does have a clear-cut trajectory that is defined by only one goal: maturity.

I hope that it is obvious that I am not arguing in favor of immaturity, either. But I do wonder what the cognitive effect is on adolescents who experience the repeated and privileged pattern of growth in their novels and their films. What happens when brains are trained to read for goal-oriented growth? Do readers themselves become so focused on achieving the end-goal — adulthood! — that they diminish their own adolescent experience? Do teenaged readers learn to devalue the time they spend as teenagers, before they have "grown up"? Do teenagers develop false or limited impressions about what maturity actually is? And are there negative implications on self-esteem? On values? On cognitive functioning?

Metaphors about growth are varied, but they are often entailed by embodiment, and they clearly influence the ways that authors and critics script conceptualizations of growth in adolescent literature. Thus, when we examine the interaction between cognition and conceptualization, we can begin to understand how the embodied experientialism of growth to adulthood has profoundly influenced the literature, literary criticism, and historical study of adolescence.

References

Primary Sources (Books)

Alcott, Louisa May. 1968. *Little Women*. Boston MA: Little, Brown (first published 1867, 1868).

Alexie, Sherman. 2007. *The Absolutely True Diary of a Part-Time Indian*. New York NY: Little, Brown.

Almond, David. 1999. *Skellig*. New York NY: Delacorte (first published 1998).

Almond, David. 2010. *My name is Mina*. New York NY: Delacorte.

Anderson, Laurie Halse. 2010. *Speak*. Harrisonburg VA: Donnelley and Sons (first published 1999).

Anonymous. [Sparks, Beatrice.] 1971. *Go Ask Alice*. New York NY: Avon.

Asher, Jay. 2007. *Thirteen Reasons Why*. New York NY: Penguin.

Bray, Libba. 2009. *Going Bovine*. New York NY: Delacorte.

Cormier, Robert. 1977. *I Am the Cheese*. New York NY: Pantheon.

Hamilton, Virginia. 1982. *Sweet Whispers, Brother Rush*. New York NY: Philomel.

Hinton, S. E. 1967. *The Outsiders*. New York NY: Dell.

Hughes, Monica. 2000. *Keeper of the Isis Light*. New York NY: Simon (first published 1980).

Johnson, Angela. 2003. *a cool moonlight*. New York NY: Dial.

Mahy, Margaret. 2002. *Memory*. New York NY: HarperCollins (first published 1987).

McDonald, Meme & Pryor, Boori Monty. 2002. *Njunjul the Sun*. Crows Nest NSW: Allen.

Montgomery, L. M. 2004. *Anne of Green Gables*. New York NY: Sterling (first published 1908).

Mosley, Walter. 2005. *47*. New York NY: Little.

Shusterman, Neal. 2007. *Unwind*. New York NY: Simon.

Twain, Mark. 2002. *Adventures of Huckleberry Finn*. Berkeley CA: University of California Press (first published 1885).

Yang, Gene Luen. 2006. *American Born Chinese*. New York NY: First Second Books.

Primary Sources (Films)

Andrews, Mark & Chapman, Brenda. (Directors). 2012. *Brave*. USA: Pixar.

Bird, Brad. (Director). 2004. *The Incredibles*. USA: Pixar.

Bird, Brad. (Director). 2007. *Ratatouille*. USA: Pixar.

Docter, Pete. (Director). 2001. *Monsters, Inc*. USA: Pixar.

Docter, Pete. (Director). 2009. *Up*. USA: Pixar.

Lasseter, John. (Director). 1995. *Toy Story*. USA: Pixar.

Lasseter, John. (Director). 1999. *Toy Story 2*. USA: Pixar.

Lasseter, John. (Director). 2006. *Cars*. USA: Pixar.

Lasseter, John. (Director). 2011. *Cars 2*. USA: Pixar.

Scanlon, Dan. (Director). 2013. *Monsters University*. USA: Pixar.

Stanton, Andrew. (Director). 2003. *Finding Nemo*. USA: Pixar.

Stanton, Andrew. (Director). 2008. *WALL·E*. USA: Pixar.

Stevenson, Robert. (Director). 1964. *Mary Poppins*. USA: Disney.

Unkrich, Lee. (Director). 2010. *Toy Story 3*. USA: Pixar.

Secondary Sources

Abaius, Cole. 2009. *Discuss: Is Pixar sexist? Film School Rejects*. <http://www.filmschoolrejects.com/features/discuss-is-pixar-sexist.php> (4 June 2010).

Abel, Elizabeth, Hirsch, Marianne & Langland, Elizabeth. 1983. *The Voyage In: Fictions of Female Development*. Hanover NH: University Press of New England.

Adams, Gerald & Berzonsky, Michael. 2006. *Blackwell Handbook of Adolescence*. Malden MA: Blackwell. DOI: 10.1002/9780470756607

Allen, Theodore W. 2002. *The Invention of the White Race, Vol. I: Racial Oppression and Control*. New York NY: Verso (first published 1994).

Ariès, Philippe. 1962. *Centuries of Childhood: A Social History of Family Life*. Translated from French by Robert Baldick. New York NY: Random House (first published 1960).

Aristotle. 2012. *Generation of Animals*. <http://ebooks.adelaide.edu.au/a/aristotle/generation/book1.html> (15 November 2013).

Armitage, Ella S. 1885. *The Childhood of the English Nation; or, The Beginnings of English History*. London: Longman.

Baxter, Kent. 2008. *The Modern Age: Turn-of-the-Century American Culture and the Invention of Adolescence*. Tuscaloosa AL: University of Alabama Press.

Berk, Laura. 1991. *Child Development*, 2nd edn. Boston MA: Allyn and Bacon.

Berk, Laura. 2010. *Development through the Lifespan*, 5th edn. Boston MA: Allyn and Bacon.

Blackford, Holly. 2012. *The Myth of Persephone in Girls' Fantasy Literature*. New York NY: Routledge.

Blakemore, Sarah-Jayne & Choudhury, Suparna. 2006. Development of the adolescent brain: Implications for executive function and social cognition. *Journal of Child Psychology and Psychiatry* 47: 296–312. DOI: 10.1111/j.1469-7610.2006.01611.x

Bodenhausen, Galen V. & Macrae, C. Neil. 1998. Stereotype activation and inhibition. In *Stereotype Activation and Inhibition*, Robert S. Wyer Jr,. (ed.), 1–52. Mahwah NJ: Lawrence Erlbaum Associates.

Borges, Jorge Luis. 2000. The analytical language of John Wilkins. Translated from Spanish by Ruth L. C. Simms. In *Other Inquisitions: 1937–1952*, 101–105. Austin TX: University of Texas Press (first published 1964).

Bromance, n. 2013. *Oxford English Dictionary Online*. <http://www.oed.com/view/Entry/378903?redirectedFrom=bromanceand> (8 Nov. 2013).

Buckley, Jerome Hamilton. 1974. *Season of Youth: The Bildungsroman from Dickens to Golding*. Cambridge MA: Harvard University Press. DOI: 10.4159/harvard.9780674732728

Cadden, Mike. 2000. The irony of narration in the young adult novel. *Children's Literature Association Quarterly* 25: 146–154. DOI: 10.1353/chq.0.1467

Cadden, Mike. 2012. But you are still a monkey: *American Born Chinese* and racial justice. Paper presented at Ethics and Children's Literature: A Symposium. Greencastle IN.

Chanady, Amaryll. 1995. The territorialization of the imaginary in Latin America: Self-affirmation and resistance to metropolitan paradigms. In *Magical Realism: Theory, History, Community*, Lois Parkinson Zamora & Wendy B. Faris(eds.), 125–144. Durham NC: Duke University Press.

Chaney, Jen. 2007. Are the Pixar movies an animated Boys Town? *Washington Post.* <http://voices.washingtonpost.com/celebritology/2007/06/are_the_pixar_movies_an_animat.html> (4 June 2010).

Christenbury, Leila, Bomer, Randy & Smagorinsky, Peter. 2009. *Handbook of Adolescent Literacy Research.* New York NY: Guildford Press.

Clark, Beverly Lyon. 2003. *Kiddie Lit: The Cultural Construction of Children's Literature in America.* Baltimore MD: Johns Hopkins University Press.

Clodd, Edward. 1887. *The Childhood of the World: A Simple Account of Man's Origin and Early History.* New York NY: Macmillan.

Coats, Karen. 2001. Keepin' it plural: Children's studies in the academy. *Children's Literature Association Quarterly* 26: 140–150. DOI: 10.1353/chq.0.1324

Coats, Karen. 2004. *Looking Glasses and Neverlands: Lacan, Desire, and Subjectivity in Children's Literature.* Iowa City IA: University of Iowa Press.

Coats, Karen. 2011. Transforming children's minds: Cognitive poetics and children's poetry. Paper presented at Transforming Childhood: Discourses and Practices. Moscow, Russia.

Cott, Jonathan. 1981. *Pipers at the Gates of Dawn: The Wisdom of Children's Literature.* New York NY: Random.

Dalsimer, Katherine. 1986. *Female Adolescence: Psychoanalytic Reflections on Works of Literature.* New Haven CT: Yale University Press.

Dennis, Felix. 2012. *Brave*: Actually a box-office disappointment? The Week. <http://theweek.com/article/index/229760/brave-actually-a-box-office-disappointment> (10 September 2012).

Engel, Manfred. 2008. Variants of the Romantic *Bildungsroman*. In *Romantic Prose Fiction* [Comparative History of Literatures in European Languages XXIII], Gerald Gillespie, Manfred Engel & Bernard Dieterle (eds.), 263–295. Amsterdam: John Benjamins.

Eyben, Emiel. 1993. *Restless Youth in Ancient Rome.*New York NY: Routledge (first published 1977).

Faris, Wendy B. 2004. *Ordinary Enchantments: Magical Realism and the Remystification of Narrative.* Nashville TN: Vanderbilt University Press.

Fauconnier, Gilles. 2003. *Mappings in Thought and Language.* Cambridge: CUP (first published 1997).

Fauconnier, Gilles & Turner, Mark. 1998. Conceptual integration networks. *Cognitive Science* 22: 133–187. DOI: 10.1207/s15516709cog2202_1

Fauconnier, Gilles & Turner, Mark. 2002. *The Way We Think: Conceptual Blending and the Mind's Hidden Complexities.* New York NY: Basic.

Fiedler, Leslie. 1958. From redemption to initiation. *New Leader* 41: 22.

Fludernik, Monika. 2010. Narratology in the Twenty-First Century: The cognitive approach to narrative. *PMLA* 125: 924–930. DOI: 10.1632/pmla.2010.125.4.924

Foucault, Michel. 1994. The Order of Things: An Archaeology of the Human Sciences. Translated from French by Alan Sheridan. New York NY: Knopf (first published 1970).

Foucault, Michel. 1995. Discipline and Punish: The Birth of the Prison. Translated from French by Alan Sheridan. New York NY: Vintage Books (first published 1975).

Frith, Uta, Happé, Francesca & Siddons, Frances. 1994. Autism and Theory of Mind in everyday life. Social Development 3: 108–124. DOI: 10.1111/j.1467-9507.1994.tb00031.x

Furay, Conal & Salevouris, Michael J. 1988. The Methods and Skills of History. Arlington Heights IL: Davidson.

Griswold, Jerry. 1992. Audacious Kids: Coming of Age in America's Classic Children's Books. Oxford: OUP.

Griswold, Jerry. 2006. Feeling Like a Kid: Childhood and Children's Literature. Baltimore MD: Johns Hopkins University Press.

Grosz, Elizabeth. 1994. Volatile Bodies: Toward a Corporeal Feminism. Bloomington IN: Indiana University Press.

Grow, v. 2012. Oxford English Dictionary Online. <http://www.oed.com/view/Entry/81904?rske y=vYlXJqandresult=2andisAdvanced=false> (18 January 2013).

Hanawalt, Barbara A. 1993. Growing Up in Medieval London: The Experience of Childhood in History. Oxford: OUP.

Handy, adj. 2012. Oxford English Dictionary Online. <http://www.oed.com/view/Entry/83957> (24 August 2012).

Hanscom, Michael. 2006. Is Pixar a "boys only" club? Eclecticism. <http://www.michaelhanscom.com/eclecticism/2006/05/20/is-pixar-a-boys-only-club/> (4 June 2010).

Hart, F. Elizabeth. 2001. The epistemology of cognitive literary studies. Philosophy and Literature 25: 314–334.

Heidegger, Martin. 2008. Being and Time. Translated from German by John Macquarrie and Edward Robinson. New York NY: Harper (first published 1927).

Herman, David. 1997. Scripts, sequences, and stories: Elements of a postclassical narratology. PMLA 112: 1046–1059. DOI: 10.2307/463482

Herman, David. 2002. Story Logic: Problems and Possibilities of Narrative. Lincoln NE: University of Nebraska Press.

Herman, David. 2007. Storytelling and the sciences of mind: Cognitive narratology, discursive psychology, and narratives in face-to-face interaction. Narrative 15: 306–34. DOI: 10.1353/nar.2007.0023

Herman, David. 2011. Cognitive narratology. The Living Handbook of Narratology. <http://hup.sub.uni-hamburg.de/lhn/index.php/Cognitive_Narratology> (21 September 2012).

Hirsch, Marianne. 1989. The Mother/Daughter Plot: Narrative, Psychoanalysis, Feminism. Bloomington IN: Indiana University Press.

Hirschfeld, Lawrence A. 1996. Race in the Making: Cognition, Culture, and the Child's Construction of Human Kinds. Cambridge MA: The MIT Press.

Hollindale, Peter. 1997. Signs of Childness in Children's Books. Stroud, Glos.: Thimble.

Holmes, Linda. 2009. Dear Pixar, from all the girls with band-aids on their knees. Monkey See <http://www.npr.org/blogs/monkeysee/2009/06/dear_pixar_from_all_the_girls.html> (30 January 2013).

Howe, Susanne. 1966. Wilhelm Meister and his English Kinsmen: Apprentices to Life. New York NY: AMS.

Hump, v. 2013. Oxford English Dictionary Online. <http://www.oed.com/view/Entry/89428?rsk ey=XXVfmXandresult=2andisAdvanced=false> (7 January 2013).

Hunt, Peter. 1994. An Introduction to Children's Literature. Oxford: OUP.

Johnson, James. 1959. The adolescent hero: A trend in modern fiction. *Twentieth Century Literature* 5: 3–11. DOI: 10.2307/440734

Johnson, Mark. 1990. *The Body in the Mind: The Bodily Basis of Meaning, Imagination, and Reason*. Chicago IL: University of Chicago Press.

Kokkola, Lydia. 2013. *Fictions of Adolescent Carnality: Sexy Sinners and Delinquent Deviants* [Children's Literature, Culture and Cognition 1]. Amsterdam: John Benjamins.

Kristeva, Julia. 1982. *Powers of Horror*. New York NY: Columbia University Press (first published 1980).

Kümmerling-Meibauer, Bettina. 2011. Emergent literacy and children's literature. In *Emergent Literacy: Children's Books from 0 to 3* [Studies in Written Language and Literacy 13], Bettina Kümmerling-Meibauer (ed.) 1–14. Amsterdam: John Benjamins. DOI: 10.1075/swll.13

Kümmerling-Meibauer, Bettina. 2012. Emotional connection: Representation of emotions in young adult literature. In *Contemporary Adolescent Literature and Culture: The Emergent Adult*, Mary Hilton & Maria Nikolajeva (eds.), 127–138. Farnham, Surrey: Ashgate.

Kümmerling-Meibauer, Bettina. 2013. Introduction: New perspectives in children's film studies. *Journal of Educational Media, Memory, and Society* 5: 39–44. DOI: 10.3167/jemms.2013.050203

Kuznets, Lois R. 1984–85. Family as formula: Cawelti's formulaic theory and Streatfeild's "Shoe" books. *Children's Literature Association Quarterly* 9: 147–149, 201.

Labovitz, Esther Kleinbord. 1987. *The Myth of the Heroine: The Female Bildungsroman in the Twentieth Century: Dorothy Richardson, Simone de Beauvoir, Doris Lessing, Christa Wolf*. Frankfurt: Peter Lang.

Lakoff, George & Johnson, Mark. 1980. *Metaphors We Live By*. Chicago IL: University of Chicago Press.

Lakoff, George & Johnson, Mark. 1999. *Philosophy in the Flesh: The Embodied Mind and Its Challenge to Western Thought*. New York NY: Basic.

Lakoff, George & Turner, Mark. 1989. *More Than Cool Reason: A Field Guide to Poetic Metaphor*. Chicago IL: University of Chicago Press. DOI: 10.7208/chicago/9780226470986.001.0001

Langacker, Ronald W. 2006. Cognitive grammar: Introduction to concept, image, and symbol. In *Cognitive Linguistics: Basic Readings*, Dirk Geeraerts (ed.), 29–68. Berlin: Mouton de Gruyter. DOI: 10.1515/9783110199901.29

Lee, Sung-Ae. 2011. Lures and horrors of alterity: Adapting Korean tales of fox spirits. *IRCL* 4: 135–150. DOI: 10.3366/ircl.2011.0022

Lepore, Lorella & Brown, Rupert. 1997. Category and stereotype activation: Is prejudice inevitable? *Journal of Personality and Social Psychology* 72: 275–287. DOI: 10.1037/0022-3514.72.2.275

Lerer, Seth. 2008. *Children's Literature: A Reader's History from Aesop to Harry Potter*. Chicago IL: University of Chicago Press. DOI: 10.7208/chicago/9780226473024.001.0001

Lerner, Richard M. & Steinberg, Laurence. 2004. *Handbook of Adolescent Psychology*, 2nd edn. Hoboken, NJ: John Wiley. DOI: 10.1002/9780471726746

Leseur, Geta. 1995. *Ten is the Age of Darkness: The Black Bildungsroman*. Columbia MO: University of Missouri Press.

Lesnik-Oberstein, Karín. 1994. *Children's Literature Criticism and the Fictional Child*. Oxford: Clarendon.

Lévi-Strauss, Claude. 1984. Structure and form: Reflections on a work by Vladimir Propp. In *Vladimir Propp: Theory and History of Folklore* Translated from French by Ariadna Y. Martin

& Richard P. Martin, Anatoly Liberman (ed.), 167–188. Minneapolis MN: University of Minnesota Press.

Light, v.1. 2012. *Oxford English Dictionary Online*. <http://www.oed.com/view/Entry/108177?> (29 August 2012).

Locke, John. 1836. *An Essay Concerning Human Understanding*, 27th edn. London: Tegg. <http://books.google.com/books?id=vjYIAAAAQAAJandprintsec=frontcover#v=onepage andqandf=false> (19 November 2013, first published 1690).

Lukens, Rebecca. 1982. *A Critical Handbook of Children's Literature*, 2nd edn. Oxford OH: Scott-Foresman.

Lyotard, Jean-François. 1984. The Postmodern Condition: A Report on Knowledge. Translated from French by Geoff Bennington & Brian Massumi. Minneapolis MN: University of Minnesota Press.

MacKenzie, Robin. 2007. Maturity and modernity in Fromentin's *Dominique*. *Nineteenth-Century French Studies* 35: 352–366. DOI: 10.1353/ncf.2007.0019

Mackey, Margaret. 2010. Reading from the feet up: The local work of literacy. *Children's Literature in Education* 41: 323–339. DOI: 10.1007/s10583-010-9114-z

Mackey, Margaret. 2011. The embedded and embodied literacies of a young reader. *Children's Literature in Education* 42: 289–307. DOI: 10.1007/s10583-011-9141-4

Mackey, Margaret. 2012. The emergent reader's working kit of stereotypes. *Children's Literature in Education* <http://link.springer.com/article/10.1007%2Fs10583-012-9184-1?LI=true> (26 October 2012).

MacLeod, Anne Scott. 1997. The journey inward: Adolescent literature in America, 1945–1995. In *Reflections of Change: Children's Literature Since 1945*, Sandra L. Beckett (ed.), 125–129. Westport CT: Greenwood.

Macrae, C. Neil, Bodenhausen, Galen V. & Milne, Alan B. 1995. The dissection of selection in person perception: Inhibitory processes in social stereotyping. *Journal of Personality and Social Psychology* 69: 397–407. DOI: 10.1037/0022-3514.69.3.397

Mallon, Ron. 2006. "Race": Normative, not metaphysical or semantic. *Ethics* 116: 525–551. DOI: 10.1086/500495

Marcus, Mordecai. 1960. What is an initiation story? *Journal of Aesthetic and Art Criticism* 19: 221–24. DOI: 10.2307/428289

Maslow, Abraham H. 1943. A theory of human motivation. *Psychological Review* 50: 370–396. DOI: 10.1037/h0054346

Mature, v. 2012. *Oxford English Dictionary Online*. <Retrieved from http://www.oed.com/view/Entry/115115?rskey=EVFKkkandresult=2andisAdvanced=false> (18 January 2013).

McCallum, Robyn. 1999. *Ideologies of Identity in Adolescent Fiction: The Dialogic Construction of Subjectivity*. New York NY: Garland.

Mercadal, Dennis. 1990. *A Dictionary of Artificial Intelligence*. New York NY: Van Nostrand.

Merleau-Ponty, Maurice. 1962. Phenomenology of Perception. Translated from French by Colin Smith. New York NY: Humanities Press (first published 1945).

Mills, Charles W. 1998. *Blackness Visible: Essays on Philosophy and Race*. Ithaca NY: Cornell University Press.

Mills, Charles W. 1999. *The Racial Contract*. Ithaca NY: Cornell University Press.

Mintz, Steven. 2004. *Huck's Raft: A History of American Childhood*. Cambridge MA: Belknap.

Moreton-Robinson, Aileen. 2005. Whiteness, epistemology and indigenous representation. In *Whitening Race: Essays in Social and Cultural Criticism*, Aileen Moreton-Robinson (ed.), 75–88. Canberra ACT: Aboriginal Studies Press.

Mosley, Walter. (n.d.) In his own words: On writing 47. Hachette Book Group. <http://faith-wordsbooks.com/Walter_Mosley_%281014487%29_Article%284%29.htm> (15 February 2013).

Murphy, Gregory L. 2002. *The Big Book of Concepts*. Cambridge MA: The MIT Press.

Natov, Roni. 2003. *The Poetics of Childhood*. New York NY: Routledge.

Nikolajeva, Maria. 1996. *Children's Literature Comes of Age*. New York NY: Routledge.

Nikolajeva, Maria. 2000. *From Mythic to Linear: Time in Children's Literature*. Lanham MD: Scarecrow.

Nikolajeva, Maria. 2002. *The Rhetoric of Character in Children's Literature*. Lanham MD: Scarecrow.

Nikolajeva, Maria. 2009. *Power, Voice, and Subjectivity in Literature for Young Readers*. New York NY: Routledge.

Nikolajeva, Maria. 2012. Reading other people's minds through word and image. *Children's Literature in Education* 43: 273–291. DOI: 10.1007/s10583-012-9163-6

Nisbet, Robert. 1970. Genealogy, growth, and other metaphors. *New Literary History* 1: 351–363. DOI: 10.2307/468261

Nodelman, Perry. 1985. Interpretation and the apparent sameness of children's novels. *Studies in the Literary Imagination* 18(2): 5–20.

Nodelman, Perry. 1988. *Words about Pictures*. Athens GA: University of Georgia Press.

Norenzayan, Ara, Atran, Scott, Faulkner, Jason & Schaller, Mark. 2006. Memory and mystery: The cultural selection of minimally counterintuitive narratives. *Cognitive Science* 30: 531–553. DOI: 10.1207/s15516709cog0000_68

Oliner, Adam J. 2000. The cognitive roots of stereotyping. <http://adam.oliner.net/comp/stereo-typing.html> (18 November 2013).

Ovid. 2012. *The Metamorphoses, Books I–VII*. <http://www.gutenberg.org/files/21765/21765-h/21765-h.htm> (10 October 2012).

Oziewicz, Marek. 2007. "Let the villains be soundly killed at the end of the book": C.S. Lewis's conception of justice in the Chronicles of Narnia. In *Past Watchful Dragons: Fantasy and Faith in the World of C. S. Lewis*, A. H. Sturgis (ed.), 41–66. Altadena CA: The Mythopoeic Press.

Oziewicz, Marek. 2011. Restorative justice scripts in Ursula K. Le Guin's *Voices*. *Children's Literature in Education* 42: 33–43. DOI: 10.1007/s10583-010-9118-8

Papalia, Diane E., Olds, Sally Wendkos & Feldman, Ruth Duskin. 2006. *Human Development*, 10th edn. McGraw-Hill Higher Education. <http://highered.mcgraw-hill.com/sites/0073133809/student_view0/> (30 January 2014).

Paul, Lissa. 1987. Enigma variations: What feminist theory knows about children's literature. *Signal* 54: 187–201.

Peck, David. 1989. *Novels of Initiation: A Guidebook for Teaching Literature to Adolescents*. New York NY: Teachers College Press.

Piaget, Jean & Inhelder, Bärbel. 1969. The Psychology of the Child. Translated from French by Helen Weaver. New York NY: Basic (first published 1966).

Pixar. n.d. *Pixar*. <http://www.pixar.com/index.html> (10 May 2010).

Pollock, Linda. 1983. *Forgotten Children: Parent-Child Relations from* 1500–1900. Cambridge: CUP.

Pratt, Annis. 1981. *Archetypal Patterns in Women's Fiction*. Brighton: Harvester.

Premack, David & Woodruff, Guy. 1978. Does the chimpanzee have a theory of mind? *The Behavioral and Brain Sciences* 1: 515–526. DOI: 10.1017/S0140525X00076512

Propp, Vladimir. 1968. Translated from the Russian by Laurence Scott. *Morphology of the Folktale,* 2nd edn. Austin TX: University of Texas Press.

Reynolds, Kimberley. 2007. *Radical Children's Literature: Future Visions and Aesthetic Transformations in Juvenile Fiction.* Houndmills, Basingstoke: Palgrave.

Richardson, Alan. 2004. Studies in literature and cognition: A field map. In *The Work of Fiction: Cognition, Culture, and Complexity,* Alan Richardson & Ellen Spolsky (eds.), 1–29. Burlington VT: Ashgate.

Rosenberg, Teya. 2001. Magical realism and children's literature: Diana Wynne Jones's Black Maria and Salman Rushdie's Midnight's Children as a test case. *Papers: Explorations in Children's Literature* 11: 14–25.

Rousseau, Jean-Jacques. 2012. *Emile.* <http://www.gutenberg.org/cache/epub/5427/pg5427. html> (10 October 2012, first published 1762).

Russell, David. 2001. *Literature for Children: A Short Introduction,* 4th edn. New York NY: Longman.

Said, Edward. 2003. *Orientalism.* New York NY: Penguin (first published 1978).

Schank, Roger & Abelson, Robert. 1975. Scripts, plans, and knowledge. In *Proceedings of the Fourth International Joint Conference on Artificial Intelligence,* 151–157. San Francisco CA: Kaufmann.

Schultz, James A. 1995. *The Knowledge of Childhood in the German Middle Ages,* 1150–1350. Philadelphia PA: University of Pennsylvania Press.

Shakespeare, William. 1974. *The Riverside Shakespeare,* G. Blakemore Evans (ed.). Boston MA: Houghton.

Sizemore, Christine Wick. 2002. *Negotiating Identities in Women's Lives: English Postcolonial and Contemporary British Novels.* Westport CT: Greenwood.

Smedley, Audrey. 2007. *Race in North America: Origin and Evolution of a Worldview,* 3rd edn. Boulder CO: Westview.

Smith, Melissa Sara. 2010. The Anxiety of Time in Young Adult Literature: Writing the Adolescent Body. PhD dissertation, Illinois State University.

Smith, Stacy L. n.d. Gender on screen and behind the camera in family films. Geena Davis Institute on Gender and Film. <http://www.seejane.org/downloads/FullStudy_ GenderDisparityFamilyFilms.pdf> (20 December 2010).

Smith, Stacy L. & Choueiti, Marc. n.d. Gender disparity on screen and behind the camera in family films: The executive report. Geena Davis Institute on Gender and Film. <http://www. seejane.org/downloads/FullStudy_GenderDisparityFamilyFilms.pdf> (17 October 2012).

Smith, Stacy L. & Cook, Crystal Allene. n.d. GDIGM major findings overview: Based on gender stereotypes: An analysis of popular films and TV. Geena Davis Institute on Gender and Film. <http://www.thegeenadavisinstitute.org/downloads/GDIGM_Main_Findings.pdf> (20 December 2010).

Sommerville, C. John. 1982. *The Rise and Fall of Childhood.* Beverly Hills CA: Sage.

Spacks, Patricia Meyer. 1981. *The Adolescent Idea: Myths of Youth and the Adult Imagination.* New York NY: Basic.

Stange, G. Robert. 1954. "Expectations Well Lost": Dickens' fable for his time. *College English* 16: 9–17. DOI: 10.2307/371614

Steinberg, Laurence. 2005. Cognitive and affective development in adolescence. *Trends in Cognitive Science* 9: 69–74. DOI: 10.1016/j.tics.2004.12.005

Stephens, John. 1992. *Language and Ideology in Children's Fiction.* New York NY: Longman.

Stephens, John. 2011. Schemas and scripts: Cognitive instruments and the representation of cultural diversity in children's literature. In *Contemporary Children's Literature and Film: Engaging with Theory*, Kerry Mallan & Clare Bradford (eds.), 12–35. Houndmills, Basingstoke: Palgrave Macmillan.

Stephens, John & McCallum, Robyn. 1998. *Retelling Stories, Framing Culture: Traditional Story and Metanarratives in Children's Literature*. New York NY: Garland.

Stewart, Susan L. 2013. A new holocaust: The consumable youth of Neal Shusterman's *Unwind*. In *Contemporary Dystopian Fiction for Young Adults: Brave New Teenagers*, Carrie Hintz, Balaka Basu & Katherine Broad (eds.), 159–174. New York NY: Routledge.

Stone, Lawrence. 1974. The massacre of the innocents. *New York Review of Books* 21: 25–31.

Swales, Martin. 1978. *The German Bildungsroman from Wieland to Hesse*. Princeton CT: Princeton University Press.

Tennyson, G. B. 1968. The *Bildungsroman* in nineteenth-century English literature. In *Medieval Epic to the "Epic Theater" of Brecht*, Rosario P. Armato & John M. Spalek (eds.), 135–146. Los Angeles CA: University of Southern California Press.

Townsend, John Rowe. 1983. *Written for Children: An Outline of English-language Children's Literature*. New York NY: Lippincott.

TransWorld Surf RSS. <http://surf.transworld.net/broism-dictionary/> (4 November 2013).

Trites, Roberta Seelinger. 1997. *Waking Sleeping Beauty: Feminist Voices in Children's Novels*. Iowa City IA: University of Iowa Press.

Trites, Roberta Seelinger. 2000. *Disturbing the Universe: Power and Repression in Adolescent Literature*. Iowa City IA: University of Iowa Press.

Trites, Roberta Seelinger. 2007. *Twain, Alcott, and the Birth of the Adolescent Reform Novel*. Iowa City IA: University of Iowa Press.

Turner, Mark. 1991. *Reading Minds: The Study of English in the Age of Cognitive Science*. Princeton NJ: Princeton University Press.

Turner, Mark. 2002. The cognitive study of art, language, and literature. *Poetics Today* 23: 9–20. DOI: 10.1215/03335372-23-1-9

Vaillant, George. 2000. Adaptive mental mechanisms: Their role in a positive psychology. *American Psychologist* 55: 89–98. DOI: 10.1037/0003-066X.55.1.89

Vandergrift, Kay. 1980. *Child and Story: The Literary Connection*. New York NY: Neal-Schuman.

Vidali, Amy. 2010. Seeing what we know: Disability and theories of metaphor. *Journal of Literary and Cultural Disability Studies* 4: 33–54. DOI: 10.1353/jlc.0.0032

Vygotsky, Lev. 1933. Play and its role in the mental development of the child. Marxists Internet Archive Library. Translated from the Russian by Catherine Mulholland. <http://www.marxists.org/archive/vygotsky/works/1933/play.htm> (2 June 2010).

Wall, Barbara. 1991. *The Narrator's Voice: The Dilemma of Children's Fiction*. New York NY: Macmillan.

Waller, Allison. 2009. *Constructing Adolescence in Fantastic Realism*. New York NY: Routledge.

West, Cornel. 1999. Race and modernity. In *The Cornel West Reader*, 55–86. New York NY: Basic Civitas.

West, Elliott. 1989. *Growing Up with the Country: Childhood on the Far Western Frontier*. Albuquerque NM: University of New Mexico Press.

White, Barbara A. 1985. *Growing Up Female: Adolescent Girlhood in American Fiction*. Westport CT: Greenwood.

White, Hayden. 1978. The historical text as literary artifact. In *Tropics of Discourse: Essays in Cultural Criticism*, 81–100. Baltimore MD: Johns Hopkins University Press.

Wiegman, Robyn. 1995. *American Anatomies: Theorizing Race and Gender*. Durham NC: Duke University Press.

Wilson, Adrian. 1980. The Infancy of the History of Childhood: An Appraisal of Philippe Ariès. *History and Theory* 19: 132–153. DOI: 10.2307/2504795

Wojcik-Andrews, Ian. 2013. Elder quests, kid ventures, and kinder quests. *Journal of Educational Media, Memory, and Society* 5(2): 61–74. DOI: 10.3167/jemms.2013.050205

Wolf, Virginia L. 1985. Laura Ingalls Wilder's Little House books: A personal story. In *Touchstones: Reflections on the Best in Children's Literature*, Vol. I, Perry Nodelman (ed.), 291–300. West Purdue IN: Children's Literature Association.

Wollstonecraft, Mary. 2002. *Vindication of the Rights of Woman*. <http://www.gutenberg.org/cache/epub/3420/pg3420.html > (10 October 2012, first published 1792).

Wordsworth, William. 1807. *Poems, in Two Volumes*, Vol. 2. London: Longman. <http://books.google.com/books?id=pzgJAAAAQAAJandprintsec=frontcover#v=onepageandqandf=false> (18 November 2013).

Zamora, Lois Parkinson & Faris, Wendy B. (eds.). 1995. *Magical Realism: Theory, History, Community*. Durham NC: Duke University Press.

Zunshine, Lisa. 2002. Rhetoric, cognition, and ideology in A L. Barbauld's *Hymns in Prose for Children (1781)*. *Poetics Today* 23: 123–39. DOI: 10.1215/03335372-23-1-123

Zunshine, Lisa. 2006. *Why We Read Fiction: Theory of Mind and the Novel*. Columbus OH: University of Ohio Press.

Index